HAND BOOK OF PLASTIC MATERIALS AND PROCESSING TECHNOLOGY

HAND BOOK OF PLASTIC MATERIALS AND PROCESSING TECHNOLOGY

Written By

EIRI Board of Consultants and Engineers

ENGINEERS INDIA RESEARCH INSTITUTE

4449, Nai Sarak, Main Road, Delhi - 110006 (India)
Ph: +91-11-43658117, Mob: +91-9289151047, +91-9811437895
* E-Mail: eiri@eiriindia.org
*Website: www.eiriindia.org

PRINTED & PUBLISHED BY

ENGINEERS INDIA RESEARCH INSTITUTE

4449, Nai Sarak, Main Road, Delhi - 110006 (India)
Ph: +91-11-43658117, Mob: +91-9289151047, +91-9811437895
* E-Mail: eiri@eiriindia.org
*Website: www.eiriindia.org

Distributors:

Industrial Technologies, India
Roop Nagar, Delhi-110007
and
EIRI PROJECT CONSULTANTS AND PUBLISHERS
Nai Sarak, Delhi-110006

ISBN: 9788189765262

Revised and Enlarged Edition

Printed in New Delhi (INDIA)

Rs. 1475/- US$150

Printed & Published by "Engineers India Research Institute",
4449 Nai Sarak, Main Road, New Delhi -110006

Preface

Plastics are an important part of everyday life; products made from plastics range from sophisticated products, such as prosthetic hip and knee joints, to disposable food utensils. One of the reasons for the great popularity of plastics in a wide variety of industrial applications is due to the tremendous range of properties exhibited by plastics and their ease of processing. Plastic properties can be tailored to meet specific needs by varying the atomic makeup of the repeat structure; by varying molecular weight and molecular weight distribution; by varying flexibility as governed by presence of side chain branching, as well as the lengths and polarities of the side chains; and by tailoring the degree of crystallinity, the amount of orientation imparted to the plastic during processing and through copolymerization, blending with other plastics, and through modification with an enormous range of additives (fillers, fibers, plasticizers, stabilizers). Given all of the avenues available to pursue tailoring any given polymer, it is not surprising that such a variety of choices available to us today exist. Materials are often classified as either metals, ceramics, or polymers. Polymers differ from the other materials in a variety of ways but generally exhibit lower densities, thermal conductivities, and moduli. Polymeric materials are used in a vast array of products. In the automotive area, they are used for interior parts and in under-the-hood applications. Packaging applications are a large area for thermoplastics, from carbonated beverage bottles to plastic wrap. Application requirements vary widely but, luckily, plastic materials can be synthesized to meet these varied service conditions. It remains the job of the part designer to select from the array of thermoplastic materials available to meet the required demands.

These materials have many different chemical and physical forms, such as cross-linked versus non-cross-linked, crystalline versus amorphous, and rubbery versus glassy. More recently, structural polymers having liquid crystalline order have become important. Structural polymers are rarely used in the pure form but often contain additives in small quantities, such as antioxidants, stabilizers, lubricants, processing aids, nucleating agents, colorants, and antistatic agents or, in larger quantities, plasticizers or fillers. There is rapid growth in the areas of blends and composites. In composites, a material of fixed shape, such as particles (filler) or fibers, is dispersed in a polymer matrix. The filler or fiber may be an inorganic material or another organic polymer. Blends (or alloys) on the other hand consist of two or more polymers mixed together and differ from composites in that the geometry of the phases is not predetermined prior to processing. Some polymers are used for many different purposes. A good example is poly (ethylene terephthalate), or PET, which was originally developed as a textile fiber. It is now used in film and tape (virtually all magnetic recording tape is based on PET), as a molding material, and as the matrix for glass-filled composites. One of its largest uses is for making bottles, especially for soft drinks. PET is also used in blends with other polymers, such as polycarbonate.

Hand book of Plastic Materials and Processing Technology contains chapters on: *Introduction of plastic materials, Polyethylene, Linear low density polyethylene (lldpe), Polypropylene, Copolymers of ethylene, Polystyrene, Acrylic plastics: poly (methyl methacrylate), Acrylic fibres, Poly (vinyl acetate), Polymers derived from poly (vinyl acetate), Poly (vinyl chloride), Polytetrafluoroethylene (PTFE), Coumarone indene resins, Polyacetals and polyetheres (acetal resins), Polyamides, Polyimides, Polyesters, Polyurethanes, Polycarbonates, Epoxy resins, Cellulose plastics, Phenolic resins, Amino resins, Silicones, Additives for plastics, Polybutylene terephthalate, Polyethersulphone, Nylon, Polyvinyliden E fluoride, Polyphenylene sulphide, Rubber reinforced polypropylene, Thermoplastic polyetherester, Fibre reinforced thermoplastics, Polyurethane plastics, Speciality thermoplastics, Styrene plastics, Polyolefin plastics, Plastic processing technology, Amino acid by protein hydrolysis, Epoxy resin/ power, Household plastic products, Nylon granules from nylon waste, Poly vinyl acetate emulsion, Phenolic resin, Polyol from propylene oxide and Unsaturated polyester resin.*

ENGINEERS INDIA RESEARCH INSTITUTE
4449, Nai Sarak, Main Road, Delhi - 110006 (India)
Ph: +91-11-43658117,
Mob: +91-9289151047, +91-9811437895
* E-Mail: eiri@eiriindia.org
*Website: www.eiriindia.org

CONTENTS AND SUBJECT INDEX

1

Introduction of Plastic Materials

Material systems which can be conveniently made to flow or deform into a desired shape or form, usually under heat and / or pressure, are commonly known as plastics. The binding material in a given plastic product is invariably a polymer or resin. A resin is defined as a material, organic in nature and of either synthetic or natural origin, which has the capacity to produce a thin coherent film either from its melt or from its solution. A resin may be polymeric (characterized by high molecular weight and a characteristic repeat (chemical) unit in the structure) or non-polymeric (characterized by low molecular weight) in nature. According to the resin concept as above almost all polymers may be considered as resin, but all resins are not polymers. Conventionally, however, resins are brittle materials showing different degrees of hardness under ambient conditions. Rosin and shellac are two important natural resins, and among the relatively low molecular wieght ($M < 2000$) synthetic resins, the coumarone-indene resins and the so-called petroleum resins are important. These resins and their derivatives find widespread use as tackifiers and as improvers of adhesion, gloss, hardness, etc. in many adhesive and coating formulations based on different polymers. Most commercially important structural resins are, however, thermosetting polymers covering such products as the phenolic (phenol-formaldehyde) resins, amino (urea-formaldehyde and melamine-formaldehyde resins, alkyd (polyester) resins, epoxy resins, etc.

The technology of a polymer begins with the polymer itself, which is the base material of a plastic, rubber, adhesive, coating or related item that we see around us. The synthetic polymer industry can be either coal-based or petroleum-based. Ethylene, an important monomer and an intermediate for some other monomers may also be obtained by dehydration of alcohol. The developing trends in the decades after 1950 switched the technology of monomer synthesis for almost all kinds of polymer in favour of petroleum as the basic raw material, so much so that today's monomers and polymers are widely recognized as petrochemicals.

2

Polyethylene

Polyethylene of different density ranges can be obtained by chain polymerization of ethylene, the simplest olefinic monomer. The observed chemical nature and physical properties of the polymer depend largely on the nature of the catalyst used and conditions employed during polymerization. Polyethylenes obtained by polymerization of ethylene are mostly branched polymers, the chemical nature and frequency of branches being largely dependent on reaction conditions and the mechanism involved. Polyehtylenes of commerce are available in two major density ranges and the classified products are commonly known as : (a) low density polyethylene, LDPE (density range, 0.915-0.95 g/cm), and (b) high density polyethylene, HDPE (density range, 0.945-0.96 g/cm).

Low density Polyethylene (LDPE)

LDPE is produced by free radical polymerization of ethylene under very high pressure (1500-3000 atm), using oxygen, peroxides or zao-compounds as initiators. The development of a commercial process of this kind was associated with numerous technical difficulties. Highly exothermic nature of the polymerization requires strict control of reaction variables (pressure, catalyst concentration, temperature, monomer purity, flow velocity in the reactor, etc.) in order to ensure safety and do prevent run-away reactions and explosion. The early ICI process, commercialized in 1939, employed oxygen (air) as the catalyst. The polymerization reaction, simply, written as

$$nCH_2 = CH_2 \rightarrow -(CH_2-CH_2)_n-$$

is expected to be favoured under high pressures and low temperature from thermodynamic consideration. On kinetic consideration, however, a temperature range of 170-250° is usually employed. At a lower temperature, the radical generation process is far too slow for commercial production of the polymer.

To get high molecular weight, ethylene of high purity is required. Traces of oxygen catalyzes the polymerization process. The allowable oxygen at a pressure of 2000 atm and 165°C Is about 0.075% If this limit is crossed, explosive decomposition reaction occurs yielding hydrogen, methane and carbon in the main. The conditions are so chosen as to permit and favour only polymer formation at commercially viable rates. High pressure increases local concentration of the gaseous monomer in the vicinityof the transient chain radicals, and thereby brightens the propect of obtaining high molecular weight for the polymer product. Higher temperature, however, tends to lowr molecular weight.

A pressure of the range of 1500-2000 atm is obtained by compressing refined ethylene, usually in two or three successive stages. For continuous operation, the reactants are passed through narrow-bore tubular reactors or stirred reactors, fitted with efficient heat-transformer system. Conversion In the ragne of 10-30% is normally achieved after which the unreacted monomer is flashed out and recovered and the viscous molten polymer is extruded out in the form of strands or ribbons, cooled and granulated.

In the conventional activation with oxygen, the formation of some unknown peroxide/hydroperoxide must be considered as the source that furnishes the radicals for chain initiation or subsequent decomposition, which apparently takes place fast enough only above 150°C. The heat of polymerization of ethylene (800-1000 cal/g) is considerably higher than that of other monomers, e.g., styrene (164 cal/g). In addition to many difficulties inherent in high pressure reactions, that control of temperature consequent to this high heat of polymerization is one of the most important problems in the polymerization of ethylene by the high pressure technique.

Chain branching (frequency, branch-length and distribution) as well as molecular weight and molecular weight distribution can be coveniently varied and controlled by varying the temperature , pressure, nature of inititator and its concentration and other additives such as solvents/non-solvents or suitable chain transfer agents, and by injecting the initiators at different points in the reactor.

High Density Polyethylene (HDPE)

Use of coordination catalysts or supported metal oxide catalysts allows polymerization of ethylene at a much lower pressure as well as at a relatively low temperature; the polymers thus produced are by the large linear, having much fewer branches than found in the product obtain by the high pressure free radical process. The HDPE synthesis is conveninetly done by (i) the Ziegler process using and aluminium trialkyl-$TiCl_4$ complex as the catalyst dispersed in a hydrocarbon solvent such as n-heptane and employing a slightly elevated pressure and temperature in the range of 70-100°C, (ii) the Phillips process, using CrO_3 (5%) supported on finely divided silica-alumina (75-90% silica) base as the catalyst; the catalyst is activated by heating to about 250°C, dispersed in a hydrocarbon solvent such as cyclohexane and polymerization of ethylene is done employing a pressure of 15-30 atm and a temperature in the range of 130-150°C, or (iii) the Standard Oil (Indiana) process using a dispersion of molybdenum oxide catalyst containing sodium and calcium metal or their hydrides as promoters in a hydrocarbon solvent, employing a pressure in the range of 49-80 atm and a temperature range of 220-250°C. The Ziegler process yields polymers of density of about 0.945 g/cm while density as high as 0.96 g/cm. On completion of reaction in the Ziegler process, the catalysts is destroyed using water or alcohol with traces of an acid and the polymer is collected by filtration or contrifugation, which is then washed and dried. The processes using metal oxide catalysts may be either fixed bed, moving-bed or slurry processes. On completion of the reaction, the polymer formed and evenly distributed in the paraffin or cycloparaffin diluent in the high reaction temperature is separated from the catalyst fragements and then recovered and isolated by cooling and/or solvent evaporation.

Structure and Properties of Polyethylenes

The differences in the density range of LDPE and HDPE as mentioned earlier have their origin in the inherent difference in the mechanistics which are consequential in giving rise to significant structural differences in these polymers. The structural differences relate to differences in molecular weight and molecular weight distribution and differences in degrees of chain branching in the main. Due to the high chain transfer (polymer transfer-"back biting" mechanism, Sec. 3.15.4) in the radical polymerization effected under high pressure, the resultant polymer, LDPE has nearly 20-50 branches (both long and short branches) per 1000 linear carbon atoms in the chain molecules.

The loss of molecular symmetry due to the high degree of 'branching results in lower density range (0.915-0.94 g/ cm^3) and lower softening or melting temperature (110-117°C) for LDPE. The low pressure polymers, HOPE, are by and large linear, having only 2-5 short branches or side chains per 1000 carbon atoms in the main chain, thus having a higher density range (0.945-0.96g/ cm^3) and higher melting temperature (125-130°C) compared to LDPE. The theoretical linear (unbranched polymer) polymethylene, —$(CH_2)_n$— as obtained from diazomethane $CH_2\langle\overset{N}{\underset{N}{\|}}$ using BF_3 - Et_20 catalyst at about O°C through elimination of N_2 on polymerization [$nCH_2N_2 \rightarrow (CH_2)n— + nN_2$] is, however, characterized by high molecular weight with a density as high as 0.98 g/ cm^3 and a melting temperature of 137°C.

Polyethylenes and other polyolefins are graded by what is known as the melt flow index (MFI), i.e., the weight in grams extruded by piston action through a standard opening under a standard load in a standard plastimeter at 190°C over a specified time period *(See also* Sec. 10.5). MFI gives a rough guide to processability of different grades of polymers of a given kind or monomeric origin. For a given kind of polymer, a higher MFI indicates lower molecular weight and vice versa. LDPE comes in a wide MFI range (0.3-70), but for HDPE, the useful MFI range is much lower (0.02-2.5). The tensile strength of LDPE ranges between 1500-2500 psi and that for HDPE is in the range of 3000-5000 psi. The Izod impact strength for LDPE is as high as 10 ft lb per inch of notch, while that for HDPE is much lower (1.5-5 ft lb per inch of notch).

Polyethylenes are chemically paraffinic in nature, inert to non-oxidizing acids, alkalies, water and many aqueous solutions and organic solvents. HDPE is usually more resistant to chemicals than LDPE. There is no singular solvent for polyethylenes at room temperature. LDPE dissolves in toluene at or above 60°C, while HDPE dissolves at temperatures about 20-30°C higher in the same solvent. With larger amorphous regions, LDPE is more permeable to gases than HDPE. Both LDPE and HDPE are prone to aerial oxidation, which is quite severe at processing temperatures. LDPE is more prone to oxidation than HDPE (if free from metallic impurities) in view of higher concentrations of tertiary hydrogen (at branch sites) in LDPE. Uncontrolled oxidation leads to measurable incorporation of carbonyl and peroxy groups which make the polymer more prone to degradation and embrittlement due to absorption of heat and UV light. Polyethylenes generally show poor environmental stress cracking resistance, LDPE being poorer in this respect than HDPE. However, improved processing conditions and better design result in low stresses being imparted to products, thus ensuring desired long service life and performance for them. The stress cracking problem is less critical with relatively high molecular weight (relatively low MFI) and high density materials.

Polyethylenes are very good insulating materials and in this respect they compare favourably with other dielectric materials. Being adequately flexible, LDPE is extensively used as an insulator in wires and cables.

Uses and Applications of Polyethylenes

Polyethylenes, being thermoplastic in nature, are conveniently processed by injection moulding, blow moulding, rotational moulding, extrusion and thermoforming techniques. They find extensive uses and applications as moulded or formed objects, films, sheets, bottles and containers, pipes and tubes, and in wire insulation and cables. Films, commonly made from LDPE, find application in packaging, waterproofing, irrigation and water management including canal lining and mulching, and in coating and lamination. Various additives such as fillers, pigments and colouring matters, antioxidants, slip additives, anti-block and antistatic agents, UV -absorbers, blowing agents and flame retardants are mixed or blended with polyethylene, polypropylene and other polyolefins for various reasons. For high voltage cables application and for heat resistant films or moulded objects, polyethylene is preferably cross-linked using selected chemical cross-linking agents, such as peroxides or by irradiation with high speed electrons or Y-rays. Factors contributing to widespread application of polyethylenes are low cost, easy process ability by variety of techniques, excellent chemical inertness and electrical insulation properties, low temperature toughness and flexibility, good clarity of thin films, heat sealability, non-toxic nature and low water vapour permeability. The major limiting factors in this respect are low softening point or heat distortion temperature, proneness to environmental stress cracking, poor scratch resistance, low tensile strength and high gas permeability.

Chlorosulphonated Polyethylene

The high molecular symmetry of polyethylene (LDPE) may be broken by treating the polymer with chlorine in presence of small quantity of sulphur dioxide, thereby introducing some $-So_2\,Cl$ groups and -Cl atoms along the polymer chain as shown in the reaction scheme (2.2).

$$\sim CH_2-CH_2-CH_2-CH_2 \sim + SO_2 + Cl_2$$

$$\rightarrow -\!\!\left[\left[(CH_2)_n-\underset{|\atop Cl}{CH}\right]_2-CH_2-\underset{|\atop SO_2Cl}{CH}\right]_y- \qquad (2.2)$$

Random introduction of chlorine atoms in the chain to the extent of one chlorine atom for at least seven carbon atoms *($n \geq 6$)* gives a useful rubbery product. For an average product, $x = 12$. The SO_2Cl groups provide sites for cross-linking or vulcanization. The vulcanization is conveniently done with certain metal oxides such as PbO as shown in the reaction scheme (8.3). This polyethylene-derived rubber is popularly known as 'Hypalon' in the trade.

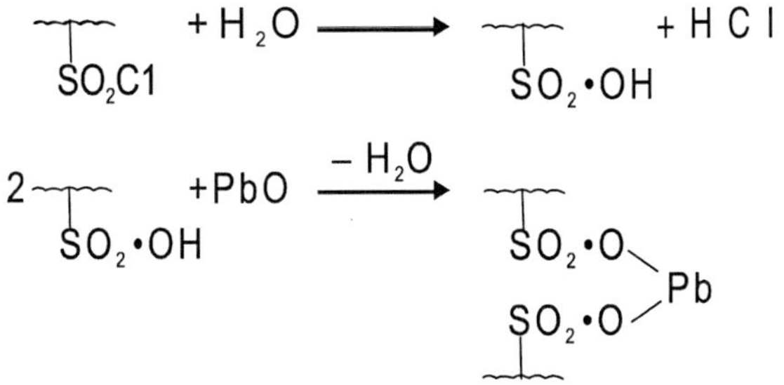

The chlorosulphonated polyethylene (CSP) rubbers are superior to many hydrocarbon (diene) rubbers in ozone resistance. They are also among the best chemical-resistant rubbers and have good resistance to heat-aging and flexing.

Chlorination of polyethylene to different degrees (up to about 40% chlorine) is also practised to obtain different products-thermoplastic or elastomeric. The reaction is carried out at an elevated temperature in solution or in suspension using either LDPE or HDPE. With HDPE, chlorination in aqueous suspension at or above 120°C gives a convenient elastomer that can be vulcanized by peroxides.

3

Linear Low Density Polyethylene (LLDPE)

The understanding of a link between different kinds and degrees of branching and different ranges of densities as exemplified by LDPE and HDPE has led to the more recent development of a mechanistically linear polyethylene of a low density range by a copolymerization approach. The product, a linear copolymer of ethylene and a minor proportion of an α-olefin such as l-butene, l-hexene or l-octene, appears as a branched polyethylene having controlled proportions of uniform short chain branching along the chain. Uniform short branches appear in the chain at each point of the α-olefin comonomer incorporation. This linear grade of polyethylene, having a low density range (0.915-0.934 g/ cm^3) is commonly known as Linear Low Density Polyethylene (LLDPE) and it can be synthesized employing the Ziegler process or the Phillips process.

Structurally, LDPE and HDPE may also be considered, as copolymers of ethylene and minor proportions of α-olefins, in view of the presence of significant long and short branches in LDPE and very limited short branches in HDPE. While LDPE and HDPE, if so considered as copolymers, are copolymers by incidence and not by definition or design, LLDPE has the distinction of being a copolymer primarily by definition and design.

LLDPE displays a superior balance of toughness, stiffness, stress cracking resistance and electrical properties over LDPE. With favourable production economics and progressive acceptability in the market, LLDPE may soon take over up to 30-50% of the traditional LDPE market throughout the world.

There are significant differences between the rheological behaviours of LDPE and LLDPE which pose some resistance towards acceptance of LLDPE by many LDPE end product manufacturers. It is, however, most likely that on grounds of superior performance, most non-film applications of LDPE will finally switch over to LLDPE. Judicial blends of LDPE and LLDPE are also being developed for various applications. The melting points of commercial grades of LLDPE are in between the melting points of commercial LDPE and HDPE.

4

Polypropylene

The polypropylene of commerce is isotactic polypropylene. Its synthesis became possible through the commercial utilization of coordination polymerization during 1957-60. Propylene, the monomer, is obtained from the cracking of petroleum products (nlatural gas, light oil or naphtha). The separation of propylene from propane in the C_3 fraction is difficult and is achieved by fractional distillation in a carefully designed distillation plant. Propylene of high purity is required for polymer synthesis.

Synthesis of Polypropylene

The synthetic approach for polypropylene is much the same as that for the production of HDPE by the Ziegler process. The same reactor can be used to polymerize ethylene, propylene or other α-olefins with some modifications, if necessary. For propylene, the reaction condition should be so chosen as to overwhelmingly favour formation of the isotactic polymer. The catalyst may be prepared from $TiC1_4$ and aluminium triethyl combination dispersed in naphtha. Propylene is charged into the reactor under pressure. Nearly 80-85% conversion is achieved in 8-10 h at 60°C. The reaction variables are molar ratio of catalyst components, catalyst concentration, reaction temperature and monomer pressure. Hydrogen may be used as a chain terminating or transfer agent for control of molecular weight.

About 3-10% atactic polymer is also formed along with the formation of the isotactic polymer in the main. After the reaction reaches 80-85% conversion stage, the ingredients are transferred into a flash drum to purge off the unreacted monomer which is then recycled. The atactic product is soluble in the solvent naphtha. The solution is decanted off after centrifugation whereby most of the atactic material is removed. The residue is then treated with methanol acidified with traces of HCl to decompose and dissolve the catalyst. The polymer is then centrifuged, washed, dried and collected.

Structure and Properties of Polypropylene

Polypropylene (PP) is the lightest homopolymer known, its density being 0.90 g/ cm^3. With a rigid, short methyl group attached to every alternate carbon atom in the linear molecular chains and the highest order of steric regularity (isotactic), polypropylene, as commercially produced, is comparatively more rigid, stiff and stronger than HDPE. Its melting point is nearly 45-50°C higher than the melting point of HDPE. Having a much higher concentration of tertiary carbon atoms in its chains, PP is much more prone to oxidation or aging than HDPE and LDPE.

Commercial PP is nearly 90-97% isotactic. The degree of isotacticity or the isotactic index is given by the percentage of the polymer that is insoluble in *n*-heptane. Isotactic PP is much less crystalline than HDPE. The high melting point (≥170°C) of PP allows the moulded objects to be steam sterilized. Its high strength (tensile strength: 4500-5500 psi, elongation at break 100-300%), high melting point and low density is advantageous in many applications. PP, however, becomes brittle close to 0°C. In this respect, PP is inferior to polyethylene. But PP has a much superior hinge property. The problem of brittleness is very well overcome by block copolymerization of propylene with minor proportions (5-15%) of ethylene. PP is generally free from environmental stress cracking problems. Its specific heat is lower than that of polyethylene but higher than that of polystyrene. PP melt is more non-Newtonian than polyethylene melt. The melt viscosity of PP is also more sensitive to change of temperature. It is also graded by melt flow index for processing purposes. Generally, PP shows lower moulding shrinkage than polyethylene. If free from catalyst fragments, PP and polyethylene are similar in electrical properties.

PP exhibits higher clarity (less opacity) than HDPE, mainly because the amorphous and crystal densities are closer for PP than for polyethylene. Biaxially oriented polypropylene (BOPP) shows a high degree of clarity and biaxial stretching also produces polymers of much improved tensile strength. PP is used in the form of moulded and formed objects, sheets and films, bristles, monofilaments and fibres, covering such items as luggage, frames containers and different packaging items, ropes, textiles, tows and nets, pipes and tubes, etc. Typical mouldings also include components of automobile and home appliances industry, machine parts and components, sterilizable health-care and hospital equipment, kitchenware, furniture, etc.

New Generation Polyolefins

Polyolefins, viz. polyethylene (PE~ polypropylene (PP) and higher poly(a-olefins) and olefin copolymers are commercially produced by chain polymerization of selected monomers or monomer combinations. The exact mechanism of polymerization, rate of polymerization, polymer microstructure, molecular weight and molecular weight distribution very much depend on the nature of the olefin monomer, catalyst, co-catalyst, temperature and pressure and also on the nature of other additives such as hydrogen as chain transfer agent or chain length regulator, solvents and comonomers. Free radical catalysts such as organic peroxides on the one hand and selected (supported) metal oxide catalysts ($Cr0_3$, $Mo0_2$ etc.) or some transition metal halide ($TiCl_4$/$TiCl_3$) catalysts along with a selected aluminium alkyl acting as a co-catalyst forming what is known as the Ziegler-Natta catalysts on the other, are most commonly used for olefin polymerization so far.

Today, metallocene catalysts are drawing the attention of all concerned with production and use of polyolefins, in view of overwhelming advantages that they offer in terms of much higher rate of polymerization, uniform structure and uniform polymer melt-rheology in view of the polymer having substantially narrower molecular weight distribution. Metallocene catalysts are based on Zr /Ti complexes with organic ligands such as the cyclopentadienes (Cp) in conjunction with aluminoxanes (oxyaluminium compounds). Characteristically, metallocenes are single site catalysts (SSC) providing nearly 100% active sites against only 1-3% active sites for the conventional Ziegler-Natta catalyst systems, indeed providing a tremendous improvement in catalyst activity. Metallocene catalyzed processes much like the Ziegler-Natta catalyzed processes, are also low-pressure polymerization of ethylene, propylene and other a-olefins, though of higher sophistication in many respects.

The mechanism of formation of the active species in the metallocene catalyst system comprising, say, cyclopentadienyl (Cp) metal (M = Ti or Zr) halide (X), structure I, and methyl aluminoxane, structure (II) may be schematically shown as:

Gas phase, slurry and solution processes have been in practice for industrial polymerization of ethylene and higher olefins. The gas phase

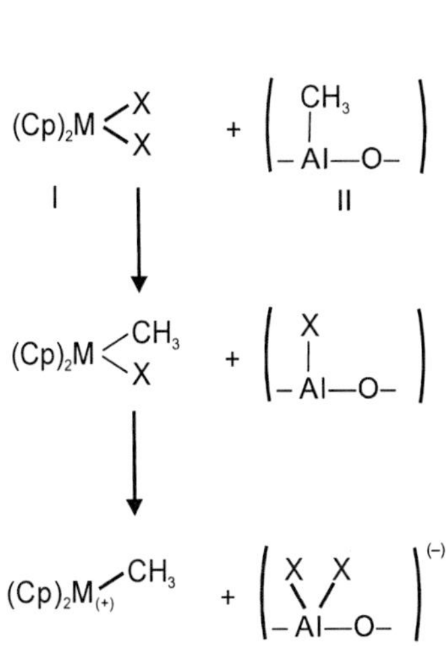

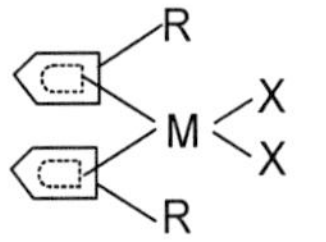

$(Cp)_2M$

I

processes are usually more versatile. Low density polyethylene (LDPE) of density range 0.91-0.94 g/ cm^3 are produced by the high pressure process of two types, viz. tubular process and autoclave process; the tubular and autoclave processes are almost similar except the reactor type and pressure requirement. Pressure requirement in the autoclave reactor (continuous stirred tank reactor, CSTR) is usually lower than that employed in the tubular reactor. Depending on the particular product to be manufactured, measured doses of selected free radical (peroxide) catalysts, assorted co monomers and modifiers such as hydrogen, if required, are also to be fed to the high pressure rectors along with ethylene monomer.

Slurry phase polymerization encompasses the largest group of HDPE technologies. Excellent temperature control is a major advantage of the slurry process. However, for the production of LLDPE, by using an α-olefin comonomer (3-6%) along with ethylene as the bulk monomer, swelling of the copolymer produced in the slurry medium may pose some problem causing lowering of polymer production rate and in its density range. Long jacketed loop reactors and continuous stirred tank reactors are most widely used for slurry polymerization that is commonly operated at 30-40 atm pressure and at 85-110°C temperature.

Solution phase processes have some distinctive advantages over slurry processes in that the molecular weight distribution (MWD) can be better controlled along with easy control of the process variables in the inherent homogeneous phase. High polymerization temperature also permits high reaction rates and high polymer throughputs in the reactor. The solution process tends to produce polymers of relatively wide density range and high melt index. A pressure of 100 atm and a temperature of Isoac are commonly maintained in the solution (CSTR) process. Because of the short residence time and high polymer concentration, reactors of smaller size, including tubular reactors put in series or parallel to the CSTR, may be used for control of MWD of the relevant HDPE or LLDPE products.

The distinctive advantage of the gas phase polymerization process is the elimination of polymer separation, diluent recovery or handling and polymer drying steps. The gas phase process is also not constrained by solubility, swelling and viscosity characteristics but it suffers from the disadvantages like limitation of reaction operating temperature to resin softening point, agglomeration of polymer particles due to generation of local hot spots and heat transfer limitation etc.

Polyolefin synthesis is slowly changing from a semi-empirical art to an exact science due to improved understanding of nature of active centres, stereoregulating mechanisms, control of polymer architecture including monomer sequence distribution." and process parameter-polymer composition-product properties relationship.

Bimodal and broad MWD LLDPEs are commonly produced in a low pressure gas phase process at a much lower cost than that of the high cost high-pressure LDPE process. Often LLDPE penetration into LDPE market is constrained by its performance deficiencies in respect of clarity and in extrusion coating. The gas phase higher a-olefin (Octene-l) LLDPE holds high promise in respect cost-performance benefit. These new LLDPEs will not only expand the total market of low-pressure, polyethylene (HDPE) but also take a larger market share of the high pressure product, LDPE.

Metallocene based new (third) generation polyolefin technology has the potential to provide a much better control over chain length, chain branching, tacticity, compositional homogeneity and MWD, all resulting in improved / controlled rheology and morphology of the product polymers and copolymers so produced. The new generation polyolefin manufacturing processes (slurry, bulk or solution and gas phase) using high performance catalyst systems have improved the reactor productivities by two to three fold (showing scope for even higher productivities) and substantial increase in manufacturing capabilities for specific product grades. Binary random copolymers and di, tri or quadri block or random copolymers providing wide scope for improvements in product properties and processing characteristics have been developed and further refinements are in the process of development. Metallocene based technology had its beginning in the early nineties and it is still in the process of development and is expected to change the polyolefin scenario in the new millennium. It is likely to be further extended to polymerization of vinylic and diolefinic monomers too.

Newly developed metallocene based LLDPE has a characteristically narrow molecular weight distribution and the potentiality of higher comonomer incorporation compared to LLDPE produced by the Ziegler-Natta and Chromium catalysts. The metallocene LLDPE exhibits a lower and sharper melting point, better hot tack and improved heat-seal, clarity and impact properties. Narrow MWD, however, may pose *Some* processing difficulties which are meticulously overcome by controlled incorporation of a higher α-olefin (providing longer branches).

Metallocene based polypropylene (PP) synthesis offers option to change each property of the polymer on molecular level, independent of each other, and also enabling synthesis of syndiotactic PP that is not obtained by supported titanium based Ziegler-Natta catalysts. Elastomeric PP consisting blocks of atactic and isotactic stereosequences can be synthesized through unprecedented control over the microstructures. The liquid-pool) using liquefied propylene) and gas-phase PP processes are not only advantageous on account of productivity and production economy, they are also advantageous due to elimination of catalyst residue and atactic removal steps.

Reactor-made polyolefin alloy is an important area of commercial relevance and significance due to its better performance characteristics compared to blends / alloys made by post-reactor blending processes. The reactor PP alloys are made by repeated sequential introduction of different monomers during polymerization of propylene. The properties of such polyolefin alloys are controlled by the chemical structure and physical state of the different phases provided by the sequential blocks. These products are commercially produced on small scales by what is known as the Catalloy process. These novel flexible, tough and impact resistant clear PP based alloy resins are developed to compete with non-olefinic (plasticized) polymers, such as poly(vinyl chloride). Use of styrene in sequential monomer addition in the Catalloy process along with propylene may produce polymer alloys with higher heat. distortion temperatures, stiffness and chemical resistance. Such polyolefinic resins are viewed as suitable competitors of polyamides, polyacetals polyphenelene oxide and polycarbonates. Future developments are aimed at working of computer controlled swing reactors enabling production of HDPE, LLDPE and random or block copolymers of ethylene, propylene and higher olefins using a single reactor by appropriately changing feed monomer, catalyst, solvent and other additives and manipulating physical process parameters.

5

Copolymers of Ethylene

Among the copolymers of ethylene, those between ethylene and propylene and between ethylene and vinyl acetate have reached a stage of widespread development and application. Other important copolymers involving ethylene and some other α-olefin such as l-butene, include the wide range of linear low density polyethylene (LLDPE). The α-olefin copolymers are produced by the Ziegler or Phillips process, while copolymers of ethylene with vinyl acetate, maleic anhydride and acrylate monomers and industrially produced by radical polymerization.

Stereo block copolymers of propylene and ethylene (4-15% ethylene) show improved impact properties. Though copolymeric in nature, they are essentially considered as polypropylenes of minor chemical modifications. When the two monomers are used in nearly equal or 60 : 40 proportions, products commonly known as ethylene-propylene rubbers (EP rubbers) are formed on copolymerization. EP rubbers are more aging resistant than diene rubbers, being devoid of unsaturations and they are conveniently vulcanized by peroxides, e.g., dicumyl peroxide. Carbon black is used with EP rubber to develop moderate to high tensile strength and moctulus. Low dose of sulphur (0.3 phr) is often used along with a peroxide (23 phr) as the curative and Ca-stearate is preferred to stearic acid as the activator.

Ethylene vinyl acetate (EVA) copolymers are available in different grades varying in vinyl acetate (VA) content (3-48%). Those containing low V A content (3-5%), are considered as modified low density polyethylenes. Their high surface tack, disadvantageous in conventional film applications, is taken advantage of in meat packaging as stretch films as well as for cling-wrap purposes. In higher vinyl acetate compositions, EVA copolymers are used as wax additives, wax coatings, hot melt adhesives and elastomers. Selected grades of hydrolyzed EVA, commonly designated as EVOH, offer excellent barrier properties with respect to gas (oxygen) permeability.

Copolymerization of ethylene with carboxylic monomers such as maleic anhydride, methacrylic acid, etc., by the high pressure process produces materials which are used as thermosetting materials but processed like thermoplastics. When treated with metal salts, oxides or alkoxides (Zn, Ca, Mg, etc), ionic (metal carboxylate) cross-links, stable under ambient conditions, are readily established. The ionic crosslinks get weakened with rise in temperature and their influence disappears at the processing (melting) temperatures, thus permitting reshaping. On cooling after reshaping, the ionic cross-links are regrouped and reformed and the thermosetting character reappears. Such polymers with “meltable” cross-links are known as “ionomers”.

6

Polystyrene

Monomer Synthesis

Polystyrene is another high tonnage, general purpose thermoplastic polymer. The monomer, styrene, or vinyl benzene, $CH_2 = CH{\cdot}C_6H_5$ is made from benzene and ethylene in two steps. The first step involves alkylation of benzene (formation of ethyl benzene) through reaction with ethylene in the presence of a Friedel-Crafts Catalyst such as $AlCl_3$.

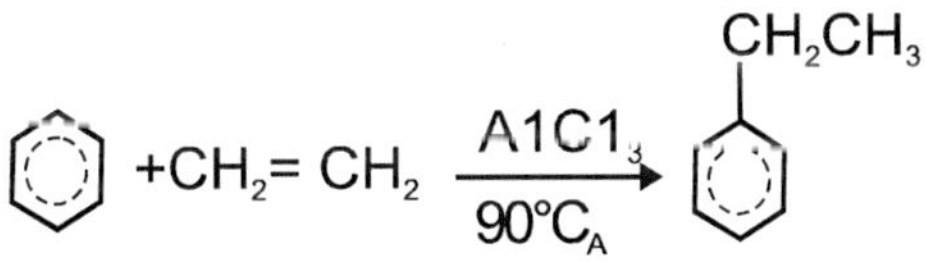

(6.1)

In a subsequent step, ethyl benzene is dehydrogenated to styrene by heating its stream over iron oxide or magnesium oxide catalyst at about 600°C. Styrene, isolated from the dehydrogenation product by distillation, is stabilized by addition of traces of a phenolic stabilizer, such as t-butyl catechol and then stored in a cold storage for longer shelf-life.

Polymerization of Styrene

Polymerization of styrene is mostly done following the bulk polymerization or suspension polymerization techniques. The bulk polymerization is done in two stages. In the first stage, the stabilizer-free monomer containing dissolved initiator is allowed to polymerize at about 80°C in one or more "prepolymerizer" batch reactors, each fitted with an efficient stirrer and an outer jacket for circulation of heat transfer fluid until a conversion of about 30% is reached. The viscous monomerpolymer mixture is then forced into the top of a tower reactor (nearly 25-40 ft in height and 10-15 ft in diameter) which is fitted with heating and cooling jackets and coils for external and internal control of temperatures respectively. The temperature down the tower changes from 100°C at the top to nearly 180-200°C at the bottom. The melt containing polystyrene and traces of the monomer passes through an extruder at the bottom from which it emerges as narrow strands or filaments which are then cooled, granulated and packed.

Structure and Properties of Polystyrene

Commercial polystyrene is a radically initiated linear atactic polymer. It is amorphous and transparent. It comes in different grades such as general purpose grade, high molecular weight grade and heat resistant grade. Removal of last traces of unreacted monomer (from 5-0%) improves the softening point or heat distortion temperature from nearly 70°C to about 100°C. The polymer is hard, brittle and transparent at room temperature. It is soluble in aromatic hydrocarbon solvents, cyclohexane and chlorinated hydrocarbons. The polymer has a density of 1.054 g/ cm^3, a refractive index of 1.59-1.60 and a *Tm* value of 240°C. It sounds like metal when dropped. It decomposes at elevated temperature into a mixture of volatiles, a significant part of which is the monomer which can be identified from its characteristic smell *(See* Table 6.1).

Polystyrene, being hydrocarbon in nature, has very low moisture absorption; this feature coupled with its good mould ability, dimensional stability and low moulding shrinkage makes polystyrene an ideal polymer for injection moulding and for thermoforming. As a rigid thermoplastic, it has moderate tensile strength (6000-8000 psi) and very low elongation at break (1-3%). The major limitations of the polymer are its brittleness and very low impact strength (Izod 0.2-0.35 ft lb in-l notch) and low heat distortion temperature (~80°C).

Polystyrene has poor outdoor weathering resistance and a tendency to yellowing and crazing on long use. It possesses very good electrical insulation characteristics and a low dielectric loss factor at moderate frequencies.

Modification to High Impact Grades

There have been many attempts to improve impact properties of polystyrene, but those achieved through use of rubbery additives and through copolymerization approach have been commercially successful and widely practised. Rubber modified polystyrenes are used to nearly the same extent as straight polystyrene. Rubbers commonly in use for the purpose are styrene-butadiene rubber (25-30% styrene content) or simply polybutadiene rubber. Simple blending of the rubbery polymer with polystyrene done on two-roll mills or in the latex form brings only marginal improvements in impact strength. Much better improvements are achieved by polymerization of styrene in an emulsion of the rubbery polymer or in solution containing the rubbery polymer, through what may be termed as a graft copolymerization approach. To derive the best effect, the rubber used should be semicompatible with polystyrene and should have limited degrees of cross-linking. The rubber should be dispersed in fine discrete droplets within the polystyrene matrix, the rubbery phase comprising only 5-20% of the total volume of the resinrubber composite. Such high impact grade polystyrenes may have two to five times the impact resistance of straight polystyrene, but they exhibit nearly half the tensile strength and a much lower softening point. They also show inferior aging resistance and require stabilization through incorporation of adequate doses of antioxidant stabilizers.

Styrene-Acrylonitrile (SAN) Copolymers and ASS Resins

To obtain a styrene-based polymer of higher impact strength and higher heat distortion temperature at the same time, styrene is copolymerized with 20-30% acrylonitrile. Such copolymers have better chemical and solvent resistance, and much better resistance to stress cracking and crazing while retaining the transparency of the homopolymer at the same time. In many respects SAN copolymers are also better than poly(methyl methacrylate) and cellulose acetate, two other transparent thermoplastics.

ABS resins are terpolymers of acrylonitrile, butadiene and styrene, prepared by interpolymerization (grafting) of styrene and acrylonitrile on polybutadiene or through blending of SAN copolymers with butadiene-acrylonitrile (Nitrile) rubber. Impact improvement is far better if the rubber in the blend is lightly cross-linked. The impact resistance of ABS resins may be as high as 6-7 ft lb. per inch of notch.

Processing, Uses and Applications of Polystyrene

Polystyrene and related copolymers, terpolymers and blends are widely processed by injection moulding, blow moulding, thermoforming and extrusion techniques. Expanded polystyrene finds extensive use in packaging and shock absorbing applications, in thermal insulation and as acoustic improvers in halls and auditoria. Largest outlet of polystyrenes is in the packaging field. High impact grades are suitable for use as toys, games and sports articles, casings and cabinets for electrical electronic gadgets and equipments and inner liners of refrigerators. ABS resins have emerged as engineering plastics for toughness, strength and durability and are being increasingly used as housewares and as housings for domestic and industrial electrical equipment, automobile components, etc. Another major outlet of polystyrene is in the making of ion-exchange resins. For this, the polymer is produced in the cross-linked form by suspension polymerization technique using divinyl benzene (1-5%) as the comonomer. Modifications of the suspension resin beads by controlled sui phonation with concentrated H_2SO_4 produces cation-exchange resin. Chloromethylation of the resins with chloromethyl ether and their subsequent transformation into quaternary ammonium salts by treatment with tertiary amines followed by alkali treatment lead to the formation of anion-exchange resins.

7

Acrylic Plastics : Poly (Methyl Methacrylate)

Plastics based on acrylate and methacrylate monomers are commonly known as acrylic plastics. Most important among the acrylic plastics is poly(methyl methacrylate) prepared by the polymerization of methyl methacrylate. Monomer methyl methacrylate is prepared from acetone through the cyanohydrin route. The cyanohydrin is treated with 98% sulphuric acid in a cooled kettle to yield methacrylamide sulphate intermediate which on esterification with methanol produces methyl methacrylate. The synthetic route is shown in the reaction scheme (7.1).

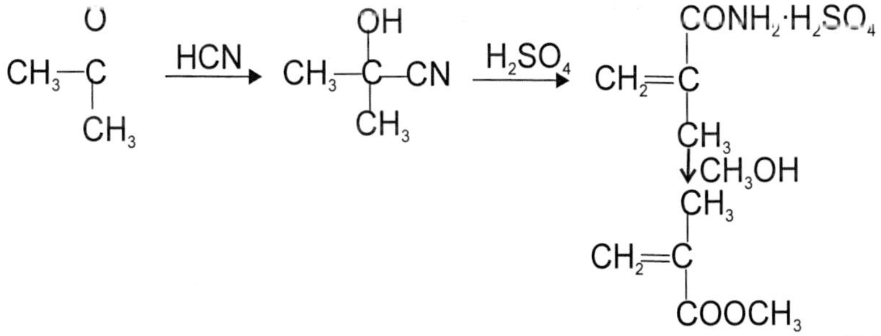

(7.1)

Moulding grade poly(methyl methacrylate) is made by bulk or suspension polymerization of the monomer, using peroxide or azonitrile initiators at about 100°C, preferably in the absence of air. For the production of cast sheets, the monomer is first converted into a prepolymer syrup of convenient viscosity and the syrup is then poured into the casting cell consisting of heat resistant, parallel, polished glass plates separated by rubber gaskets round the edges, and held together by spring loaded clamps or spring clips. Precautions must be taken to obtain sheets free of sink marks and voids. The cell is then gradually heated in a heating tunnel for 15-20h over a temperature zone of 50-100°C to complete the polymerization. Rods are made by polymerizing the syrup under pressure in vertical aluminium tubes, while tubes are prepared by polymerizing a calculated amount of syrup in an aluminium tube under nitrogen pressure, with its both ends closed. The assembly is heated as the tube is rotated horizontally at a constant rate, and the syrup polymerizes on the wall of the rotating tube. Natural shrinkage on polymerization enables easy removal of the casting.

A combination of excellent optical clarity (refractive index, 1.49), total lack of colour, some toughness and outstanding outdoor weathering behaviour makes poly(methyl methacrylate) very useful as automotive tail lamp and signal light lenses, jewellery, lenses of optical equipment and contact lenses. The polymer is very popular in display and advertisement applications; use in the building industry is also notable.

Minor proportions (5-25%) of different monomers such as n-butyl acrylate, 2-ethyl hexyl acrylate, methacrylamide, dimethyl aminoethyl acrylate, etc., are used to make coating grade poly(methyl methacrylate), usually by solution or emulsion techniques, for paints and enamel applications. Production of dentures is another important outlet of poly(methyl methacrylate). Poly(methyl acrylate) and poly(methyl methacrylate) may be saponified to form the polymeric acids which correspond to polymers of acrylic acid and methacrylic acid. They show characteristic/polyelectrolytic behaviour in aqueous solution. They are not suitable for use as formed or moulded objects, films, sheets, etc. As such or as sodium salts they are useful as thickening agents.

8

Acrylic Fibres

Fibres primarily based on polyacrylonitrile are known as acrylic fibres. Acrylonitrile monomer is produced by addition of HCN to acetylene or by dehydration of ethylene cyanohydrin formed by the addition of HCN to ethylene oxide. Acrylonitrile is a monomer which is a non-solvent for its polymer. Bulk polymerization turns out to be a case of heterogeneous polymerization and is associated with high heat generation and consequent to that, with hazards of violent explosion. The monomer is soluble in water to the extent of nearly 8% at room temperature and poly acrylonitrile of commerce is conveniently formed by heterogeneous aqueous polymerization of acrylonitrile using redox catalysts at or near room temperature. Thc polymer is obtained in the form of a fine precipitate.

Polyacrylonitrile, i.e., the homopolymer of acrylonitrile is unsuitable for many conventional thermoplastic applications as it suffers discolouration and infusibility on heating. It starts yellowing on heating and finally turns black, insoluble and infusible (Sec. 6.4.3). It is ordinarily insoluble in most common solvents. However, dimethyl formamide, dimethyl sulphoxide and tetramethylene sulphone are good solvents for the polymer. It also dissolves in aqueous concentrated solution of some salts. The polymer is dissolved in one of these solvents and then processed by wet or dry spinning techniques to produce the fibre.

To improve certain properties such as dyeability, feel and texture of the acrylic fibre, the polymer is prepared by copolymerizing 5-15% of one or more monomers, such as vinyl pyrrolidone, vinyl acetate, acrylates, acrylic/methacrylic acid, along with acrylonitrile. The incorporation of the comonomer units makes the fibre more suited for dyeing with many common dyes for textiles. Fibres from copolymers having much higher proportions (20-35%) of a comonomer, usually vinyl chloride and vinylidene chloride, are commonly known as modacrylic fibres.

The commercial acrylic fibres come in different colours and shades. They have outstanding weathering resistance. They also exhibit good resistance to chemicals, stains, insects and microorganisms. In bulkiness, feel and warmth, the acrylic fibres are very much similar to wool. They are widely blended with other fibres, particularly wool, to form various textile items.

9

Poly (Vinyl Acetate)

Vinyl acetate monomer is most conveniently prepared by catalytic addition of acetic acid to acetylene, which may be accomplished by a liquid-phase or a vapour-phase process. The vapour-phase synthesis is more in commercial practice and is accomplished by passing a mixture of acetylene and acetic acid through a reaction tube packed with such catalysts as cadmium acetate or zinc acetate at a temperature of 220-250°C. The monomer formed is purified by distillation.

$$CH{\equiv}CH + CH_3COOH \rightarrow \underset{\displaystyle OCOCH_3}{CH_2{=}\overset{}{CH}} \qquad (9.1)$$

Because of soft and gummy nature of poly(vinyl acetate), the polymer has poor dimensional stability. It rarely finds an application as moulded or formed objects and is seldom processed like common thermoplastics. The polymer is widely used in an emulsion form and hence, emulsion polymerization of vinyl acetate is widely employed for commercial purposes. The commercial emulsion polymerization is usually accomplished at a temperature of 50-70°C in a reactor with all provisions for temperature control. For desirable control of particle size and particle size distribution in the emulsion on latex and to regulate chain branching, a measured stream of the monomer and initiator is slowly and steadily added over a period of 3-4 h into the polymerization system and the polymerization is usually stopped after about 4-6 h.

Poly(vinyl acetate) as formed commercially is atactic in nature and hence amorphous and it is transparent if free from contaminants such as emulsifiers. It is soluble in benzene, acetone and chloroform. Poly (vinyl acetate) is also widely miscible with methanol. It finds widespread use as adhesives for wood, decorative laminates and related items and as a sizing material for paper and textiles; gum application (chewing gum) is also popular.

Polymers Derived from Poly (Vinyl Acetate)

Poly(vinyl acetate) is also used as the intermediate for the commercial production of (i) poly(vinyl alcohol) and (ii) poly(vinyl acetals). The monomer, vinyl alcohol, does not exist in the free state and all attempts to make it result in the formation of the stable tautomer, acetaldehyde.

$$CH_2{=}\underset{\displaystyle OH}{\underset{|}{CH}} \rightarrow CH_3{-}\underset{\displaystyle O}{\underset{|}{CH}} \qquad (9.2)$$

(i) ***Poly(vinyl alcohol)*** Poly (vinyl alcohol) is prepared by the alcoholysis of poly(vinyl acetate) as shown in reaction (9.3). The process is often inappropriately termed as "hydrolysis". Methanol is preferred over ethanol for the alcoholysis which is better carried out with alkaline catalysts (NaOH, $NaOCH_3$, etc.) than with acidic catalysts. The process is accomplished much quicker < 1 h) at a higher temperature (say, 60°C) than at or near room temperature (6-8 h at 20-25°C). The average degree of polymerization of poly(vinyl alcohol) is considerably lower than that of the parent poly(vinyl acetate) because the alcoholysis process splits the branch units formed via the acetate groups.

$$\left[CH_2{-}CH(OCOCH_3) \right]_n + nCH_3OH \rightarrow \left[CH_2{-}CH(OH) \right]_n + n\, CH_3{-}\underset{\displaystyle O}{\underset{\|}{C}}{-}OCH_3 \qquad (9.3)$$

Polymers with a degree of alcoholysis close to or higher than 85% (85% or more of the acetate groups of poly(vinyl acetate) transformed into alcohol (OH) groups) are readily soluble in water. For polymers with >90% of the substituents transformed into OH groups by alcoholysis, water-solubility follows a falling trend with increasing degree of alcoholysis.

Poly (vinyl alcohol) is normally unsuitable as a material for thermoplastic applications. It tends to decompose before melting, liberating moisture and forming chain unsaturations. Extended heating leads to discolouration and insolubilization.

Readily water soluble poly (vinyl alcohols) are made by keeping the degree of alcoholysis in the range of 80-90% and they find widespread use as thickening agents for aqueous suspensions and emulsions. Films obtained from them are useful as water-soluble packages. Tubular film forming technology has been developed for poly(vinyl alcohol). As a polyol, it behaves as a nonionic surfactant and is extensively used as a stabilizer in suspension and emulsion polymerization. It is also variously useful as a binder, adhesive and sizing agent in ceramic, paper and textile industry. Poly (vinyl alcohol) in the form of a warm aqueous solution may be wet spun into a concentrated aqueous salt (Na_2SO_4) solution containing known proportions of H_2SO_4 and formaldehyde whereby it is insolubilized through formation of formal groups and drawn into a stable fibre. Establishment of limited cross-linking through formaldehyde helps in optimizing the shrinkage property of the fibre. The fibre is useful as a textile material with washability and quick drying properties.

(ii) *Poly(vinyl acetals)* Poly(vinyl acetals) are products of interaction between poly(vinyl alcohol) and various aldehydes. Products based on reactions involving formaldehyde, acetaldehyde, propionaldehyde and butyraldehyde are separately known as poly(vinyl formal), poly(vinyl acetal), poly(vinyl propional) and poly(vinyl butyral) respectively. Reactions usually involve condensation between 1,3-hydroxyl groups of poly(vinyl alcohol) and the aldehyde molecules. Besides containing the acetal structures formed,

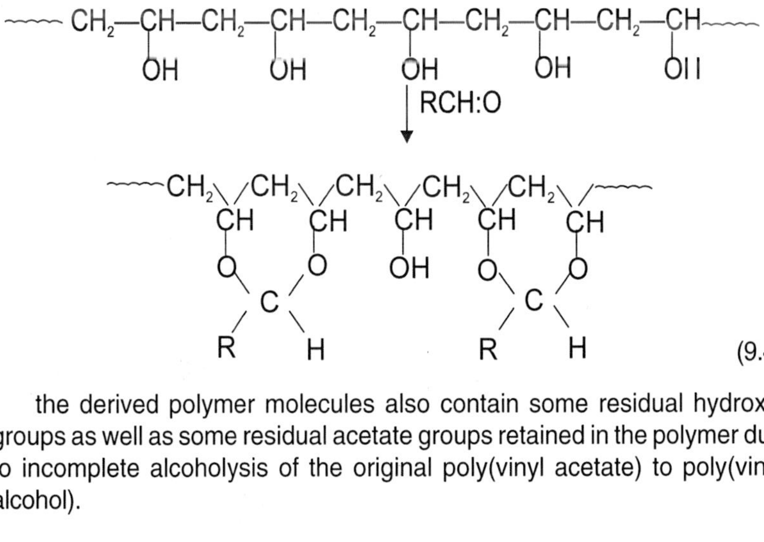

(9.4)

the derived polymer molecules also contain some residual hydroxyl groups as well as some residual acetate groups retained in the polymer due to incomplete alcoholysis of the original poly(vinyl acetate) to poly(vinyl alcohol).

Among the poly(vinyl acetals), only poly(vinyl butyral) is important considering commercial aspects. It finds extensive use as safety glass interlayer, particularly because of its outstanding clarity, toughness, photostability, moisture insensitivity and exceptional adhesion to glass. The polymer may be prepared by the direct process from poly(vinyl acetate); but for safety glass purposes it is most conveniently prepared from poly(vinyl alcohol). The catalyst most commonly used is H_2SO_4. If the reaction is done using aqueous solution of poly(vinyl alcohol) and butyraldehyde to give a homogeneous system to begin with, poly(vinyl butyral) precipitates out as it is formed. On the other hand, if one begins with an initial inhomogeneous system, i.e. a suspension of poly(vinyl alcohol) in water-ethanol mixture and requisite proportions of butyraldehyde and H_2SO_4 catalyst, one obtains a homogeneous solution at the completion of the reaction. Poly(vinyl butyral) is precipitated from the solution by addition of water under stirring conditions, washed and dried. For safety glass application, about 25% of the hydroxyl groups are usually left unreacted, and about 30-40 wt.% of a plasticizer, such as dibutyl sebacate or triethylene glycol di-2-ethyl butyrate, are commonly used.

10

Poly (Vinyl Chloride)

Poly(vinyl chloride), commonly named as PVC, is the most important of the vinyl thermoplastics considering volume of production and fields of application, the commercial products ranging from very rigid to very flexible items. The polymer is highly unstable when thermally treated at the processing temperatures and it is due to the discovery of a variety of heat stabilizers that the prospect of PVC technology became very bright and the technology reached its present height of success.

Preparation of Vinyl Chloride

Vinyl chloride monomer (CH_2 – CH. Cl) is being synthesized throughout the world on commercial scales mainly according to the following processes employing (1) acetylene, and (2) ethylene as the immediate organic raw materials. Main processes developed and in practice are:

(i) hydrochlorination of acetylene,

(ii) chlorination of ethylene to ethylene dichloride (EDC) and thermal cracking of the latter to vinyl chloride and hydrogen chloride,

(iii) the byproduct hydrogen chloride in process (ii) can be utilized in: (a) hydro chlorinating acetylene to produce more vinyl chloride straight away, or (b) in oxychlorinating more ethylene to produce EDC, and

(iv) mixed gas process starting with a dilute mixed stream of acetylene and ethylene.

Historically, vinyl chloride is definitely an acetylene derivative and as late as 1965, more than 45% of all vinyl chloride produced was still based on acetylene derived from coal via calcium carbide or from petroleum sources. However, the technology later shifted overwhelmingly in favour of ethylene.

The earliest route to vinyl chloride (VC) was from acetylene and HCl. In a typical synthesis

$$CH \equiv CH + HCl \rightarrow CH2 = CH{\cdot}Cl \tag{10.1}$$

dry hydrogen chloride free from chlorine is mixed with an equimolar proportion of dry acetylene and the mixture is then passed through a multitubular reactor packed with mercuric chloride catalyst on an activated carbon support. Temperature is maintained at 90-100°C. Vinyl chloride monomer formed is then purified and stored under nitrogen in stainless steel tanks.

As ethylene became more abundant, technology based on chlorination of ethylene to ethylene dichloride (EDC) and then cracking of EDC to vinyl chloride was developed. The byproduct HCl was recovered and utilized to make more vinyl chloride by reaction with acetylene.

$$CH_2{=}CH_2 \overset{C1_2}{} C1{\bullet}CH_2{-}CH_2 \bullet C1 \xrightarrow[500°C]{-HC1} CH_2{=}CHC1 \tag{10.2}$$

The next development was the so-called 'oxychlorination' process involving reaction of HCl with ethylene in presence of air (oxygen) to produce EDC. In a subsequent step,

$$CH_2{=}CH_2 + 2HC1 + \tfrac{1}{2}O_2 \xrightarrow{CuC1_2} C1 \cdot CH_2{-}CH_2.Cl + H_2O \tag{10.3}$$

the EDC is cracked to yield vinyl chloride and HCl. The byproduct HCl is recycled in the oxychlorination step.

Mixed gas processes based on cracking of naphtha to equimolar proportions of ethylene and acetylene have also been developed with the objective of total chlorine utilization. The mixture of the two is first reacted with HCl to form vinyl chloride, the reaction taking place between the acid and acetylene contained in the cracked gases. Vinyl chloride formed is separated from ethylene which is then chlorinated to EDC and then cracked to vinyl chloride and HCl. The mixed gas processes are competitive with the oxychlorination process.

Polymerization of Vinyl Chloride

Commercial polymerization is done by using free radical catalysts and employing bulk, suspension and emulsion techniques. Suspension and emulsion techniques are, however, most commonly employed.

Bulk polymerization is heterogeneous in view of insolubility of the polymer in the monomer. Peroxy dicarbonates are conveniently used as initiators in the bulk or suspension polymerization. Bulk polymerization may be done in rotating cylindrical reactors with tumbling steel balls inside to facilitate removal of heat of polymerization from the monomer-polymer heterogeneous system. The bulk polymerization may also be done in two stages as in the Pechiney-St. Gobain process to overcome the difficulties of heat removal and to have better control on molecular weight and particle size of the polymer. Suspension and emulsion polymerizations are done in stirred tank jacketed pressure vessels following approaches as described in Secs 4.11.3 and 4.11.4. For injection moulding, extrusion and calendering purposes, particularly for clear objects and for electrical insulation purposes, bulk and suspension grade PVC resins are used. Emulsion grades are utilized in organosols and plastisols and in some other areas, but they are unsuitable in insulation (wire and cable) industry because of the presence of traces of detergent or soap and other ionic components of the polymerization recipe in the isolated polymer (PVC).

Structure and Properties of PVC

Poly(vinyl chloride), PVC is by and large a linear polymer, colourless and thermoplastic in nature, and having a chlorine content of about 56.8%. The polymer is thermally unstable and extensive heating transforms it into a dark coloured residue resembling poly acetylene and liberating HCl as the volatile (Sec. 6.4.3). PVC is insoluble in all hydrocarbon solvents. Two of its important solvents are cyclohexanone and tetrahydrofuran. It is also soluble in ethylene dichloride and nitrobenzene. It possesses flame retardation and self-extinguishing characteristics. The polymer as produced commercially, is substantially amorphous in nature. Structural irregularities in the polymer arise due to occasional branching effect during polymerization and due to chain-end unsaturation consequent to termination by disproportionation. Technically, the polymer is graded on the basis of a solution viscosity parameter known as the K-value but not by melt viscosity or melt flow index, in view of its poor thermal stability.

Commercial polymers differ not only in molecular weight and molecular structure (degree of branching) but also in their particle characteristics such as porosity, shape, size and size distribution. The processing behaviour of the polymer is largely linked with these particle characteristics. In its massive form, PVC is a hard, horny, rigid material with a characteristic tendency to stick to metallic surfaces at elevated temperatures.

Compounding and Processing of PVC

PVC can be conveniently processed to rigid items if only it is compounded with stabilizers and lubricants. It is variously compounded with many other compounding ingredients such as fillers, plasticizers, extenders, and other process aids, impact improvers, colouring matters, etc.

Stabilizers of PVC protect it from measurable degradation at processing temperatures. Among the common stabilizers are basic lead salts such as basic lead carbonate, tribasic lead sulphate, dibasic lead phosphate, etc. Organo compounds of other metals used as stabilizers include those of cadmium, barium, calcium, zinc and tin, mostly in the form of phenates, octoates, benzoates and laurates. Some of them produce much improved effects in presence of phosphite antioxidants, such as trisnonyl phenyl phosphite. Organo-tin compounds are specially useful for producing (crystal) clear compounds and products.

All flexible applications of PVC depend on significant use of plasticizers; notable among them are the high boiling phthalates such as, dibutyl phthalate, dioctyl or diisooctyl phthalate, etc., and the phosphate plasticizers, such as trioctyl phosphate and tric{esyl phosphate. Chlorinated paraffin and the phosphate plasticizers are used in fire retardant compounds. Aliphatic esters such as dibutyl sebacate and dioctyl sebacate or adipate are specially useful for having compounds with high resilience and a low cold flex temperature.

Impact modification of rigid PVC is variously accomplished by blending with it different proportions of such polymers as nitrile rubber, ABS graft terpolymers, chlorinated polyethylene, selected polyacrylates, etc.

Compounded PVC is converted into moulded or formed objects by melt processing or by processing of PVC pastes and latices. Widespread processing techniques include injection moulding, extrusion, calendering, blow moulding and thermoforming. The processing of unplasticized (rigid) PVC is much more difficult and critical than that of plasticized PVC, primarily because of much higher temperature needed for the processing of the former at which measurable decomposition of the polymer occurs. However, trouble-free processing of rigid PVC can be done through judicious blending and compounding of lubricants, stabilizers (organotin compounds) and other process aids. Blending or compounding of different ingredients is conveniently accomplished by dry blending of powders, thus avoiding unnecessary heating in mills and mixers.

Applications of PVC

Both rigid and flexible applications of PVC have been developed. Rigid applications include chemical plants and equipments, storage tanks, building items, pipes, sheets, specific moulded objects and containers. PVC guttering and rain water piping, window frames and transparent roof sheeting are some of its building applications. Floor tiles and wall linings from plasticized PVC are also worthy of mention. Other flexible or semi-rigid applications include toys, packaging items, tubes, pipes and hoses, leather cloths, moulded objects, sheets, films, containers, footwear, belting, wire insulation and cables.

Copolymers of Vinyl Chloride

The processing temperature of PVC can be substantially lowered by plasticizer incorporation (external plasticization) or a comonomer incorporation (internal plasticization). Vinyl chloride-vinyl acetate (VC-V A) copolymers containing about 15% vinyl acetate can be processed at about 130-140°C. Gramophone records moulded from VC-V A copolymers are made from compositions containing only stabilizer, lubricant, pigment and sometimes an anti-static agent as the additives. The copolymer loaded with large proportions of filler and other essential ingredients finds significant use in flooring. Vinyl chloride copolymers with vinyl acetate (15%) or acrylonitrile (40%) as comonomers can be drawn into fibres. Copolymers of vinyl chloride (15%) and vinylidene chloride (85%) known as Saran in the trade have excellent chemical resistance including resistance to acids and alkalies and prominent self-extinguishing properties. Saran films (biaxially oriented) have excellent clarity, strength, toughness and water and gas impermeability. The copolymer can be conveniently drawn into a fibre. Saran fibres are suitable as filter cloths for filtering acidic, alkaline or corrosive chemicals.

11

Polytetrafluoroethylene (PTFE)

Among the fluorocarbon polymers, the use of polytetrafluoroethylene is relatively widespread and it is popular in certain specific areas of application. The monomer tetrafluoroethylene (bp - 76.3°C) is obtained by pyrolysis of monochlorodifluoromethane in contact with platinum at about 700°C. Monochlorodifluoromethane (bp 40.8°C) is obtained by reacting chloroform with hydrofluoric acid:

$$CHCl_3 + 2HF \rightarrow CHClF_2 + 2HCl \quad (11.1)$$

$$2CHClF_2 \rightarrow CF2{=}CF_2 + 2HCl \quad (11.2)$$

Commercial polymerization of tetrafluoroethylene is essentially aqueous polymerization accomplished by using free radical initiators (persulphate or hydrogen peroxide). An elevated pressure is maintained during polymerization. Polymer is obtained either in a granular form or in the form of a fine aqueous dispersion.

PTFE is essentially a linear polymer having a density of about 2.2 g/ cm^3. The properties of the polymer depend on its particle size and molecular weight. As manufactured; the polymer has a crystallinity> 93%. There are no solvents for it at room temperature. The degree of crystallinity of processed items depends much on the rate of cooling. Polymers of lower molecular weight are usually more crystalline. PTFE has a waxy feel and it is self-lubricant in nature, having a coefficient of friction lower than any other solid. Aerosol dispersions of low molecular weight PTFE are effective dry lubricants. PTFE shows a moderate tensile strength (2500-4000 psi) and excellent heat resistance, its melting point (*T*m) being 327°C. Its electrical insulation property, weathering resistance and chemical resistance are excellent.

Above melting point, the melt viscosity of PTFE is very high, so much so that the normal processing technology for thermoplastics is not applicable. For moulding, techniques similar to those employed in powder metallurgy or ceramic processing are used for PTFE. The process involves preforming the powder usually at room temperature under a pressure of 2000-8000 psi, sintering at 370°C and finally cooling. The dispersions can be used for casting films, dip coating, etc.

Major applications of PTFE are as seals, films, gaskets, laboratory equipments or components thereof, packings in pumps and valves, stopcocks, machine components, kitchenwares (non-stick PTFE coated pans), etc. and in electrical insulation and electronics. Its high volume cost is a constraint for its use for making large objects. Outstanding weather resistant and chemical resistant polymers are also obtained from polymerization and copolymerization of chlorotrifluoroethylene, vinyl fluoride, vinylidine fluoride and hexafluoropropylene.

12

Coumarone-Indene Resins

Coumarone and indene are two major constituents of the fraction boiling at 165-180°C obtained from fractionation of coal tar naphtha. Being aromatic in nature and bearing vinylic kind of structure attached to the aromatic ring, they closely resemble styrene. For resinification, they are polymerized in the crude naphtha without separation using sulphuric acid as the (ionic) catalyst. The commercial polymers or resins are obtained in the molecular weight range of 2000-2500, giving an average degree of polymerization of 20-25. The resins of different grades, from sticky and soft to hard and brittle, are commercially available. They are variously used as process-aids and property improvers in plastics and rubbers and in the formulation of coatings and adhesives. They are also useful as binders of different fibrous of particulate fillers, waxes, etc., for making hard thermoplastic floor tiles.

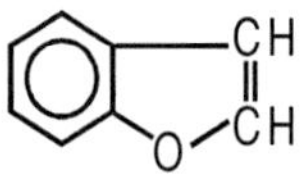

coumarone
bp 168-172°C

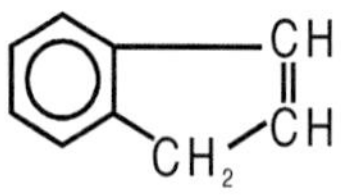

Indene
bp 182°C

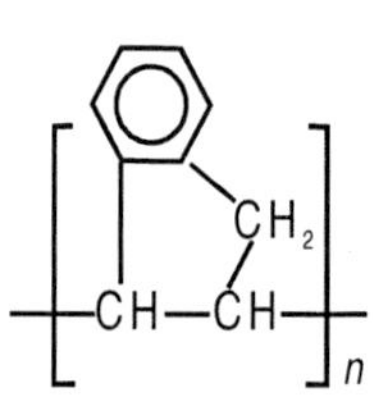

Polyindene

13

Polyacetals and Polyethers (Acetal Resins)

Hydrocarbon chain segments when interlinked with one another by (-0-) ether linkages give polymeric structures commonly known as polyethers. Polyoxymethylenes $-(-CH_2-O-)_n-$ or polyformaldehyde resins derived from formaldehyde are commonly referred to by the generic term acetal resins.

For polymerization purposes, formaldehyde of very high purity is required. Polymerization may be done by ionic mechanism in a dry inert solvent such as *n*-hexane or *n*-heptane over a wide range of temperature (–40 to +60°C). The polymer is formed under rapidly stirring conditions and is removed as a slurry. Catalysts used include Lewis acids, amines, phosphines, arsines and stibines. Heat stability of the polyoxymethylenes or the acetal resins is much improved by transforming OH end groups to acetate groups using acetic anhydride as the acetylating agent and sodium acetate as the catalyst (0.01% based on the anhydride) at about 140°C. Under these conditions acetylation is substantially complete in 5 min.

$$\sim\sim CH_2{-}P{-}CH_2{-}OH + (CH_3CO)_2O \rightarrow \sim\sim CH_2{-}O{-}CH_2OCOCH_3 + CH_3COOH \qquad (13.1)$$

Processes based on copolymerization of small amounts of ethylene oxide,

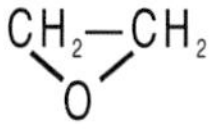 or 1,3-dioxolane 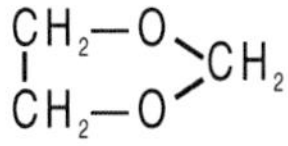 with formaldehyde have also been

commercially developed to produce thermally stable polyoxymethylenes or acetal resins. Occasional incorporation of molecules having two successive methylene groups make the polymers much less prone to degradation.

Due to their simple structures and linearity of the chains, the polyoxymethylenes are capable of crystallization just as the polyethylenes. In commercial polymers, copolymerization leading to thermal stability tends to reduce crystallinity. The density of acetal homopolymer is 1.425 g/ cm^3 while that of acetal copolymer is nearly 1.41 g/ cm^3, their crystalline melting points are nearly 180° and 160°C and tensile strengths are 10000 and 8000 psi respectively. They are considered as engineering polymers because of their high melting point and high mechanical properties and resistance to chemicals and common solvents at room temperature. They are processable like all other thermoplastics. Typical applications of acetal resins cover machine parts and components, automobile instrument panels, in the construction of pumps and pump housings, etc. The polymers are not generally suitable for use in strong acid, alkali or oxidizing chemicals. They are commonly used with the incorporation of small quantities of an antioxidant and a UV stabilizer. Their ease of fabrication, low coefficient of friction and good corrosion resistance and resistance to fatigue also make them suitable as engineering plastics.

$$CH_2-CH_2 \rightarrow -CH_2-CH_2-O-CH_2-CH_2-O- \xleftarrow{-H_2O} \underset{OH-OH}{\underset{|\quad\;\; |}{CH_2-CH_2}} \qquad (13.2)$$

Linear polyethers known as poly(ethylene oxides) are conveniently made by controlled ring opening polymerization of ethylene oxide or through polycondensation of ethylene glycol. Low molecular weight poly(ethylene oxides) of the molecular weight range 1,000-20,000 are greasy to waxy in appearance depending on molecular weight and they are readily soluble in water. High molecular weight grades (molecular weight >50,000) have melting points close to 66°C and tensile strength in the range of 1500-2000 psi. They can be processed like many thermoplastics. Poly(ethylene oxides) or poly(ethylene glycols) are particularly suitable for application requiring good water solubility together with very good to excellent film forming property. They are also used as textile sizes and thickening agents. Copolymers of epichlorohydrin and ethylene oxide are elastomeric in nature. Polyether from epichlorohydrin $\left(\overset{O}{\overbrace{CH_2-CH}}-CH_2\cdot Cl\right)$ is also elastomeric. These elastomers are conveniently vulcanized with the help of diamines or polyamines or by using lead oxides. They have good heat resistance, excellent ozone resistance, and good weathering resistance. The polyepichlorohydrins are noted for their good flame resistance.

14

Polyamides

Synthesis of linear polyamides can be made by polycondensation of bifunctional acids and amines or by polycondensation of amino acids of the type $\underset{\displaystyle H}{HOO\overset{}{C}RNH_2}$ or by ring opening polymerization of lactams of the type $(CH_2)_x\left\langle \begin{array}{l} CO \\ | \\ NH \end{array}\right.$ polyamides are commonly known in the trade by the generic term "nylon". Nylons from diacids and diamines are designated by code of two numbers, the first indicating the number of carbon atoms in a molecule of the diamine and the second indicating the number of carbon atoms in a molecule of the diacid (thus giving identity of the monomeric constituents). Polymers from amino acids or lactams are designated by a code of single number indicating the number of carbon atoms in a molecule of the amino acid or the lactam. Thus, the polyamide from caprolactam is known as nylon 6, that from hexamethylene diamine and adipic acid as nylon-66 or from hexamethylene diamine and sebacic acid as nylon 610. The polymer from ~ aminoundecanoic acid with 11 carbon atoms in its molecule is known as nylon 11.

Preparation of Poly(Hexamethylene Adipamide): Nylon 66

Nylon 66 or poly(hexamethylene adipamide) is synthesized by polycondensation of adipic acid and hexamethylene diamine. Adipic acid can be prepared by oxidation of cydohexane or cydohexanol either directly or via cydohexanone. Benzene is used as the starting material for the production of cyclohexane and cyclohexanol. The different routes of formation of adipic acid are shown in the reaction scheme (14.1). Hexamethylene diamine is conveniently prepared from adipic acid via adiponitrile as shown in the reaction sequence (14.2).

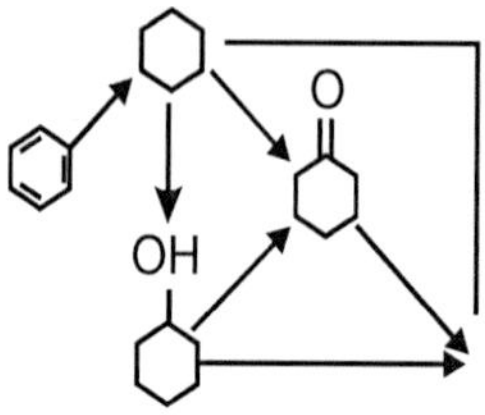

HOOC $(CH_2)_4$COOH (14.1)
Adipic acid

$$HOOC \cdot (CH_2)_4 \cdot COOH \xrightarrow{NH_3} NC \cdot (CH_2)_4 \cdot CN \xrightarrow{H_2} \underset{\text{hexamethylene diamine}}{H_2N \cdot (CH_2)_6 \cdot NH_2} \quad (14.2)$$

The first step during the synthesis of nylon 66 or poly(hexamethylene adipamide) is the formation of the nylon 66 salt. The adipic acid and the hexamethylene diamine are reacted in boiling methanol to the insoluble nylon 66 salt (mp 190°C) which precipitates out. The salt is then dissolved in water,

$$HOOC \cdot (CH_2)_4 \cdot COOH + H_2N \cdot (CH_2)_6 \cdot NH_2 \longrightarrow \underset{\text{nylon 66 salt}}{\begin{matrix} {}^{-}OOC \cdot (CH_2)_4 \cdot COO^{-} \\ H_3\overset{+}{N} \cdot (CH_2)_6 \cdot \overset{+}{N}H_3 \end{matrix}} \quad (14.3)$$

mixed with about 0.5-0.1 mole percent of acetic acid to act as the viscosity stabilizer, i.e., to limit the molecular weight, and pumped into an autoclave. The autoclave is closed and the temperature is raised to nearly 220°C. The steam generated purges the air and a pressure of nearly 250 psi is allowed to develop. After about 2 h the temperature is raised to 270-280°C and steam is bled off to maintain the pressure at 250 psi. Pressure is then reduced over a period of 1-2 h to the normal level. The molten polymer is then extruded out under nitrogen pressure through a valve at the bottom of the autoclave onto a water-cooled casting wheel forming ribbons which are then chipped into granules and stored. Nylon 610 is prepared by a similar technique via formation of the appropriate salt (mp 170°C).

Preparation of Nylon 6

Caprolactam is made from cyclohexanone oxime through reactions involving Backmann rearrangement. Nylon 6 or polycaprolactam may be made by a batch or continuous process. Caprolactam, water (acting as the catalyst) and traces of acetic acid (chain length regulator) are charged into a reactor and heated at 250°C under blanket of nitrogen for 10-12 h. Polycaprolactam formed remains in equilibrium with unreacted monomer (about 10%) which may be removed from the product by washing with water. For making large cast objects in particular, polymerization of caprolactam by ionic (chain) mechanism developed later may be employed.

Preparation of Nylon 11 and Nylon 12

Nylon 11 is prepared by self-polycondensation of co-amino undecanoic acid under melt condition at about 220°C. The- equilibrium ring-opening reaction of caprolactam during preparation of nylon 6 is easily catalyzed by water. In case of synthesis of nylon 12 from dodecyl lactam, temperature higher than 260°C is necessary for ring opening and almost 100% yield of high polymer is achieved as the condensation is not an equilibrium reaction.

Properties, Uses and Applications of the Nylon Polyamides

The nylons are polar, crystalline materials with excellent resistance to hydrocarbons. There are only a limited number of solvents for them, the most common ones being formic acid, glacial acetic acid, phenols and cresols. Dilute mineral acids are usually not much active on the nylons, but concentrated acids attack them to different extents depending on the nature of the nylon and the acid concentration. HNO_3 is mostly active at all concentrations. Resistance to alkalies is very good at room temperature.

The nylons are polymers of low specific gravity (1.02-1.14). The specific gravity of nylon 66 and nylon 6 are very close (1.14 and 1.13 respectively). The properties of the nylons are considerably affected by the amount of crystallization. The glass transition temperatures (T_g) of the nylons are below room temperature, thus making them somewhat flexible and reasonably tough despite high order of crystallinity. They have fairly sharp melting points and the homopolymers show low melt viscosities above T_m Nylons are hygroscopic; nylon 66 and nylon 6 show an equilibrium moisture content of about 8-10% at 100% relative humidity; moulded objects from them exhibit tensile strength of nearly 12,000 psi.

For better processing, the nylon granules should be dry; if necessary, the granules should be dried in an oven at 70-90°C prior to processing. Because of high crystallizing tendencies, a high mould shrinkage is generally observed, which may be reduced using high injection pressure. The shrinkage depends on the melt temperature, mould temperature, injection speed, mould design and, of course, on the type of the nylon.

High cost of the nylons restrict their use as general purpose plastics. They are particularly used where their toughness, rigidity, oil resistance, heat resistance, abrasion resistance and self-lubricating properties are of special advantage. In plastics application, their largest outlet is in mechanical engineering. They are prone to embrittlement on long exposure to direct sunlight. They tend to discolour or turn yellowish on aging. Widespread applications include gears, bearings, cams, bushes, etc. Nylon films feature low odour transmission and are useful in packaging for food stuffs, drugs, and pharmaceuticals.

Nylon 6 and nylon 66 are melt-spun into fibres or filaments and the fibres and cords made from them are extensively used as reinforcing agents for plastics and rubbers (in the construction of composites including hoses and beltings and as tyre cords). Nylon 11 and nylon 610 find application in brush tufting, wigs, outdoor upholstery, etc., because of their flexibility. Other applications of the nylons include textiles, ropes, tows, nets, pipes, tubes, rods, bottles and containers, toys, electrical components, cable sheathings, (chemical, solvent and abrasion) resistant coatings, etc.

Liquid Crystalline Polymers

Liquid crystals are highly anisotropic fluids that exist between the boundaries of solid and conventional isotropic liquid phase. A number of high polymeric substances do exist normally as liquid crystals or they form liquid crystals under specific conditions. Cases of polymeric mesomorphism that cover thermotropics, i.e., liquid crystalline polymer melts and lyotropics meaning liquid crystalline polymer solutions are known. A material of this kind is commonly referred to as a mesophase. Configurational restrictions prevalent in a polymeric mesophase allow formation of structures that readily accommodate the long range orientational order that commonly characterizes liquid crystals. For a polymeric mesophase, not only are the molecules locally parallel to each other to begin with but also the frequency of reversals of chain direction in melt or solution are expected to be low.

For structure formation in melt or solution, it is required to incorporate rigid and polarizable segments in the polymer chain. This may at the same time result in enhanced thermal stability and poor solubility making them ultimately meltable with difficulty and often with decomposition or make the polymers intractable in solvents. An optimum balance of rigidity, nature of interunit linkages and molecular weight is required to enable the polymer attain useful thermal and/or solubility characteristics.

Poly(γ-benzyl-l-glutamate) (PBLG) provides a liquid crystalline polymer that has been most extensively studied:

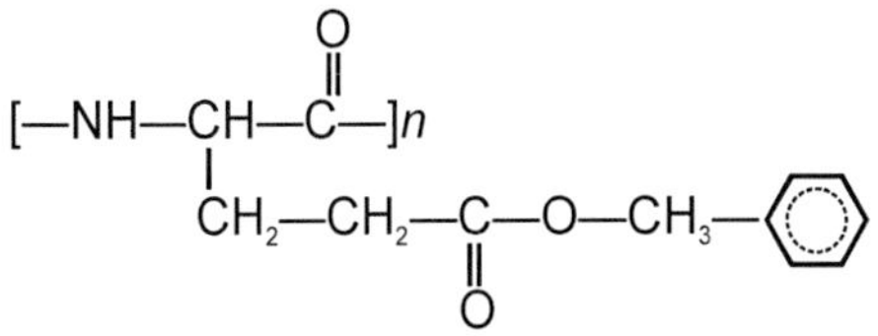

PBLG

PBLG assumes the *a* - helical conformation in a number of solvents as a result of intramolecular hydrogen bonding and favourable orientation and stacking of the pendant side chains. The polymer molecules readily assume an extended and rigid geometry and may turn into oriented and ordered clusters at sufficiently high concentrations. The formation of a lyotropic liquid crystal occurs at a critical volume fraction of polymer which is inversely proportional to the length to diameter ratio of the polymer. The random copolyester based on residues of hydroxy benzoic acid

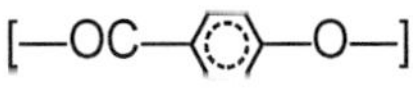 and hydroxy naphtoic acid  has a melting point of about 300°C. Above this temperature, the polymer can be processed as a thermotropic mesophase while below it, the beneficial mechanical properties are realized (high strength and modulus).

The rigid units in the molecular structure of liquid crystalline polymers (LCP) are primarily responsible for their high performance and liquid crystalline behaviour. The said rigid units are commonly referred to as mesogens and the phases with positional and / or orientational long range order in one or two directions as provided by the thermotropic or lyotropic LCP's are termed as mesophases.

The mesophase structures may be of different types depending on the nature of melting point of about 300°C. Above this temperature, the polymer can be processed as a thermotropic mesophase while below it, the beneficial mechanical properties are realized (high strength and modulus).

The rigid units in the molecular structure of liquid crystalline polymers (LCP) are primarily responsible for their high performance and liquid crystalline behaviour. The said rigid units are commonly referred to as mesogens and the phases with positional and / or orientational long range order in one or two directions as provided by the thermotropic or lyotropic LCP's are termed as mesophases.

The mesophase structures may be of different types depending on the nature of the meso gens, interunit linkages and the flexible chain segments; the mesophases may be schematically viewed as (a) cholesteric (array of layered uniaxially oriented patterns of the meso gens with different sets of parallel alignments from layer to layer caused by rotational effects, thus giving a helical arrangement of the mesogens through the layers). (b) Smectic (array of layered uniaxially oriented structures of mesogens showing them in parallelly set positions, upright or inclined with respect to the preferred direction of alignments, (c) discotic (cluster of disc-like array of main-chain or side-chain mesogens) and in this type of mesophase, the disc units in clustered stacks are linked with one another along the axial direction of the iong chains or in a direction perpendicular to the axial direction, and (d) nematic (uniaxial random spacing of the parallelly aligned mesogens, giving practically no layered arrangement (Fig. 8.1).

One may have (i) main-chain LCP's having meso genic groups incorporated end to-end into main chain and interspaced by small flexible chain units or spacer groups, and (ii) side-chain LCP's in which the meso genic groups are linked to the main flexible chains at regular intervals or chain unit spacings, as pendent groups or branch units, giving a comb-like physical feature (Fig. 8.1). If the segments linking the mesogenic units along the main chain or in the side chain are also rigid, then the LCP is difficultly processable due to high melting point; on the other hand, if the said segments are relatively flexible, the LCP shows lower melting point and easier processability.

Space groups such as $—CH=N—$,$—C=C—$, $—C:O—O—$, or $—N=\overset{\overset{O}{\uparrow}}{N}—$ act as stiff polar linkages; segments such as $—(CH_2)_n—$, $—(CH_2—CH_2—O)_n—$,$—[(CH_3)_2SiO]—$, however, act as flexible spacer groups. As few as two para-linked aromatic rings (axial ratio about three) are adequate to provide an effective mesogenic unit.

Most if not all LCPs including those main-chain polyaromatics are high performance polymers, showing high thermal and mechanical resistance properties. Some of the poly aromatics and related polyheterocyclics with favourable structures and having no flexible spacer groups between the main chain mesogenic units also exhibit electrical conductivities of the semiconducting range that can be enhanced hundred to million fold or even more by doping and for some, the conductivities may even be raised to the metallic range, thereby making it possible to obtain what is known as synthetic metals. LC displays have shown vast potential for application in digital or graphic display systems in watches, calculators, TV, computer screens and other such electronic devices. High performance easy processable LCPs are usually high cost polymers at the current stage, thus justifying their limited use in low volume special applications as thermoplastics (moulded objects and films), fibres and cords and special purpose cans, casings, containers, etc. for engineering applications and in optoelectronic devices.

Aromatic Polyamides

A number of aromatic polyamides are known to form a mesophase in concentrated solutions. Aromatic polyamide fibres, commonly known as aramid fibres, are relatively recent developments. Poly condensation between appropriate diamines (*m*-or p-phenylene diamine) and acid chlorides (isophthaloyl or terephthaloyl chloride) leads to the production of industrial

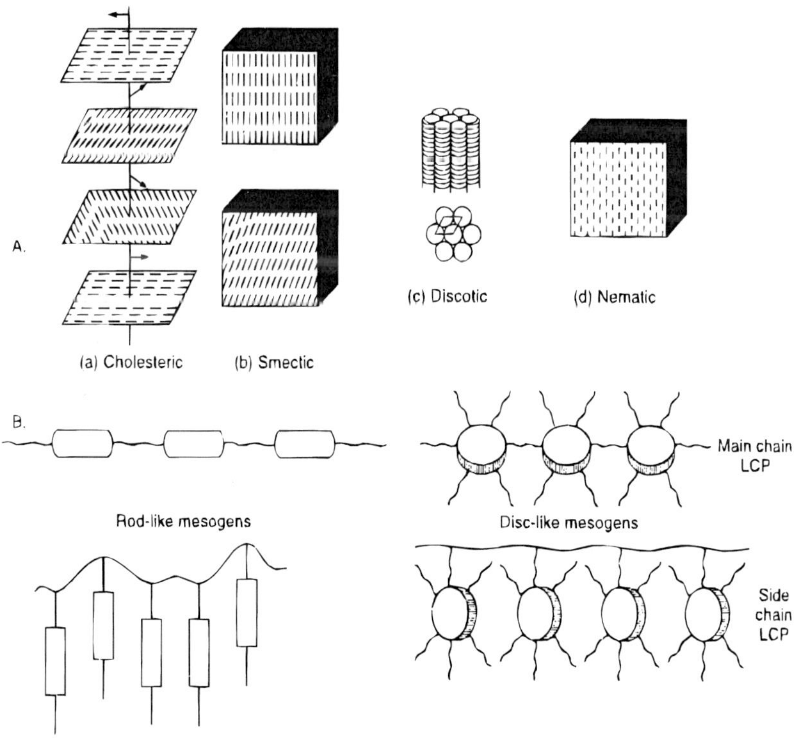

Fig. : 14.1 Schematic representation of : A. mesophasic structurs—(a) Cholesteric, (b) smectic, (c) discotic, (d) nematic; and B. liquid crystalline polymers (LCP): main-chain LCP and side-chain LCP

aromatic polyamides. The reaction product between p-phenylene diamine and terephthaloyl chloride is known by the name Kevlar (Dupont) in the market. Kevlar fibres are nearly one-fifth in density, compared to steel but are nearly equal to steel in tensile strength. The high tenacity, high modulus aramid fibres are excellent in dimensional stability. Kevlar has a $T_g > 300°C$ and a melting point of 500°C which is above its decomposition temperature in air. It is wet spun from a solution of concentrated sulphuric acid, methyl pyrdine or a mixture of hexamethylene phosphoramide, *N-N*-dimethyl acetamide and LiCl. The aromatic polyamide solutions initially show a rise in viscosity with increase in volume fraction of polymer followed by a reversal in the trend and an abrupt decrease in viscosity indicative of mesophase formation when a critical volume fraction of polymer is exceeded.

The aromatic polyamides have important practical applications. The exceptionally high degree of orientation, achieved when the lyotropic mesophase is spun or extruded, imparts exceptional high strength and moduli to aramid fibres and films.

They are useful in cables for stiffness, corrosion resistance and light weight. They are in demand in fibre reinforced composites where their price and properties lie between those of glass fibre and carbon fibre. Bullet resistant fabrics are another important area of use of the aramid fibres.

15

Polyimides

Polyimides which have reached the stage of commercial exploitation are those based on reactions between pyromellitic dianhydride and diamines, particularly aromatic diamines. The sequence of reactions involved in the two stage preparation may be written as:

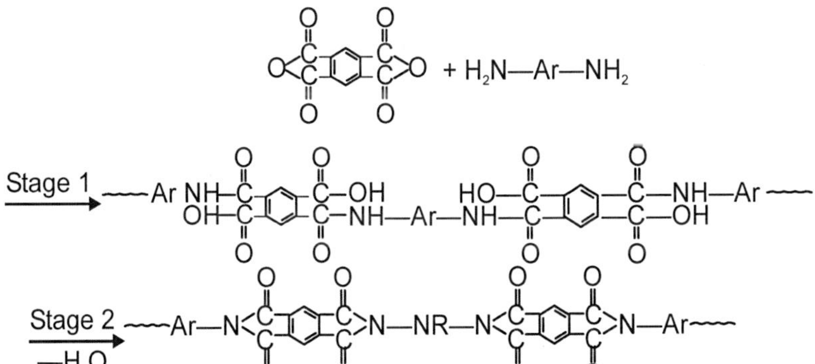

(15.1)

Polyimide

The polymer formed in stage 1 is soluble and it is converted into the thermally stable polymer, polyimide in the second stage. Premature gelation or the second stage reaction can be prevented by using dry reactants in an anhydrous system free from pyromellitic acid and keeping the temperature low (< 5O°C). The stage 1 polymer is soluble in dimethyl formamide. The diamines used to make useful polyimides are m-phenylene diamine, benzidine and 4,4-diaminodiphenylether.

The polyimides have excellent resistance to thermal and oxidative degradation, chemicals excepting strong bases, and to high energy radiations. Their applications as wire enamels, insulating varnishes. and heat resistant coating finishes have been developed. The resins are also useful in the production of heat stable laminates by impregnation of glass or carbon fibres with them and then pressing to form.

16

Polyesters

The early development in polyesters were almost entirely based on resins meant for surface coatings industry. These resins are commonly known sa "alkyd" resins, the term having been coined by combining the first part of the word alcohol and the last part of the word acid. Of the different alkyds, the glyptals based on glycerol-phthalic anhydride condensates received most attention in the early stages. A later development is the unsaturated polyester resins for use as laminating resins particularly for the production of glass fibre reinforced structural items. Another siginificant development in linear polyester subsequent to the development of fibre-forming polyamides is the discovery of polyethylene terephthalte as an excellent fibre forming polyester.

Alkyds for Oleoresinous Varnishes

The polyester resins used for surface coating applications are mostly glyptals usually modified with a drying oil. The resins are produced by extended condensation reactions involving glycerol, phthalic anhydride (acid) and (the fatty acids of) various oils such as linseed oil, soya bean oil, dehydrated castor oil and tung oil. A sizable part of the constituent C_{18} fatty acids of these oils bear conjugated unsaturations in their structures which make them" drying", i.e., they lose unsaturation, gain in viscosity and become progressively less soluble or insoluble on aging or aerial oxidation. The drying is, in fact, a case of oxidative cross-linking often highly catalyzed by such compounds as lead soaps, cobalt or manganese naphthenates, etc., commonly known as driers. The useful properties of the alkyds may be varied by varying the acid, alcohol or the oil. Other polyhydric alcohols commonly used are ethylene glycol, propylene glycol, pentaerythritol and .orbitol, and other acids used are maleic anhydride, isophthalic acid and terephthalic acid.

High or low proportions of drying oils may be used for cooking out the oleo resinous compositions. The oil length of the varnish is given by the number of gallons of drying oils per 100 lb of resin. Long oil compositions are more tough and durable and particularly more suited for outdoor applications while short oil compositions are more hard and glossy and take a higher polish.

In the initial stage of the cooking or resin making, the temperature is kept relatively low (~225°C) for a few hours and extensive ester interchange reaction is accomplished at this stage along with some degree of chain extension involving the dicarboxylic acid giving rise to increased molecular weight and higher viscosity. The ester interchange reactions lead to uniformity of molecular composition. Polymerization of the uniform mixed glycerides is better accomplished by raising the temperature to above 250°C over the final hours of the cooking. The structure of a segment of a molecule of an oil-modified alkyd (glyptal), I is shown below:

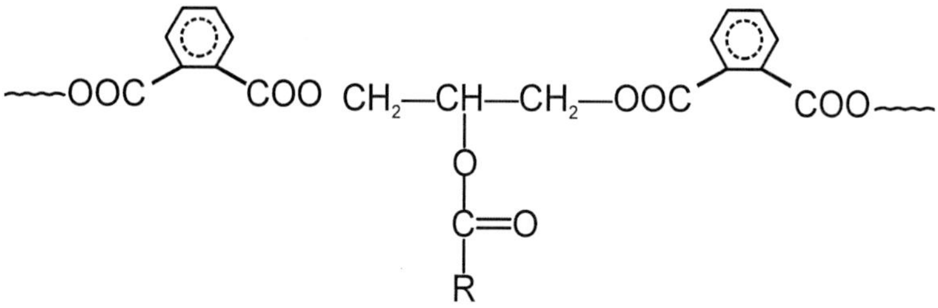

(R=C_{17} chain with conjugated unsaturation)

(I)

Segment of an oil-modified alkyd molecule

The alkyd resins are useful because of good combination of properties and a favourable cost structure. They are also widely modified with rosin, phenolic resins, urea resins, epoxy resins and such monomers as styrene to suit different property needs for different applications. Most of the hard resins are based on maleic anhydride or maleic-rosin adducts. The maleic-rosin resins are made by allowing the anhydride and glycerol to react in presence of excess of rosin.

Polyester Resins for Making Laminates and Composites

(i) *The Resin System* The laminating resins and those meant for reinforced composites are widely made by poly condensations involving varied proportions of a saturated acid (phthalic anhydride, isophthalic acid, adipic acid, etc.), an unsaturated acid, which is most invariably maleic anhydride and a glycol (ethylene glycol, diethylene glycol or 1,2-propylene glycol), whose chemical structures are given below:

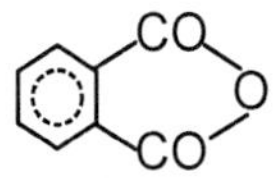

phthalic anhydride

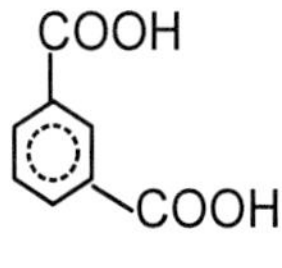

isophthalic acid

$HOOC—(CH_2)_4—COOH$

adipic acid

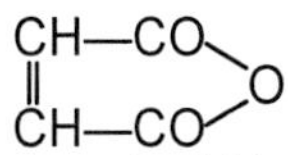

maleic anhydride

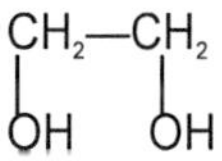

ethylene glycol

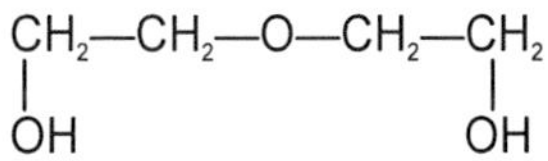

diethylene glycol

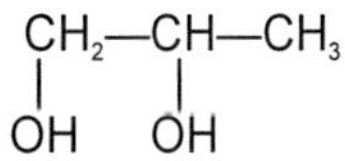

1,2-polypropylene glycol

The unsaturated polyester resins are prepared by heating the component acids and glycols for 10-12 h at about 160-200°C, under stirring conditions usually under a blanket of nitrogen. An inert atmosphere is necessary to obtain light colour for the resin and to prevent premature gelation. A slight molar excess of glycol is usually taken to allow for evaporation losses. The progress of reaction is followed by measurement of fall in acid number with time of reaction. Xylene is generally used to facilitate removal of water formed in reaction steps through azeotropic distillation. When the acid number drops in the range 25-50, xylene is allowed to boil off and heating is discontinued. The resin is then cooled to below the boiling point of styrene and pumped into a blending tank when it is appropriately blended with right proportions of styrene containing suitable inhibitors. The cooled blend is then ready for storage and shipping.

(ii) *The Curing System* The success of the laminating resins is related to the laststage curing process when the resin blend has been applied to the glass fibre or other reinforcing agents. Benzoyl peroxide dispersed in dimethyl phthalate is often used in appropriate doses for pressure moulding at elevated temperatures (-100°C). In presence of dimethyl aniline, the peroxide forms a redox combination and readily brings about satisfactory room temperature curing. Methyl ethyl ketone peroxide (m.e.k.p.) and cobalt or copper naphthenate or octoate also combine to give an efficient room temperature curing system. Depending on the nature and concentration of the curing agents and the prevalent temperature, the curing may be accomplished in a few minutes to a few hours. Mixed with fillers / glass strands, the resins are processed to finished items either by hand lay up or by compression moulding.

The cured resins formed by a graft copolymerization approach have a crosslinked structure; the polystyrene chains form the cross-links corinecting different polyester chains at the point of maleic unsaturations during the curing process, which is induced by a radical mechanism. The major utility of the saturated acid used during the resin-making is to space out the chain unsaturation and as a consequence appropriately reduce or control the cross-link density.

Film- and Fibre-Forming Polyester: Poly(Ethylene Terephthalate)

Poly(ethylene terephthalate) provides very good mouldable, film-forming and fibreforming polyester because of its high glass transition temperature (70-80°C) and high crystalline melting point (>250°C). The fibres and films must be drawn out with ease and convenience as the spun or extruded melt is cooled.

The polymer is essentially looked upon as the linear poly condensation product of terephthalic acid and ethylene glycol. The terephthalic acid is commonly prepared from *p*-xylene by an oxidation process. In view of difficulties in isolating *p*-xylene in pure form consequent to the closeness of its boiling point to the boiling points of 0- and m-xylenes and strong sublimation tendencies of terephthalic acid at polycondensation reaction temperatures, it is convenient to produce the polymer poly(ethylene terephthalate) by an ester interchange reaction between the more readily purified dimethyl terephthalate (DMT) and ethylene glycol. The overall reaction is accomplished in two stages. Ester interchange takes place in the first stage with liberation of CH_3OH as the byproduct in presence of Sb_20_3 with cobaltous acetate as the ester interchange catalyst. A reduced pressure is maintained to facilitate removal of CH_3OH. In the subsequent stage, temperature is raised and taken to a level of 250-280°C towards the end while maintaining a reduced pressure whereby the desired condensation to high molecular weight polymer with removal of the byproduct of condensation, ethylene glycol is accomplished. The molten polymer is then cooled, granulated and stored.

The commercial films [Melinex (ICI) and Mylar (DuPont)] are made by quenching the extruded sheets or films to the amorphous state and subsequently by controlled reheating and stretching of the sheet/ film nearly three fold in machine and transverse directions at 80-100°C. Controlled annealing of the biaxially oriented films at 180-200°C improves crystallinity (-40%) and reduces heat shrinkage. The films are suitable in electrical applications and packaging, and as magnetic recording tapes. The fibre is made by a melt spinning process. Poly(ethylene terephthalate) is the most important synthetic fibre to have found widespread textile applications either alone or more commonly as different blends with cotton or wool. The fibre is widely known as Terylene (ICI trade name) or "Dacron" (DuPont trade name). The polyester fibres possess good" crease resistance" and "wash and wear" properties. A sizable fraction of the polyester fibre is used as the reinforcing cord in the tyre, belting and related industry.

Microbial Thermoplastic Polyesters

(a) *Background* Polyesters of the microbial poly(hydroxyalkanoate) family are thermoplastic in nature and they have biodegradable and biocompatible properties. They can be produced from selected carbon substrates by a variety of microorganisms. Prokaryotic organisms including gram-positive and gram-negative bacteria are known to produce poly(3-hydroxybutyrate) [P(3HB)], structurally expressed as a polymer of 3-hydroxybutyric acid:

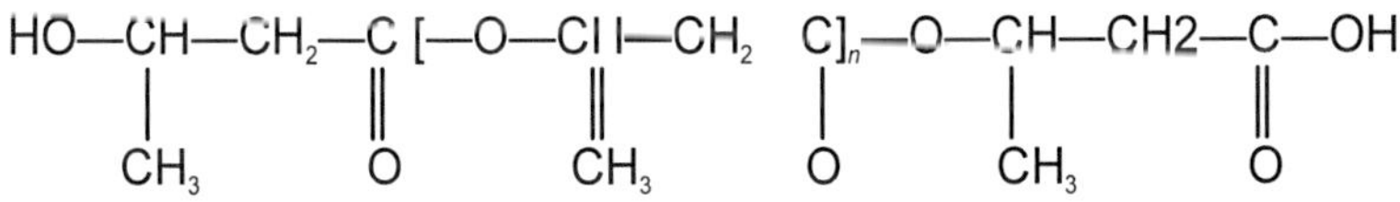

Some bacteria have further been found to accumulate poly(3-hydroxy alkanoates), [P(3HA)] by incorporating into the polymer structure repeat units other than 3hydroxybutyrate, so that the copolyester derived by the microbial process may be structurally written as:

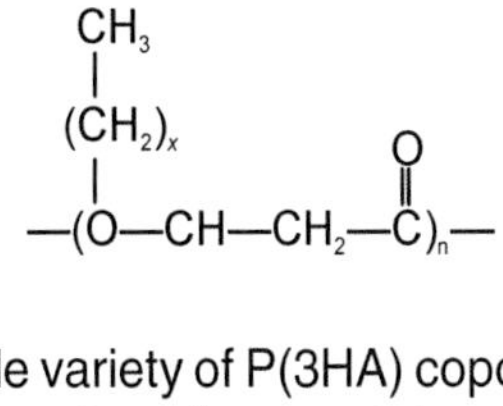

(n = 0,1,2,3)

A wide variety of P(3HA) copolymers have been reported to be isolated from different environmental sources ssuch as fresh water and marine cyanobacteria, marine sediments and sewage sludges. For use of different alkanes and alkanoic acids as the carbon sources, microbial synthesis of P(3HA) copolyesters having alkyl chain lengths from methyl to nonyl or even higher has been reported.

The physical properties of the microbial co polyesters can be regulated by controlled variation of molecular structure, covering copolymer composition and chain length. Copolyesters from hard crystalline thermoplastics to soft elastic rubbers can be made. The microbial thermoplastic polyesters having melting temperatures of 55-l80°C can be processed by common extruder and injection moulding equipments.

The microbial copolyester products such as films, fibres, moulded objects and extruded profiles can be degraded in our environment-soil, sludge and sea water. The degradation is very fast under optimal conditions. Some microorganisms such as bacteria and fungi excrete extracellular P(3HA) depoly-merases to degrade the microbial polyesters utilizing the intermediates as nutrients. Extracellular P(3HB) depolymerases have been isolated from *Pseudomonas lemoiguei* and *Alcaligenes faecalis.* The enzymatic degradation commonly occurs at the surface of the microbial polyester item and the rate of surface erosion is strongly contingent upon both the molecular structure and copolymer composition of the microbial polyesters.

(b) *Production and Isolation* The production of microbial polyesters is done by batch or continuous fermentation using selected bacterial cultures in the presence of a variety of carbon substrates such as glucose, gluconates or methanol as the feed and a salt medium containing dissolved oxygen, ammonium, sulphate, phosphate, potassium or iron ions as nutrients.

The next step is to isolate and purify the produced polymers (microbial polyester / copolyester). They can be extracted from bacterial cells using an organic solvent such as chloroform, methylene chloride, dichloroethane or propylene carbonate. Various lipids are coextracted together with the polyesters from the cells. To remove lipids, the polyesters are precipitated slowly by adding diethyl ether, hexane or lower alcohol as non-solvents. The polyesters can be further purified by reprecipitation from chloroform solution.

Alternatively, the bacterial cells are selectively destroyed and dissolved by -treatment with dilute sodium hypochlorite solution for 30-60 min; longer time may result in degradation of the polyesters as well. The isolated polyester / copolyester granules are purified and made free of lipids by washing with diethyl ether or methanol. Poly (3-hydroxybutyrate), [P(3HB)] granules can also be isolated by treating bacterial cells with enzymes that solubilize all of the cell components except P(3HB).

(c) *Application Prospects* Man's life-style at the dawn of the twenty first century is so much dependent on use of plastics in packaging, construction, health care and sanitation, agriculture, furniture, food and most industrial sectors that man is confounded with the massive problem of disposal of millions of tons of plastic wastes. The concept of biodegradable plastics is the key to solving the waste disposal problem; thus developing plastics that are biodegradable and that do not pollute the environment has become an extremely important global objective. About a million marine animals face death every year by choking on floating plastic waste items that are mistaken by them as food items or by otherwise getting entangled in non-degradable plastic debris.

Fibres and films of biodegradable microbial polyesters get completely decomposed in about eight weeks in sea water and their use or disposal in marine environments would go a long way in reducing harm and injuries to fishes, turtles, seals and other big or small marine animals caused by synthetic plastic wastes. Other important applications of biodegradable polyesters are in the making of agriculture aids including mulching films, and for making films for packaging and other related applications and of bottles and containers. Microbial (biodegradable) polyesters have high potential for use as a matrix for controlled or sustained release plantgrowth regulators such as fertilizers and other nutrients or pesticides. The chemicals are gradually released as the encapsulant polyester is degraded in soil. Blends of biodegradable polyesters or other natural polymers such as starch, gelatin, dextrin and alginates with many synthetic polymers such as the nylons, poly(ethylene oxide), poly(vinyl chloride), poly(vinyl acetate) etc hold high prospect of making biodegradable plastic items of diverse property ranges. Further, rigorous and systematic evaluation of effects of incorporation of plasticizers in and blending other polymers with the microbial polyesters hold high prospect toward making biodegradable polymer items of diverse application potentials. Possible medical applications of P(3HB) include controlled drug release, bone plates and surgical sutures. P(3HB) and other microbial polyesters show good bio-compatibility and slow resorption in biological environments *(in-vivo).* P(3HB) exhibits negligible oral toxicity and its ultimate biodegradation product, D(-)-3-hydroxybutyric acid, is a normal metabolite in human blood.

Some synthetic polyesters / copolyesters having biodegradable cross links and backbone links based on trimellitic acid or citric acid and such alcoholic systems as glycerol, castor oil, and 1,2,6 hexane triol have been recently studied and characterized and they are reported to be promising as encapsulants for control release of drugs, fertilizers and pesticides.

17

Polyurethanes

Polymers formed through interactions of isocyanate groups of di- or polyisocyanates and hydroxyl groups of monomeric or polymeric diols or polyols are commonly known as polyurethanes. The reaction between hexamethylene diisocyanate and l,4-butanediol yields a fibre-forming polyurethane (Perl on U). The reaction is better considered as rearrangement (rather than condensation) polymerization characterized by a step-growth mechanism:

$$n\text{OCN} \cdot (\text{CH}_2)_6 \cdot \text{NCO} + n\text{HO} \cdot (\text{CH}_2)_4 \cdot \text{OH}$$
$$\rightarrow \text{—[OOCNH} \cdot (\text{CH}_2)_6 \cdot \text{NHCOO} \cdot (\text{CH}_2)_4\text{]n—} \quad (17.1)$$

Different kinds and grades of polyurethanes have been developed for applications as fibres, resins, rubbers, adhesives and surface coatings. However, their applications as flexible or rigid foams are of special importance.

The reaction (17.1) for the production of *fibre-forming polyurethane* is carried out by controlled heating of the mixture of the diisocyanate and the diol at about 190-200°C, usually under a blanket of nitrogen with agitation, till the reaction is complete. The reaction is exothermic and good care must be taken to avoid overheating in the kettle. The molten polymer is then passed through metal gauge screen and extruded and cut into chips. The melt may be fed directly into the spinneret to form the filaments.

The fibre formation technology of the polyurethane (Perlon U) through melt spinning is much the same as for the nylons. However, the polyurethane begins to decompose close to and above 220°C and overheating should be avoided. The polyurethane fibre is less prone to colour development (yellowing) in air, and has a lower moisture absorption than the nylon fibres. They are comparable in tensile strength, but the polyurethane fibre has a much lower softening temperature which limits its use in the textile field. The fibre or filament finds some use as bristles, monofilaments, nets, sieves and filter cloth. The polymer is otherwise useful as a *thermoplastic resin* and is readily processed by injection moulding and extrusion. The moulded and formed objects have very good dimensional stability and good retention of electrical properties in humid conditions. Like the nylons, the polyurethane is readily dissolved by formic acid and phenols.

The *polyurethane rubbers* are made from chain extension reactions involving linear aliphatic polyesters with terminal hydroxyl groups and diisocyanates (toluene diisocynate, I,S-naphthalene diisocynate, etc.) The urethane linkages formed during chain extensions may further react with excess diisocyanates or through terminal isocyanate groups of the growing chains at a higher temperature in a mould to establish cross linking. The polyurethane rubbers have good tensile strength (~5000 psi), higher than any other rubber, and excellent tear and abrasion resistance, and they exhibit excellent resistance to oxygen and ozone. They are, however, less resistant to acids and alkalies and steaming (hydrolytic decomposition) than the conventional rubbers. They find application as oil seals, footwear soles and heels, conveyor belts, printing rollers, fabric coatings, waterproof items, tank lining in chemical plants, cable sheathing, pump impellers and diaphragms, industrial hoses, etc.

Polyurethane foams are very popular. They may be rigid, semirigid or flexible. They may be either polyester-based or polyether-based. The foam technology requires concurrent chain extension with diisocyanates, cross-linking and gas evolution. Gas evolution may be achieved by reaction between –COOH end-groups of polyesters and isocyanate groups (–COOH + OCN → -CONH- + CO_2) or more readily by reaction between isocyanate and water:

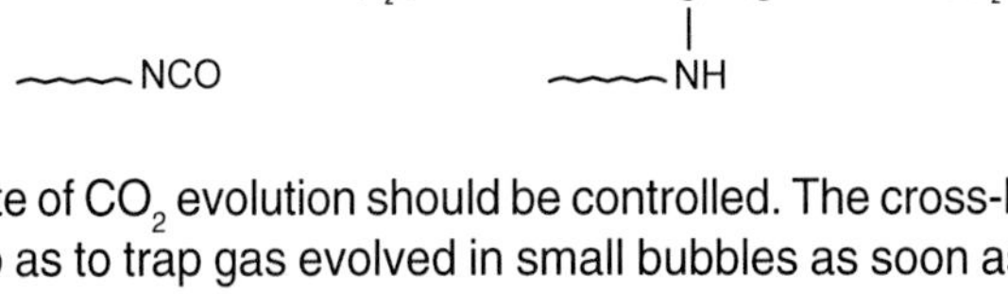

The rate of CO_2 evolution should be controlled. The cross-linking should be rapid so as to trap gas evolved in small bubbles as soon as it is formed. Loss of gas would result in poor foams. The polyurethane foams commonly known as "U" foams are extensively used as cushioning materials, soft backing or padding, sponges, paint rollers and in quilting and packaging.

Rigid foams are mostly used in the field of thermal insulation. As adhesive and surface finishes, hard polyurethane resins are suitable for metals while the soft elastomers for rubbery or leathery products. A two pack system is usually used, the curing agent being used just prior to application. Single component finishes cure in contact with moisture from air.

18

Polycarbonates

Polycarbonates are characterized by repeat units having carbonate $\left(\text{—O—}\overset{\displaystyle\text{O}}{\overset{\|}{\text{C}}}\text{—O—}\right)$ inter-unit linkages. Linear polycarbonates are formed either by reaction between dihydroxy compounds and phosgene or by means of ester interchange reaction involving dihydroxy compounds and organic carbonates (R-O · CO · O–R). The polycarbonate based on bisphenol A and diphenyl carbonate is the only one that has been developed into a commercial product of special importance.

Bisphenol A is readily produced by the condensation of acetone and phenol under acidic condition at temperatures below 70°C. An excess of phenol is used in order to achieve a high yield. Phosgene used (in the direct process or for preparing diphenyl carbonate) is prepared commercially from chlorine and carbon monoxide. Diphenyl carbonate (C_6H_5—O · CO · O—C_6H_5) is conveniently obtained by reacting phenol with phosgene in aqueous NaOH solution in presence of a tertiary amine catalyst. The diphenyl carbonate is purified by redistillation.

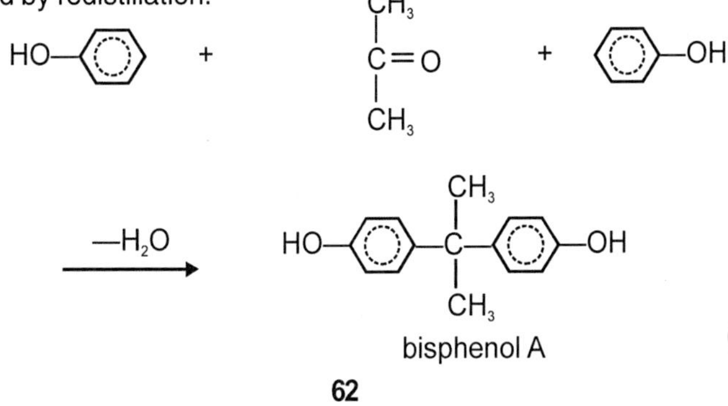

bisphenol A (18.1)

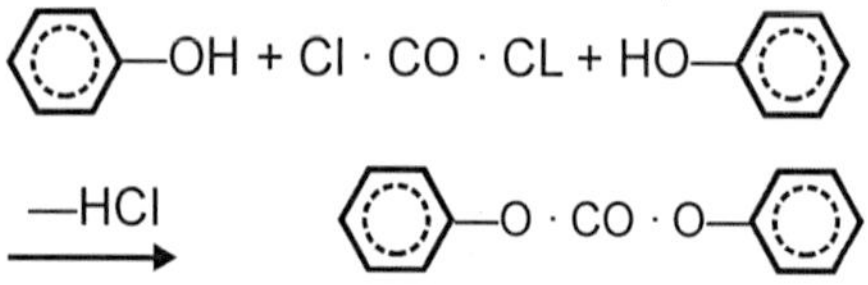

diphenyl carbonate (18.2)

The easter interchange reaction leading to polycarbonate formation is shown in reaction (18.2). The reaction is normally accomplished at nearly

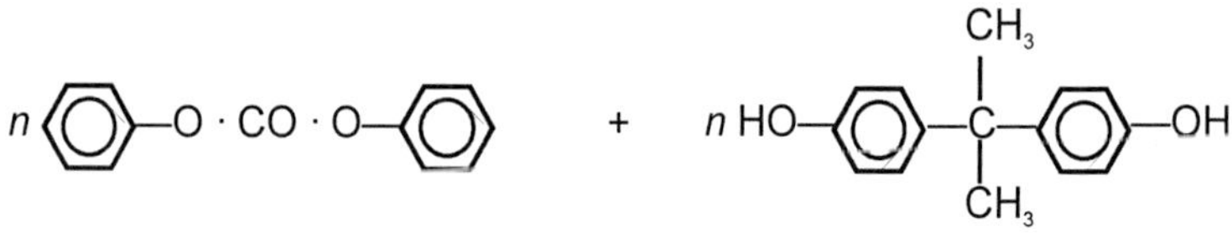

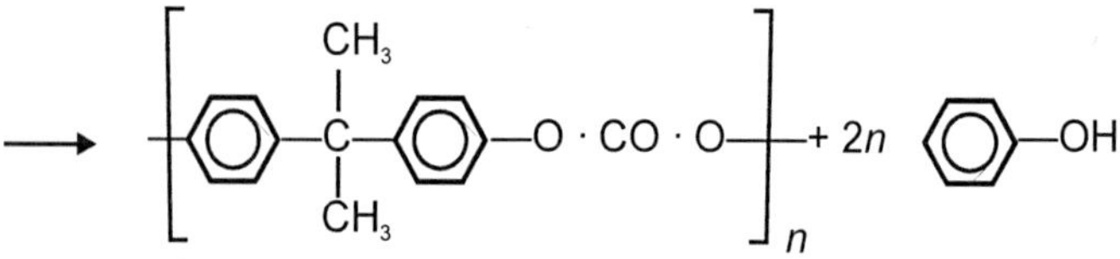

(18.3)

200°C at a reduced pressure (25 mm Hg), until about 90% of the phenol liberated has been removed. The temperature is then raised to about 290-300°C and the pressure further reduced to below 1 mm Hg. Further chain extension takes place and the melt viscosity increases significantly at this stage. The reaction is arrested at an appropriate melt viscosity and the melt is forced out of the kettle under nitrogen pressure. For convenience, the reaction is done using very high molar proportions (≥2) of the diphenyl carbonate so that the initial reaction product is the bis(phenyl carbonate) of bisphenol A. On further heating, polymerization proceeds by splitting out of the diphenyl carbonate thus producing the polycarbonate resin. Direct phosgenation of bisphenol A may be used for the production of high molecular weight polycarbonates:

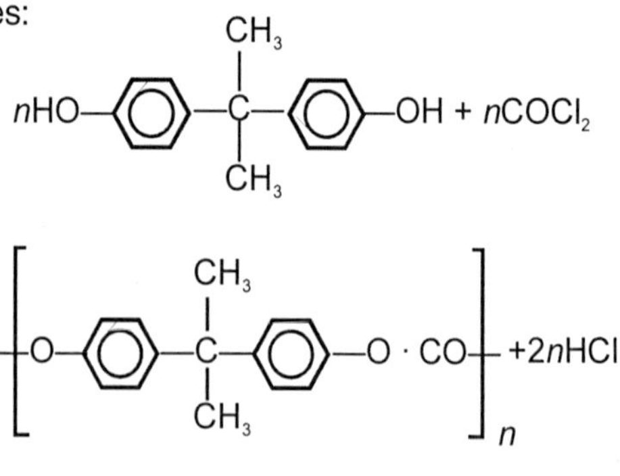

(18.4)

The reaction is better done in presence of such solvents as pyridine (which act as HCl acceptors) diluted with some other solvents as chloroform, methylene chloride or tetrachloroethane. The polymer is isolated by precipitation with methanol. The ester-interchange method is commercially more favoured as it allows avoidance of the handling of toxic and flammable solvents and thus allowing avoidance of costs of solvents and solvent recovery.

Bisphenol-A polycarbonates have densities of nearly 1.2 g/ cm^3. They exhibit tensile strengths of the order of 9,000-10,000 psi. They are characterized by very good impact resistance (12-18 ft.1b/in notch). Their creep resistance is also very remarkable and this makes them much superior to polyamides and acetal resins. The polycarbonates are however inferior in respect of stress-cracking or crazing.

The polycarbonates appear in crystal-clear grades, if prepared from high purity ingredients. The refractive index at 25°C is 1.58. Their low water absorption, good insulation properties (low dielectric constant, 2.9-3.2, and high volume resistivity, 2×10^{16} ohm em), transparency and toughness coupled with hoat and flame resistance (T_m = 225-250°C, Tg = 145°C), make them suited for many areas of application including electrical insulation.

Poly carbonates can be processed by all the usual thermoplastic processing techniques-injection moulding, extrusion, blow moulding, roto-moulding, themoforming, etc. Major applications include electric and electronic appliances, helmet, automotive lighting, protective shields, safety glass / sun glass, bottles, domestic wares, structural foams, components of camera, projector housings, etc. Factors retarding their growth are high cost, limited chemical and UV resistance and stringent processing requirements. For processing, the resin must be thoroughly dried for several hours in an oven at 110-120°C and used for processing immediately thereafter.

19

Epoxy Resins

Epoxy or epoxide resins are those resins or polymers which are produced by condensation reactions using an epoxy compound as an ingredient in the monomeric reactant mixture. The most common and widely used epoxy resins are made by allowing poly condensation involving epichlorohydrin and bisphenol A. Epichlorohydrin, .more expensive of the two, is derived from propylene via allyl chloride according the sequence of reactions given in reaction scheme 19.1. The material, a colourless liquid, is commercially available at 98% purity.

$$CH_2{=}CH \cdot CH_3 + Cl_2 \longrightarrow CH_2 = CH{\cdot}CH_2{\cdot}Cl{+}HCl$$

$$CH_2{=}CH \cdot CH_2 \cdot Cl + HOCl \xrightarrow{H_2O/Cl_2} Cl \cdot CH_2{-}CH(OH) \cdot CH_2 \cdot Cl$$

$$Cl \cdot CH_2{-}CH(OH) \cdot CH_2Cl + NaOH \longrightarrow \underbrace{CH_2{-}CH}_{O}{-}CH_2 \cdot Cl \qquad (19.1)$$

The commercial liquid resins are essentially diglycidyl ether of bisphenol A mixed with small proportions of some high molecular weight polymers. Two to three moles of epichlorohydrin are used for one mole of bisphenol A in order to obtain higher yield of the diglycidyl ether. Commercial resins show molecular weights in the range of 340-400 and seldom their molecular weights exceed the range 3000-4000. The mixture of bisphenol A and epichlorohydrin in the desired molar proportion is heated under stirring condition to about 110°C under an atmosphere of nitrogen while a 30% aqueous solution of NaOH is added dropwise continuously to neutralize the HCl liberated. After the reaction, the organic layer is removed, dried and then fractionally distilled under vacuum.

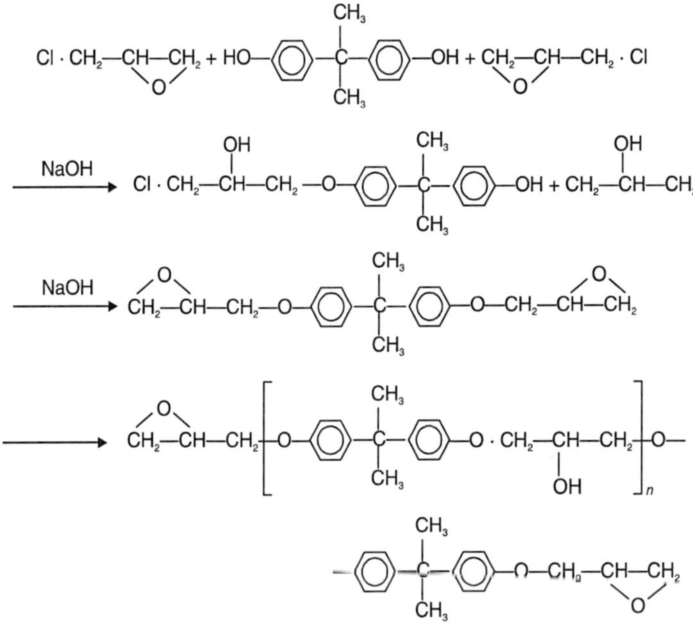

(19.2)

The quality of the epoxy resin is determined by its viscosity, hydroxyl equivalent and epoxy equivalent, and molecular weight. The hydroxyl equivalent is the weight in gram of the resin containing ono gram equivalent of hydroxyl group and is normally determined by reacting the resin with acetyl chloride. Likewise, the epoxy equivalent is the weight of the resin in gram containing one gram equivalent of epoxy group and it is normally determined by reacting a known quantity of the resin with HCl and then estimating the unreacted acid. HCl reacts with the epoxy group according to Eq. (19.3).

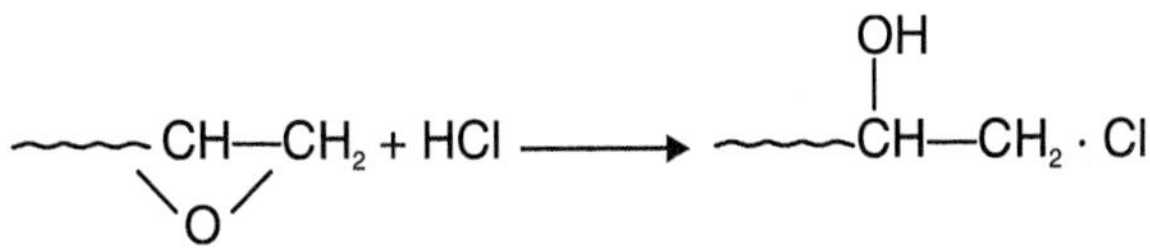

(19.3)

The cross-linking of epoxy resins is done through the epoxy or hydroxyl groups. The curing or cross-linking agents are commonly termed as hardeners or hardening agents. The hardeners commonly in use are monoamines, diamines and polyamines, acids and anhydrides [phthalic, hexahydrophthalic, maleic, pyromellitic (dianhydride), chlorendic, etc.]. With amines or acids, the reaction involves opening of the epoxide rings giving ,a-hydroxy amino or ,ß-hydroxy ester linkages:

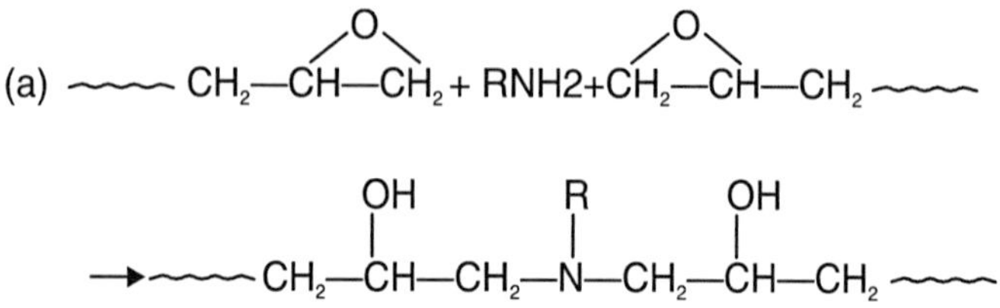

(19.3a)

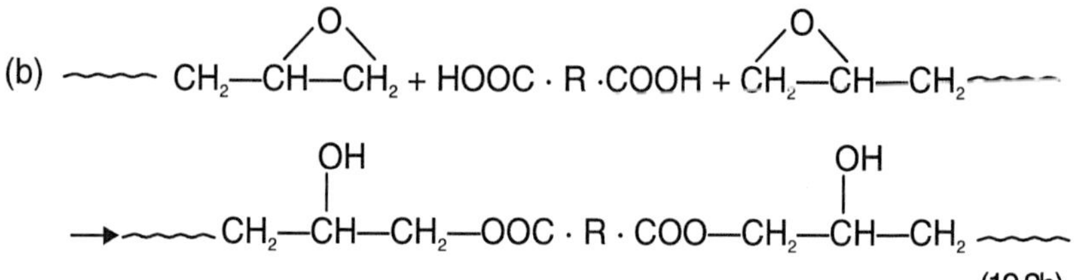

(19.3b)

The above reactions are, in fact, linear chain extension reactions. Use of diarnines and polyamines with more than two active hydrogen in the molecule leads to three dimensional networks and cross-linkages. With acids and anhydrides, reactions involving OH groups initially present or those formed on opening of the epoxide ring lead to cross-linking.

$$|\text{—OH} + \text{HOOC}\cdot\text{R}'\cdot\text{COOH} + \text{HO—}| \xrightarrow{-H_2O} |\text{—OOC}\cdot\text{R}'\cdot\text{COO—}|$$

(20.1)

The cross-linking may also be done using low molecular weight phenolic (novolac) and urea resins where the reactions may involve condensation of methylol groups with the secondary hydroxyl groups of the epoxy resin or epoxide ring opening through reaction with the phenolic hydroxyls or the amino groups of the urea resins.

Amines are fast curing even at room temperatures, and they incorporate good chemical resistance. They are, however, toxic and skin-sensitive. The anhydrides are much less toxic and give cured products of good thermal stability and high heat distortion temperature. They are effective only at elevated temperatures. Better pot life is obtained using Lewis acid hardeners, such as BF_3 and its complexes.

The epoxy resins are suitable for both moulding and laminating applications. They also find special applications as high strength adhesives and cementing agents, in the building industry and road surfacing, in surface coating and in potting and encapsulation of electronic components. The major structural and engineering applications include glass fibre reinforced cast objects and laminates and in these applications, the epoxy resins excel the polyester resins in view of their far superior heat resistance, chemicals and alkali resistance, mechanical properties and aging resistance. The epoxy's excellent adhesion, very good cohesion, low creep and low shrinkage on cure and absence of volatiles have developed the resin into an excellent adhesive, bonding or cementing material for metal-to-metal, metal-to-ceramics, metal-to-plastics and various other combinations of substrates.

The so-called phenoxy resins or the phenoxies are the extended polycondensation products of bisphenol A and epichlorohydrin of molecular weight close to 25,000, represented by a polymer structure given in the final step of reaction sequence (19.2), where *n* is nearly 100. The phenoxies are usually slightly branched and are readily cross-linked through the hydroxyl groups in the repeating units by diisocyanates.

The phenoxies exhibit very good resistance to alkalies and quite low gas permeability. Their rigidity, creep resistance, high toughness and ductility, high heat resistance and low moulding shrinkage (0.003 cm · cm^{-1}) make them suitable for special engineering applications.

Another class of polymers of related structure are the polysulphones, usually having -0- (ether) and —SO_2— (sulphone) linkages between aromatic rings, e.g., 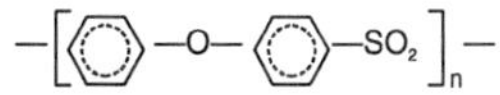 prepared by self condensation of Ar—O—Ar—SO_2Cl or polycondensation involving (Ar—O—Ar) and (ClO_2S—Ar—0—Ar—$S0_2$Cl). Commercial polysulphones have T_g > 200°C, and they are usually aromatic polyethersulphones. Polysulphones with no interunit ether links may be obtained by reacting bissulphonylchlorides with an aromatic hydrocarbon using Lewis acid catalysts:

$$\begin{array}{c} CLO_2S\text{—}Ar\text{—}SO_2Cl + H\text{—}Ar\text{—}H \\ \xrightarrow{-HCl} \text{—}[O_2S\text{—}Ar\text{—}SO_2\text{—}Ar]_n\text{—} \end{array} \qquad (19.2)$$

The processing temperatures of commercial polysulphones are above 300°C. They are rigid, tough, high tensile strength/high modulus thermostable polymers with non-burning behaviour, and they can also withstand ionizing radiations without much degradation or cross-linking and deterioration of other properties. They are, however, notch sensitive, like the polycarbonates. Their high mechanical strength, heat resistance, chemical resistance, oil resistance and good burning behaviour make them suited for many engineering applications.

20

Cellulose Plastics

Cellulose is the most abundant constituent of the vegetable or plant kingdom. The cellulose content, however varies from plant to plant. Cellulose content is over 90% in cotton and nearly 50% in an average wood, the most convenient sources of cellulose for chemical treatments and transformations are cotton linters and wood pulp.

Of the very large number of cellulose derivatives that have been prepared, only the esters and ethers are generally important. The three hydroxyl groups of the repeating anhydro-,β-glucose units are transformed into the ester or ether groups during esterification and etherification reactions, giving a theoretical degree of substitution (DS) equal to 3.0.

Cellulose esters find widespread applications as moulded plastics, artificial fibres, films, sheets, and in coatings and lamination. Among the important cellulose esters are cellulose nitrate, cellulose acetate, cellulose acetate-butyrate and cellulose propionate.

Cellulose Nitrate

Cellulose nitrate is the oldest cellulosic or cellulose derivative known and it is the only inorganic ester of cellulose of commercial importance. Nitration of cellulose is carried out by using a mixture of HNO_3 and H_2SO_4 over a specific time period under controlled conditions of temperature and mixed acid composition. The nitration can be done by batch or continuous process. The three distinct stages in the preparation of cellulose nitrate are: (i) pretreatment of cellulose, (ii) nitration, and (iii) after treatment and dehydration.

Wood pulp or cotton linters are shredded by a set of rotating blades and then dried to a very low water content < 0.5%). Water content is an important factor in the preparation of mixed acid which may vary in composition from 0-20% water, 15-50% HNO_3 and 30-60% H_2SO_4. A very low water content tends to produce high degree of nitration; H_2SO_4 plays the role of a condensing agent. In a typical batch process, 500 kg of the mixed acids are taken into a jacketed reaction vessel fitted with agitators and about 12 kg of dried cotton linters or shredded wood pulp are added keeping the temperature in the range 25-40°C. The nitration is allowed to proceed for 20-25 min. Even after nitration, the fibrous form of cellulose is retained. The nitrated product is dumped through the bottom of the reactor into a centrifuge and much of the acid mixture is removed. The ester is washed profusely with water in what is known as the drowning tank and pumped as a slurry into a vat that holds products of several nitrations. Due to minor degrees of sulphation through reaction with H_2SO_4 the nitrated product at this stage is unstable as the sulphate groups tend to split off reforming H_2SO_4 and setting off an autocatalytic decomposition process. During stabilization process, the product is boiled in water under controlled pH condition whereby removal of sulphate groups is accomplished. The cellulose nitrate is then washed, bleached if necessary, centrifuged and then dehydrated with alcohol. The transformation of cellulose (R- cell. OH) into the nitrate may be written as:

$$\text{R-cell} \cdot \text{OH} + \text{HO} \cdot \text{NO}_2 \rightarrow \text{R—cell} \cdot \text{O} \cdot \text{NO}_2 + \text{H}_2\text{O} \qquad (20.1)$$

Commercial cellulose nitrates meant for plastics and coating applications have N_2 contents in the range of 10.9-12.2% corresponding to degrees of substitution (DS) 1.8-2.3. Complete nitration leading to DS of 3.0 corresponds to a N_2 content of 14.14%. Nitrates with N_2 content ≥ 12.5% are used as explosives.

Cellulose nitrates for plastics and coating (lacquor) applications have N_2 content in the range 11.5-12.2%; they are available in a large number of viscosity grades and they are soluble in esters, ketones, ether-alcohol mixtures and glycol ethers. They are compatible with many other resins. Cellulose nitrates with 10.9-11.2% N_2 content find use in flexographic inks, lacquor coatings for paper, foils and other flexible substances. For plastics applications cellulose nitrate is invariably plasticized with nearly 25% by weight of camphor. The camphor plasticized product is known as 'celluloid'. Cellulose nitrate, alcohol and camphor are mixed in a steam-heated dough mixer until homogeneous, whereby the fibrous nature of cellulose is lost. The dough is then filtered under pressure, reduced to a low solvent content (12-16%), first by putting under vacuum and then milling on a calender. It is then sheeted into slabs and pressed into a homogeneous block of a specific size. Sheets may be sliced out from the blocks. They are then 'seasoned' to remove last traces of solvent and subjected to surface finishing operations. The high inflammability and somewhat poor chemical and solvent resistance of cellulose nitrate stand in the way of its widespread industrial application. It is no longer considered suitable in many of its earlier areas of application such as photographic and cine film, machine guards or covers, toys, etc. Curent applications include tool or knife handles, table-tennis balls spectacle frames, lacquors and printing ink; in some of these fields, celluloid is facing growing challenge from other synthetic polymers or other cellulosics such as cellulose acetate.

Cellulose Acetate

The most important organic ester of cellulose is cellulose acetate. Cellulose acetate is prepared by acetylation of cellulose using a mixture of acetic anhydride and glacial acetic acid as the acetylating agent under a controlled condition. Small proportion of H_2SO_4 is used as catalyst. In most instances cotton linter and wood pulp are used for acetylation. Acetic acid used acts as a swelling agent for the cellulose and as a homogenizing solvent or diluent for the acetate derivative formed. Three stages are associated with the homogeneous acetylation process: (a) pretreatment of cellulose, (b) acetylation and (c) hydrolysis.

Pretreatment makes cellulose swell whereby it becomes readily accessible to acetic anhydride, the actual acetylating agent. Glacial acetic acid is most commonly used for pretreatment. Cotton or wood pulp is steeped in 30-40% of its own weight of glacial acetic acid for 1-2 h.

The pretreated cellulose is then transferred into the acetylating tank and a requisite amount of the acetylating mixture consisting of acetic anhydride, glacial acetic acid and the catalyst, H_2SO_4 previously cooled to 15-20°C is poured into the tank. As the acetylation proceeds, the physical appearance of the substrate slowly changes from a mass of shredded fibre through an opaque dough like mass to finally a clear viscous solution. Temperature is controlled carefully within 45-50°C. Esterification is usually complete in 5-6 h and the primary product, characterized by a degree of substitution of 3.0, is called the primary cellulose acetate; theoretical acetic acid yield of the primary acetate is 62.5% which corresponds to an acetyl content of 44.8 percent.

The primary acetate is soluble in chlorinated hydrocarbons (such as chloroform, trichloroethane or methylene chloride), dioxane or nitromethane and insoluble in acetone. The primary acetate obtained under the conditions detailed above contains some sulphate groups, and it exhibits a viscosity not much suited for spinning. The primary acetate or the triacetate obtained as a viscous solution in the acetylating mixture is then diluted with aqueous acetic acid and all the sulphate groups as well as part of the acetate groups are hydrolyzed. The hydrolysis is accomplished over several hours to several days depending on temperature employed and degree of hydrolysis desired. As the desired degree of hydrolysis or degree of substitution is reached, the cellulose acetate is precepitated by addition of water to the stirred solution. The product is then filtered, washed and dried. It is commonly known as secondary cellulose acetate or the diacetate. The theoretical acetic acid yield corresponding to the diacetate is 48.8% which is equivalent to 35.0% acetyl content. The cellulose diacetate or the secondary acetate is soluble in acetone and insoluble in chloroform.

Even through the secondary acetate is soluble, it is thermally unstable and decomposes below its softening point. It can be conveniently processed and moulded if only it is plasticized with a suitable plasticizer such as, diethyl phthalate and triphenyl phosphate. Other compounding ingredients used are UV-stabilizers, extenders, lubricants and colouring matters. A major outlet of cellulose acetate is in the area of sheets, films and membranes. Its exceptional clarity makes it suited for photographic films. Injection moulded items include tooth brush handles, combs, etc. Films are useful in packaging and wrapping. The toughness, low flammability (compared to cellulose nitrate), good clarity and favourable cost structure of cellulose acetate are advantageous. On the other hand, its high water absorption, poor solvent and chemical resistance and limited heat resistance and dimensional stability are its limitations.

The diacetate is dry spun from acetone solution into fibre, and it is less prone to wrinkling than regenerated cellulose (viscose) fibres. It also soils less and is known as the acetate rayon. The acetate fibre is less prone to creasing and it is washable more readily than regenerated cellulose fibres. The primary acetate can be dry spun from methylene chloride solution and the relevant fibre is suitable for apparels.

Mixed organic esters of cellulose have also been developed commercially. The important mixed esters are cellulose acetate-butyrate and cellulose acetatepropionate. The cellulose acetate-butyrates meant for plastics application (injection moulded objects) have nearly 12-20% acetyl and 30-40% butyryl content. Cellulose acetate-butyrate is more suitable than cellulose acetate for movie films. Its excellent appearance and clarity, toughness and ease of mouldability are of special advantage. It is also of lower density than cellulose acetate. The mixed ester is competitive with cellulose acetate in most of its thermoplastic applications on property considerations. However, the polymer emits smell of butyric acid under processing conditions. The mixed ester is used in the making of automobile parts, tool handles, toys, telephone housings and pipes. Other cellulose esters that have been commercially exploited are cellulose propionate and cellulose acetate-propionate.

Cellulose Ethers

Cellulose ethers are conveniently prepared by allowing selected alkyl chlorides to react with alkali cellulose in presence of alkali at a specific temperature over a specific time period.

$$\text{R-cell} \cdot \text{OH} + \text{R'Cl} + \text{NaOH} \rightarrow \text{R-Cell} \cdot \text{O} \cdot \text{R'} + \text{NaCl} + H_2O \qquad (20.2)$$

For making ethyl cellulose, the alkyl chloride used is ethyl chloride. The reaction is done at 60°C for several hours and the temperature is raised to 125-140°C towards the end. Ethyl alcohol and ethyl ether are formed as byproducts and are removed by distillation. Ethyl cellulose is precipitated by adding hot water; it is then centrifuged, washed and dried.

The completely substituted product (DS = 3.0) exhibits an ethoxyl content of 54.88%. With a DS value of 0.8%-1.2, the ethyl cellulose is water soluble. Highly or fully substituted product is, however, soluble in non-polar solvents (aromatic hydrocarbons). Ethyl cellulose is used in hot melt strippable coating formulations, and surface coating formulations (paints, varnishes and lacquers). Water soluble grades were developed for use in textile and paper sizing and the alkali soluble grades were developed as permanent textile finishes. The cellulosic thermoplastics have been gradually losing their place and importance in many areas of application due to progressive availability of and developments in superior synthetic resins.

Other cellulose ethers of some importance include methyl cellulose (DS 1.6-2.0) which.is employed as a thickening agent, and an emulsifying and paper sizing agent being soluble in cold water. It has also limited use in leather tanning operation and ceramic processing. Hydroxy ethyl cellulose prepared by reaction of alkali cellulose with ethylene oxide also finds applications similar to those for methyl cellulose.

Sodium carboxymethyl cellulose is another important cellulose ether. It is produced by reacting alkalicellulose with sodium salt of chloracetic acid:

$$\text{R-Cell} \cdot \text{ONa} + \text{Cl} \cdot CH_2 \cdot \text{COONa} \rightarrow \text{R-Cell} \cdot \text{O} \cdot CH_2\text{COONa} + \text{NaCl} \qquad (20.3)$$

On acidification the acid form known as the carboxy methyl cellulose (CMC) is obtained. Na-CMC of DS in the range 0.5-1.0 are water soluble and are commercially useful. They find use in synthetic detergents (soil suspending agent) and as stabilizers or viscosity modifiers in aqueous suspensions and emulsions. They also find applications as textile or paper sizing agents, surface active agents and polyelectrotyles. Pure Na-CMC is physiologically inert and is commonly employed as thickening agent in food, pharmaceutical and cosmetic products.

Regenerated Cellulose

One simple way of solubilizing cellulose is to transform the alkali cellulose or soda cellulose (R—Cell. ONa) into sodium cellulose xanthate by reacting it with CS_2. The xanthate made appropriately is soluble in dilute aqueous alkali, which on acidification decomposes; the xanthate structure is broken and cellulose structure is regenerated. This is the basic approach to the production of regenerated cellulose. The main reactions involved may be shown as:

$$\text{R—Cell} \cdot \text{OH} + \text{NaOH (18\%)} \longrightarrow \text{R—Cell} \cdot \text{ONa} + H_2O \qquad (20.3)$$

$$\text{R—Cell} \cdot \text{ONa} + CS_2 \longrightarrow \text{R—Cell} \cdot \text{O—}\overset{\overset{\displaystyle S}{\|}}{C}\text{—SNa} \qquad (20.4)$$

$$\text{R—Cell—O—}\overset{\overset{\displaystyle S}{\|}}{C}\text{—SNa} + H^+ \longrightarrow \text{R—Cell—OH} + CS_2 + Na^+ \qquad (20.5)$$

The solution of sodium cellulose xanthate in dilute alkali is commonly known as the viscose solution. Fibre made from wet spinning of viscose solution in an acid / salt bath is known as the viscose rayon.

In the initial step, cellulose (cotton linter or wood pulp) is steeped in 18% aqueous NaOH at room or lower temperatures. This helps appropriate swelling of the cellulose which is at the same time converted into soda-cellulose. The excess alkali is then pressed out and the soda-cellulose formed is shredded and allowed to age at 25-30°C for 2-3 days to accomplish desirable extents of oxidative degradation of the cellulose substrate. The aged soda-cellulose crumbs are then reacted with liquid or gaseous CS_2 at about 25-30°C for 2-3 h whereby the mass becomes sticky and somewhat gelatinous, assumes a deep orange colour and emits a bad odour. After the desired extent of xanthation is accomplished, excess CSz is removed by applying vacuum and the mass is dissolved in dilute aqueous NaOH solution (4%). The odour and colour of these viscose solution is attributed to some sulphurous byproducts formed during xanthation.

The viscose solution is then allowed to stand at a low temperature (IS-20°C) for a few days and a process known as ripening follows. The unstable sodium cellulose xanthate undergoes decomposition and a complex sequence of reactions and physical changes take place during ripening at the end of which coagulation of viscose becomes easy and almost spontaneous. The ripened viscose is then filtered and spun into fibre or made into transparent film. The coagulation or regeneration bath is made up of an appropriate aqueous solution of H_2SO_4, Na_2SO_4 and glucose. The fibre made from viscose is known as viscose rayon and the film made is known as cellophane.

The low or normal tenacity viscose rayon (2-2.5 g/ denier) was once developed almost solely as an apparel fibre. But it is no longer useful in this field because of subsequent developments of much better fibre forming synthetic polymers. High tenacity viscose rayons (3-6 g/ denier) are produced by high degrees of stretching of the fibre after spinning. Because of high order of crystallinity, very low elongation (poor flexibility) and low moisture absorption, the high tenacity rayon is almost exclusively used as tyre cords but not as a textile material. In tyre cord application too, the viscose rayon is facing stiff challenge from the synthetic fibres, particularly polyesters and nylons.

For the production of cellophane films, the viscose solution is extruded as a film which is then immersed in the Na_2SO_4/H_2SO_4 bath. Xanthate-splitting and regeneration of cellulose takes place in the bath and the film is passed through washing, bleaching and de sulphurizing baths. Plasticization and finishing of the film is achieved by passing it finally through a bath containing ethylene glycol or glycerol. Cellphane or regenerated cellulose films or foils are popular in wrapping applications and useful as membranes for displays.

21

Phenolic Resins

The reaction between different phenols and aldehydes leads to the formation of what is known as phenol-aldehyde resins; or simply phenolic resins or the phenolics. The simplest of these reactants, viz. common phenol and formaldehyde are most commonly employed in the making of different grads of phenolic (phenol-formaldehyde) resins. Other phenols used are cresols, resorcinol and *p-tertbutyl* phenol. Among aldehydes other than formaldehyde, only furfural has been used commercially to a limited degree. Resins from phenol and formaldehyde are also commonly known as p-f resins.

Chemistry of Resin Formation

For resinification with aldehydes, common phenol is recognized to function as a trifunctional compound (the 2 ortho-positions and the para-position are the three reactive sites). In most resinification reactions involving formaldehyde, formalin solution (nearly 37% aqueous formaldehyde) is used and the aqueous formaldehyde is considered to remain in this solution as methylene glycol ($CH_2 = 0 + H_2O \rightarrow HO \cdot CH2 \cdot OH$). Thus, phenol—formaldehyde resinification system is a tri-bi functional system and the resinification that proceeds by a polycondensation process invariably leads to the ultimate formation of a space network, i.e. three dimensional crosslinked polymer. The first step in the resinification reaction producing monomethylol phenols may be written as:

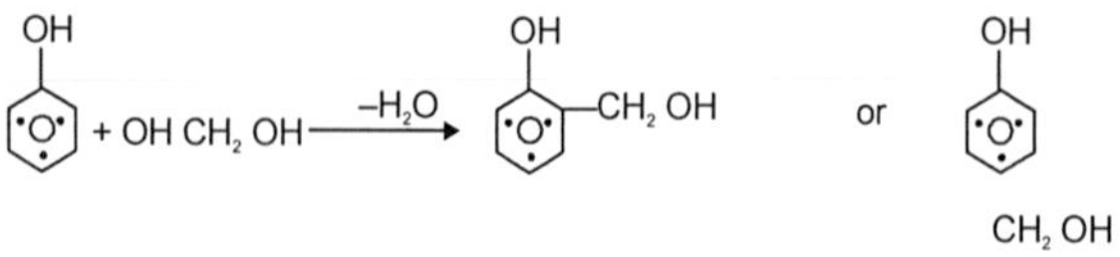

(21.1)

The reaction is catalyzed by both acids and bases. Basic catalysts (Na_2CO_3, NaOH, NH_4OH, etc.) and higher molar proportions of formaldehyde favour formation of di- and trimethylol pehnols in the subsequent steps e.g.

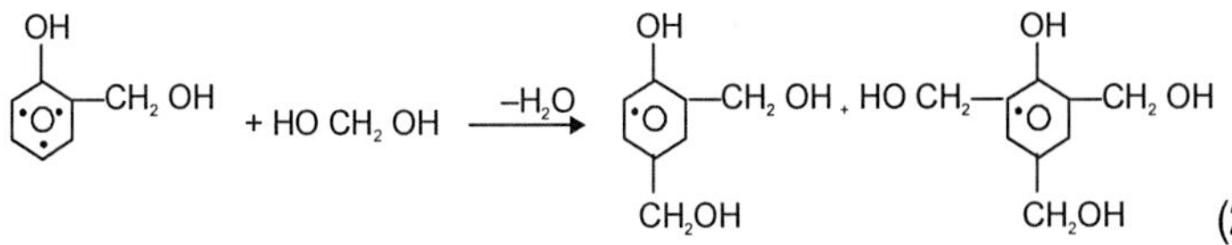

(21.2)

The initial reaction products or the resinoids and the reactants further react among them leading to chain extension and resin formation giving progressively increasing molecular weight. Acids are, however, more powerful catalysts. Acid catalysts (mineral or organic acids) and higher molar proportions of phenol favour immediate reaction involving two phenol molecules for each formaldehyde molecule resulting in the production of 2,4-dihydroxydiphenylmethane as the primary isolable product in the early stages. The early stage resinoids readily react with additional formaldehyde to form larger monomethylol derivatives which immediately

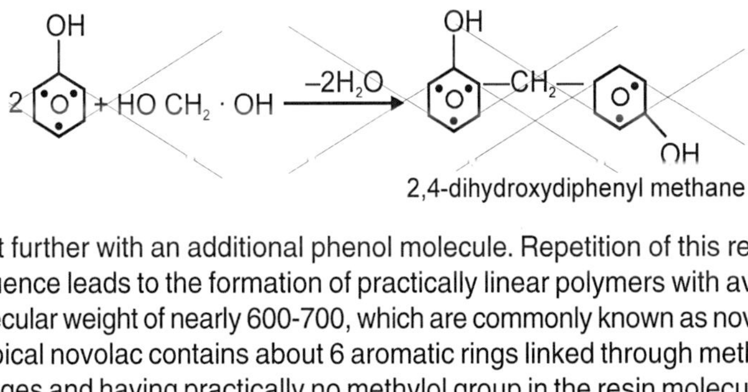

(21.3)

2,4-dihydroxydiphenyl methane

react further with an additional phenol molecule. Repetition of this reaction sequence leads to the formation of practically linear polymers with average molecular weight of nearly 600-700, which are commonly known as novolacs. A typical novolac contains about 6 aromatic rings linked through methylene linkages and having practically no methylol group in the resin molecule, (II). Novolacs are thus permanently soluble and fusible.

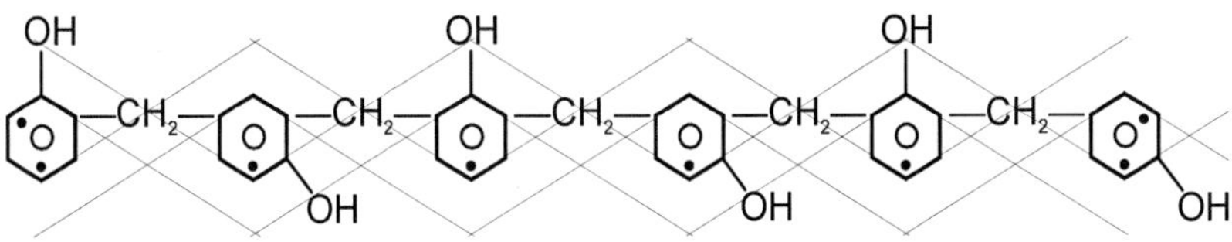

(II)

Average novolac molecule

If additional formaldehyde is made available and the resin is thermally treated, cross-linking reactions between novolac chains via the formation of methylol groups along with chain extensions take place ultimately rendering the resins insoluble and infusible. A segment of a typical cross-linked structure, (III) is shown below:

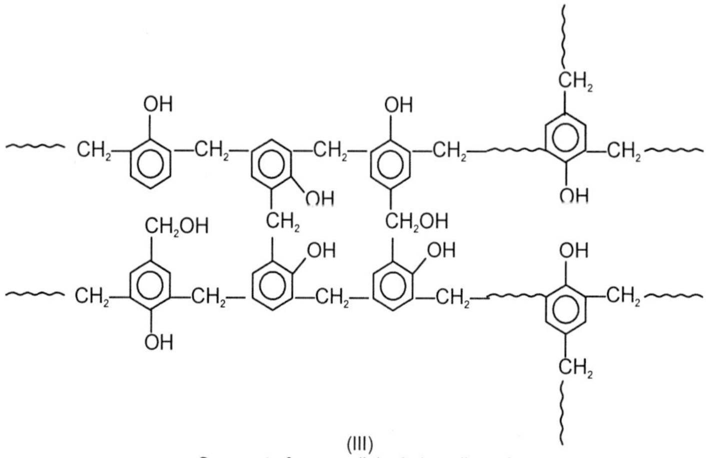

(III)
Segment of a cross-linked phenolic resin

The cross-linking of the novolacs in the second step in presence of additional formaldehyde is better accomplished using a basic catalyst. The overall technology of the novo lacs is a two step process; the first step corresponds to the formation of the linear, soluble and fusible resins using phenol and formaldehyde, usually in 1 : 0.8 molar proportions and the second step corresponds to heating the linear resin in presence of what is known as a hardener or cross-linking agent which decomposes under heat and pressure

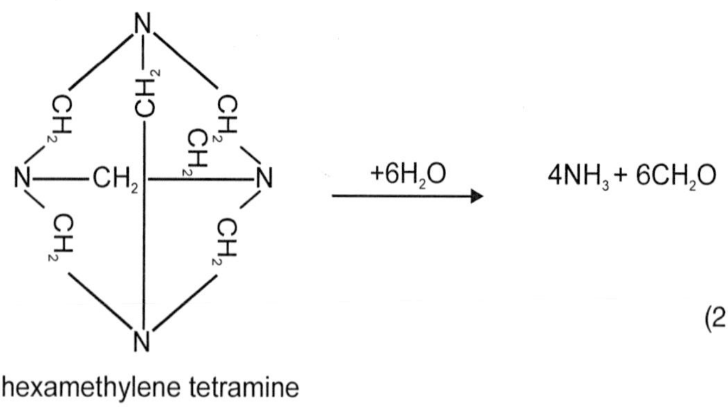

(21.4)

hexamethylene tetramine

to liberate formaldehyde and bring about cross-linking through establishment of methylene bridges. Hexamethylene tetramine or simply hexa, most commonly used as the cross-linking agent, decomposes under heat and using the moisture present to generate formaldehyde (the curing agent) and ammonia (the curing ca,talyst).

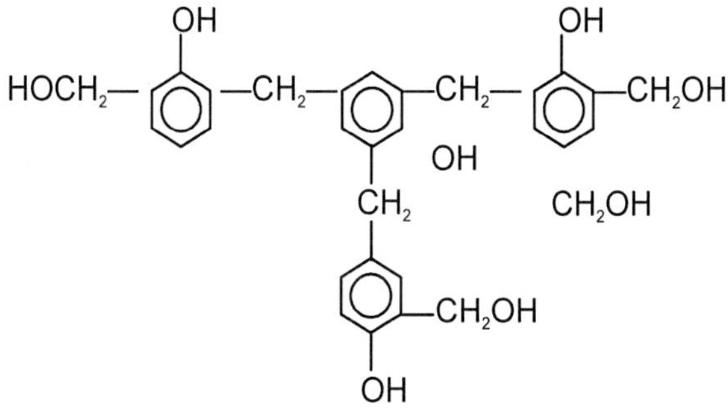

(IV)

Resole or A-stage phenolic resin

By contrast, the resinification using basic or alkaline catalysts ultimately leading to the production of insoluble, infusible, cross-linked polymer products is a one step process. The resinoids or chain molecules formed initially and at intermediate stages of growth carry appreciable number of methylol groups. If the reaction is stopped in the early stages, a low molecular weight product soluble in alkali or alcohol is obtained. It is commonly known as *resole* or the A-stage resin. A typical resole producing larger and mildly cross-linked resin molecules known as *resitol* or the B-stage resin. The resitol is insoluble in alkali and alcohol, but is partly or completely soluble in acetone. Resitols are still heat-fusible, and on further heating they turn into fully cured or cross-linked resin known as *resite* or the C-stage resin. The C stage resin is totally insoluble and infusible, and is segmentally represented by structure (III) shown earlier in this section. There are also evidences that under conditions of higher molar proportions of formaldehyde and alkaline catalysts, reaction between phenol alcohols initially formed leads to measurable formation of methylene ether bridges at temperatures as low as 70-100°C. Heating of the ethers in subsequent step or during cross-linking results in transformation of the methylene ether bridges to methylene bridges by splitting off formaldehyde, at least in part,

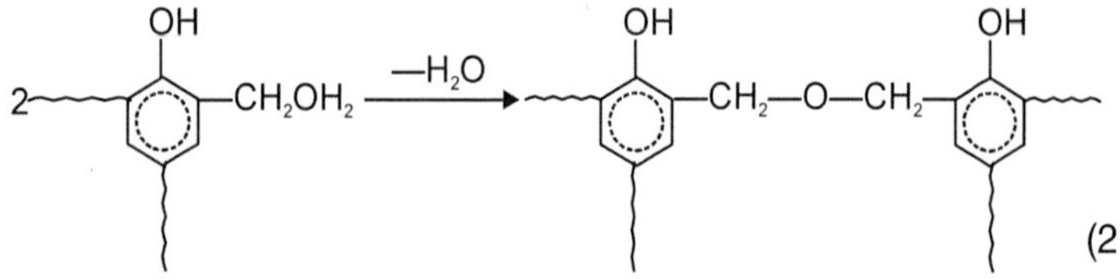

(21.5)

which may then react at other reactive sites ultimately leading to the establishment of additional cross-linkages.

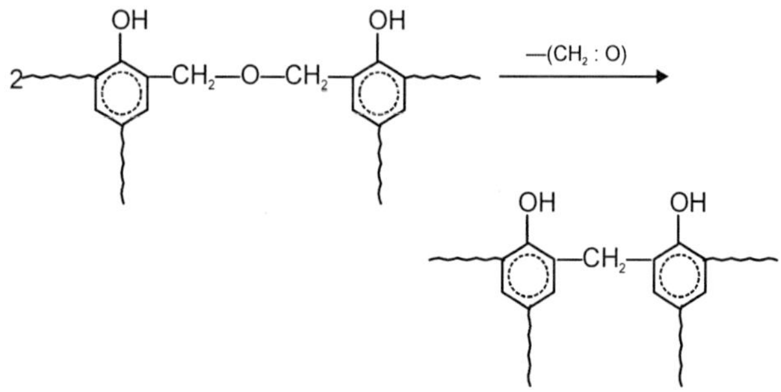

(21.6)

Commercial Production

Commercial resinification reactions for the production of resol~ or novolac, using appropriate proportions of phenol and formaldehyde and an appropriate catalyst are done at nearly 100°C in stainless steel jacketed (to permit heating or cooling) kettles. each fitted with an efficient stirrer and a condenser with provisions for reflux. After adequate progress of the reaction, water is removed usually under reduced pressure and under controlled temperature conditions and the molten or high viscous resin is discharged by opening the main discharge outlet valve at the bottom of the kettle.

Phenolic Moulding Powders

Novolacs are commonly used for preparation of moulding powders by judicious blending or mixing with the resin a host of compounding ingredients such as filler (usually wood flour or saw dust, 40-60 phr), hardener (hexa 10-12 phr), accelerators or curing catalysts (CaO, MgO, 2-5 phr), lubricant (stearic acid or Ca/ Zn stearate, 1-2 phr) and pigments (2-5 phr). During curing at high temperatures (160-165°C or higher) the phenolics darken considerably due to additional reactions involving the methylene ether linkages and phenolic OH groups leading to the formation of quinone methide and related structures. The pigments used in the phenolic moulding-powders are limited to blacks, browns and dark greens, blues, reds and oranges. Fillers are used to impart useful properties and to produce good mouldings. Saw dust has the additional advantage of reducing the cost. The phenolic moulding powders are usually moulded by compression moulding techniques using a pressure of 1500-3000 psi and a temperature of 160-170°C. The bulk factor of the moulding powder is given by the ratio of the density of the moulding to the apparent density of the powder fed into the mould. A convenient bulk factor for efficient moulding is normally obtained by what is known as preforming or pelletizing. Both preforming and preheating help in optimizing the moulding cycle. Preheating also reduces shrinkage and required moulding pressure. The curing is usually accomplished in 30-60 s for small and thin objects.

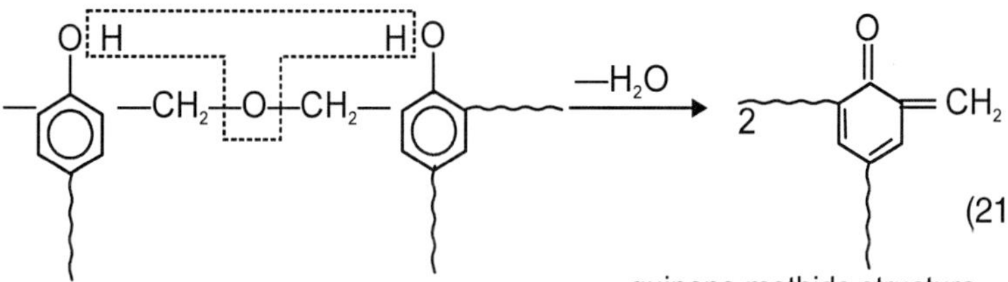

(21.7)

quinone methide structure

The most well-known applications of the phenolics are in areas of electrical insulation such as switches and plugs. The phenolics have better heat and moisture resistance than the urea-formaldehyde mouldings. Phenolic mouldings are also used to make knobs, handles, telephones, instrument cases, automobile components, caps and closures of containers, etc.

Phenolic Laminates

Laminating phenolic resins are usually the resoles. Caustic soda catalyzed resoles are suitable for mechanical and decorative laminates while ammonia-catalyzed resoles are suitable for electrical laminates. The reinforcements in the laminates are either paper, fabric or wood vineer. Resoles having a high methylol content made by using high formaldehyde to phenol ratio are water-soluble and a high degree of impregnation is possible using the aqueous solution. Spirit soluble resoles are also used for impregnation wherever necessary, convenient or advantageous. The continuously impregnated sheets are dried in a vertical or horizontal drying oven; the solvent evaported may be recovered if necessary and the resin advances to a desirable high degree of polymerization. The resin impregnated dry sheets are then cut into pieces and laminates are prepared by plying up the pieces and pressing in (multi-daylight) compression press between metal plates at 150-160°C and under pressure of 1000-2000 psi.

The phenolic (paper) laminates are extensively used for high voltage electrical insulation purposes. The laminates properly made through the right selection of the resin and reinforcement exhibit high strength, stiffness rigidity and good machinability and they are used in many engineering applications such as gears, bearings, bushings, etc. Plywoods and particle boards find use in the building and furniture industry. The laminates are also used in chemical plants and in the construction of transport vehicles and aircrafts.

Cast Phenolics

The casting grade phenolic resins are different from those meant for other applications. They are prepared from highly pure grades of phenol and formaldehyde (formalin) using more than 2 moles of formaldehyde (typically 2.2-2.5 moles) per mole of phenol and employing alkaline catalyst. To minimize colour formation, a stainless steel resin kettle is used and a milder temperature (70-75°C) is maintained. Highly methylolated hydrophilic resin molecules are formed and they remain uniformly dispersed in the water without separation or layer formation. The nearly water-white resin solution is then mixed with lactic acid to neutralize the alkaline catalyst and then the water content is reduced to nearly 5-10% by applying vacuum at 80-85°C. The viscous resin, light straw in colour, is then mixed with glycerol, a mould lubricant and colouring matter and poured into appropriate moulds and allowed to cure slowly at a temperature of 70-75°C over a period of 2-10 days. With growth in sizes of the resin molecules, ultimately leading to the formation of the C-stage resin, water present tends to separate out in fine droplets.

Glycerol used helps to disperse the entrapped water and thus helps minimize loss of transparency. Post-baking improves the dimensional stability of the cast phenolics. The curing time may be significantly lowered by using small amounts of an acidic catalyst into the resin mix just before casting. For their attractive colours and transparency self-lubricating properties and good machinability, the cast phenolics are used as objects of art and jewellery and as handles of tools and umbrella, knobs, etc. Cast phenolics have, however, become of much less commercial relevance in view of the widespread developments of cheaper and much improved materials in the form of vinyl and related thermoplastics, over the decades following the Second World War.

Miscellaneous Applications of Phenolic Resins

Foamed objects based on phenolic resins have gained importance, particularly in structural applications in the building industry. Resins based on para substituted phenols are used in surface coating formulations; *p-tertbutyl* phenol and p-phenyl phenol are reacted with formaldehyde to produce oil-soluble grade phenolics. Resorcinol-formaldehyde resins are extensively used as suitable bonding or coupling agents aimed at achieving good adhesion between reinforcing cords and rubber in the tyre, hose and belting industry. Other applications, taking advantage of the binding or adhesion capacity of the phenolics include brake linings, abrasives, sand core bonding and shell moulds for metal castings, grinding wheels, high performance refractory items etc. Another important application of the phenolics is in the area of making ion-exchange resins via sulfonation (cation exchanger) and chloromethylation followed by quaternization by treatment with ter-amines followed by alkali treatment (anion exchanger)

22

Amino Resins

Resins or plastics based on products of interactions between amines or amides and aldehydes are commonly known as amino resins or aminoplastics. Of the different amino resins prepared and used, the urea-formaldehyde (u-f) resins are the most important in all respects. Next in importance are the melamine-formaldehyde (m-f) resins.

Urea-Formaldehyde Resins

Urea-formaldehyde resins are prepared by reactions between urea and formaldehyde, usually carried out in two stages. The resinification is usually carried out in the first stage under a mildly alkaline condition in the temperature range of 30-45°C leading to the formation of monomethylol urea, and dimethylol urea. They are colourless and extensively soluble in water.

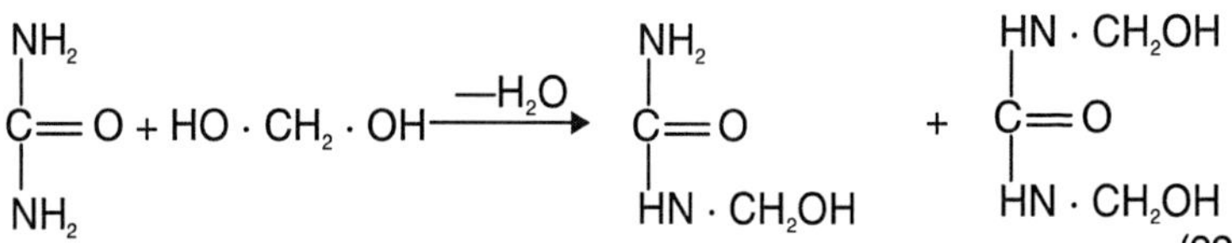

(22.1)

The relative proportions of mono- and di-methylol ureas would depend on the molar ratio of urea to formaladehyde (u : f). Urea is potentially tetrafunctional and use of nearly 1.5 to 2 moles of formaldehyde for each mole of urea has been found to yield useful resins. There should be enough formaldehyde to permit measurable and significant formation of dimethylol urea. Both monomethylol urea and dimethylol urea are isolable in the pure form. They further react amongst each other and with higher condensation products leading to chain extension and ultimately to the formation of high polymers. The polymerization is conveniently carried out in the second stage under acidic condition, the acid acting as a strong catalyst for the polymerization, leading to the formation of insoluble, infusible cross-linked products. The chain extension and cross-linking are accompanied with loss of water and formaldehyde. A segment of a typical cross-linked species is shown below (structure V).

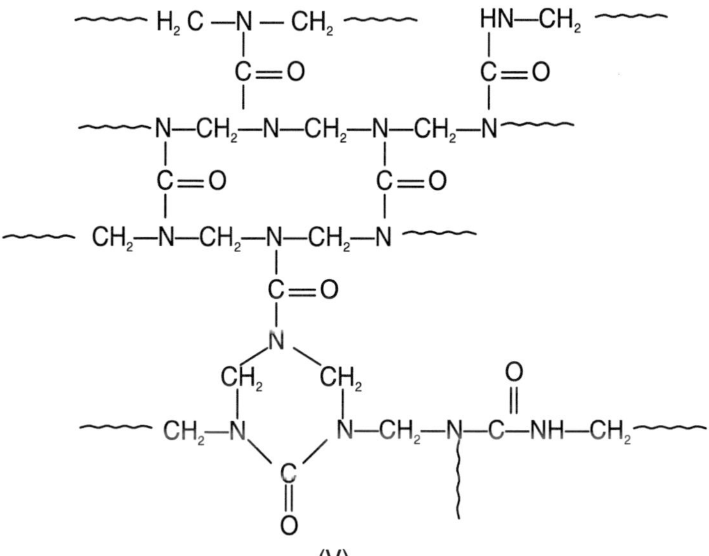

(V)

Segment of a typical cross-linked structure of urea-formaldehyde resins

The first stage resinification using appropriate molar proportions of urea and formaldehyde (37% formalin, adjusted to a *pH* of nearly 8.0 with NaOH) is done in a stainless steel reactor for about 30-90 min at a temperature of 30-45°C. Any drop in *pH* is usually adjusted by the addition of small amounts of ammonia or hexamine, The first stage or the A-stage resin is a water soluble mixture of monomethylol and dimethylol urea and some unreacted urea and formaldehyde.

The aqueous solution is then used straight away for the preparation of moulding powder. Cellulosic fillers in the form of bleached wood pulp are almost universally used to obtain widest range of bright colours or white objects. The pulp, resin solution and other additives are mixed together and heated at 60-70°C for 2-3 h to allow impregnation and further growth in size of the resin molecules. The resin impregnated pulp is then dried in a rotary drier for nearly 2 h at 100°C to a water content of about 5% and the resin advances to the B-stage in the process. The mixture is then milled in a ball mill and the pigments or colouring matters are added at this stage. For efficient and rapid curing of the resin to C-stage at moulding temperatures, a latent catalyst (1-2%) such as ammonium sulphamate, trimethyl phosphate etc., is mixed with the resin-filler systems. The catalyst decomposes at moulding temperatures to liberate an acid that accelerates the cross-linking reactions. To improve the shelf-life, the moulding powders are stored in a cool place. Incorporation of a small amount of a stabilizer such as hexamine in the moulding powder further improves the shelf-life. About 1% of a metal stearate (Zn, Al, Mg) is used as the lubricant in the moulding powder.

Moulding is commonly done by the compression, transfer or screw injection technique. Compression moulding is done employing a temperature of 150-160°C and a pressure of 1000-3000 psi over a time period of 20-60 s depending on the size and thickness of the moulding following the procedure described for the phenolic moulding powders. Typical end-uses are housewares (cups, bowls, saucers, etc.) housings for domestic appliances, electrical plugs and switches, telephones sets, caps and closures, vacuum flask cups and jugs, buttons, trays, knobs, lampshades, kitchen and bathroom fittings, etc.

The cured urea resins are hard and rigid and resistant to stain and scratching. They are non-inflammable but they char around 200°C. They exhibit good impact properties and excellent electrical insulation properties under dry conditions. They (u-f) resins do not impart taste and odour to food and drinks with which they may come in contact.

Urea-formaldehyde resins also find extensive use as wood adhesives and in the manufacture or plywood and laminates. The adhesive resins are prepared in the water soluble form, stabilized by maintaining the *pH* at 7.5 and a solid content of nearly 50-70% according to requirement by allowing partial dehydration using vacuum distillation. The resin may also be spray. dried to a stable powder. The high formaldehyde resins exhibit greater clarity, but they are more expensive due to the higher cost of formaldehyde. The resins are hardened under acidic conditions. In plywood manufacture, the more common hardening agent used is ammonium chloride (1.5 parts per 100 parts of resin solution) which acts as an acid donor. The resin/hardener mixture is used to impregnate the wood veneers, which are then plied together and pressed at nearly 100-110°C using a pressure of 200-1000.psi.

The plywoods are extensively used indoors but are unsuitable for outdoor work. A major outlet of the u-f resin bonded plywood is in the packaging field.

Urea-formaldehyde and related resins also find widespread use in the finishing of cotton textiles. The fabric is passed through the aqueous solution of methylol urea containing metal salts as hardeners and the resin-soaked fabric is heated in an oven at 140-160°C whereby the resins are hardened *in situ.* The process imparts good crease resistance to the fabric. Mercerization (steeping in NaOH solution) before resin treatment imparts improved combination of properties, particularly with respect to tear and tensile strengths along with crease resistance. Butylated urea resins show a good degree of thermoplasticity and they are soluble in organic solvents. They are used along with alkyd resins in the formulation of stoving enamels or air-drying lacquors. Simultaneous condensation of urea, formaldehyde and a monohydric alcohol such as butanol in presence of an acidic catalyst involve etherification and resinification at the same time. The alkoxy groups formed improve the solubility of the resin in surface coating solvents (make the resin oilsoluble) and by blocking the methylol groups they also reduce the tendency of the resin to get cross-linked.

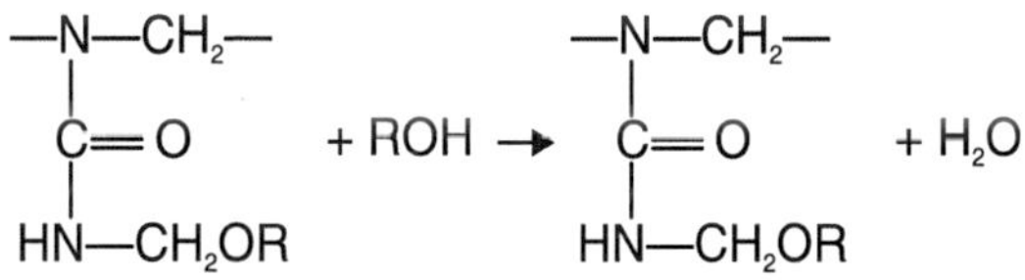

(22.2)

Melamine-Formaldehyde Resins

The other amino resin of commercial importance is melamine-formaldehyde (m-f) resin. Melamine may be obtained by heating urea under pressure, or more conveniently by heating dicyandiamide,

$$\underset{\text{urea}}{6CO(NH_2)_2} \xrightarrow[\text{400-600 atm}]{\text{400-600°C}} \underset{\text{melamine}}{C_3H_6N_6} + 3CO_2 \qquad (22.3)$$

preferably in presence of ammonia at about 300°C under pressure. Dicyandiamide is produced by heating cyanamide (NH_2CN) which in turn is obtained from calcium cyanamide, $CaCN_2$.

$$CaCN_2 \xrightarrow{[H^+]} H_2N\,CN \xrightarrow{70°–80°C} H_2N \cdot \underset{\underset{NH}{\|}}{C}\,NH \cdot CN$$

Cynamide Dicyandiamide

↓

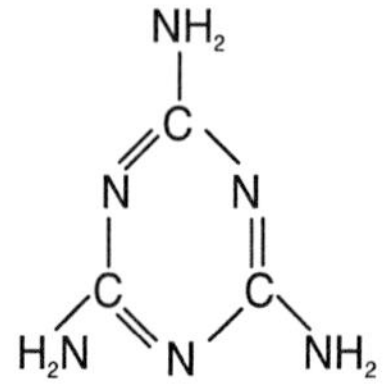

Melamine (22.4)

Resinification reaction between melamine and formaldehyde is very much dependent on the melamine to formaldehyde molar ratio and on the *pH* of the medium. Initial reactions lead to the formation of a mixture of water soluble methylol melamines. Depending on the prevalent reaction conditions, methylol derivatives up to six methylol groups per molecule (melamine is potentially hexafunctional) may be obtained.

Methylol-methylol condensation may subsequently lead to some methylene ether linkages:

$$\sim\sim \underset{|}{N}—CH_2OH + HOCH_2—\underset{|}{N} \dashrightarrow \sim\sim \underset{|}{N}—CH_2—O—CH_2—\underset{|}{N}\sim\sim + H_2O \quad (22.6)$$

However, major reactions leading to formation of methylene bridges are :

$$\sim\sim \underset{|}{N}—CH_2OH + \underset{|}{HN} \sim\sim \xrightarrow{—H_2O} \sim\sim \underset{|}{N}—CH_2—\underset{|}{N}\sim\sim \quad (22.7)$$

$$\sim\sim \underset{|}{N}—CH_2—O—CH_2—\underset{|}{N} \sim\sim \xrightarrow{—CH_2\,:\,O} \sim\sim \underset{|}{N}—CH_2—\underset{|}{N} \sim\sim \quad (22.8)$$

Commercial resinification reactions are done in much the same manner as employed for urea resins; pH is adjusted to 8-8.5 using Na_2CO_3 and an initial molar ratio of 1 : 3 for melamine to formaldehyde is used. The methylolation is done at a temperature of 80-85°C. The aqueous solution of the methylol melamines may be directly used for the finishing of fabrics,

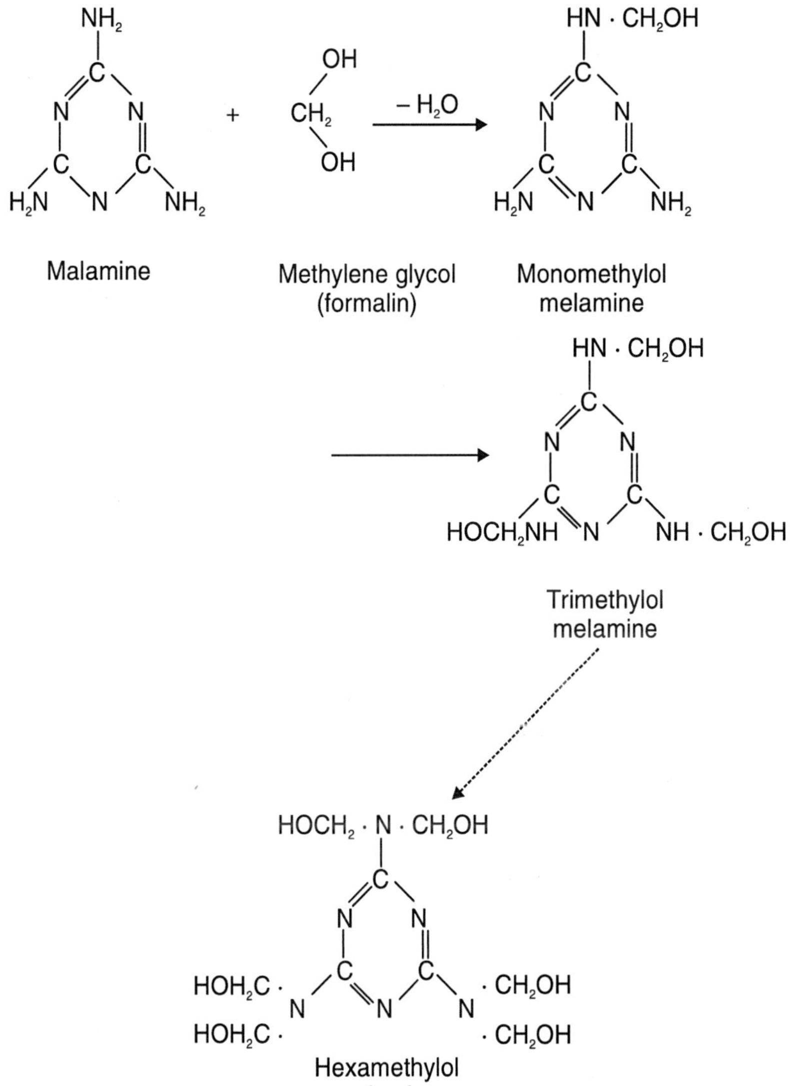

(22.5)

leather and paper. Spray drying of the soluble resins gives a product of higher stability.

The m-f moulding powders are made from the aqueous resin syrup produced by partial dehydration of the initial aqueous resin solution by vacuum distillation and using an initial melamine-formaldehyde molar ratio of 1 : 2. The resin syrup is intimately mixed with fillers, pigments, lubricants, stabilizers and with an accelerator if necessary in a suitable mixer, dried in an oven at 100-110°C and then ball milled into a powder. Common fillers employed are bleached wood pulp (a-cellulose), asbestos, silica or glass fibre. The m-f mouldings are superior to (u-f) mouldings with respect to hardness, scratch resistance, heat resistance, stain resistance and water resistance (the m-f mouldings having much lower moisture absorption). The m-f resin imparts better electrical insulation properties to the mouldings under humid or damp conditions and at higher temperatures. Principal applications include dinnerware, housings of home appliances, handles and knobs, bathroom fixtures, etc. They are moulded by compression, transfer or screw-injection techniques. For compression moulding, temperatures in the range 150-170°C and pressure of the order of 2000-8000 psi are commonly employed.

The high cost of the melamine resins limits their use in the production of common, general purpose laminates where p-f and u-f resins are more competitive. However, the exceptional hardness, scratch and stain resistance, solvent resistance and heat stability qualities of the m-f resins are taken advantage of in making special purpose and decorative laminates in which only the surface layers are impregnated with the m-f resins and the inner or base layers with phenolic resins. For the production of electrical grade laminates the condensation catalyst used is triethanolamine rather than sodium carbonate. The electrical grade laminates are usually made by impregnating electrical-grade glass cloth with the triethanolamine catalyzed resin.

23

Silicones

Polymers in which the chain backbone consists of repeat units having organic side groups linked with silicon atoms are commonly known as silicones or polyorganosiloxanes. The polyorganosiloxanes are usually prepared by allowing chlorosilanes such as $Cl_2Sir_1R_2$ to react with water to form the corresponding hydroxy compounds which subsequently condense with each other leading to the production of polymer molecules.

Only dichlorodialkyl silanes yield linear polymer; monochloro silanes fail to produce any polymer and trichloromonoalkyl silanes yield network polymers. The intermediate silanes, R_nSiX_{4-n} (n = 0—4), where X is a hydrolyzable group or atoms such as chlorine or alkoxy, may be made by direct synthesis involving reactions between alkyl/ aryl halides and elementary silicon, e.g.,

$$2CH_3Cl + Si \xrightarrow[Cu]{250\text{-}280°C} Si\,(CH_3)2C_2 \qquad (23.2)$$

When methyl chloride is used, the major product under the most favourable condition is dimethyldichlorosilane (70-75%); the minor constituents in the crude product being methyltrichlorosilane (8-10%) and trimethylchlorosilane (5-6%). They are separated by fractional distillation.

Silicone fluids are linear (low) polymers or cyclic condensation products of silanols obtained by hydrolysis of a predetermined mixture of chlorosilanes in excess water under vigorous agitation. Initial products give an approximately equal mixture of cyclic compounds (mainly tetramer) and linear low polymers. To stabilize the viscosity and to obtain higher proportions of linear polymers, it is required to equilibrate the fluid by heating with dilute H_2SO_4. Chain length is controlled by using the desired proportions of the monofunctional trimethylchlorosilane as the "blocking agent". The equilibration may take several hours at 100-150°C. The oil is separated from the aqueous layer and neutralized by washing with sodium carbonate solution. Silicone fluids of different viscosity grades are all colourless, odourless, water repellent and non-toxic products of high thermal stability showing very narrow deviation in physical properties, e.g. viscosity, over a wide range of temperature (-70 to 200°C). They are used as polish additives, as release agents during the moulding of certain plastics and rubber goods and in the die casting of metals, and as greases. They are useful as antifoam additives, in drug formulations, as additives in paints and other surface coatings and as water repellent finishes in the textiles, paper and leather industry.

Silicone rubbers or *elastomers* are very high molecular weight linear siloxane polymers prepared from the difunctional monomer, dichlorodimethyl silane (or from its cyclic tetramer) often mixed with minor proportions of dichloromethyl phenyl silane. The elastomer may be vulcanized with peroxides such as benzoyl peroxide. Filler incorporation is necessary to produce vulcanizates of some strength (up to 2000 psi), since unfilled polymers are soft and they have negligible strength. Silica fillers are preferably used for reinforcement. Silicone rubbers with vinyl side groups (0.02-0.5 mole % of other organic side groups-methyl and phenyl) may be more readily cured using less reactive peroxides such as dicumyl peroxide giving more elastic vulcanizates. The silicone rubbers are much more expensive than other synthetic rubbers and they exhibit room temperature physical and mechanical properties inferior to those exhibited by other synthetic rubbers. The silicone rubbers are characterized by good resistance to weathering and lubricating oils, high compression set (20-50% after 24 h at 150°C), very high air permeability and excellent low temperature (-80°C) flexibility. Special purpose rubbers as they are, they are used in wire and cable insulation demanding fire resistance and in gaskets and seals. The physiological inertness of the silicones is taken advantage of in such applications as sterilizable blood transfusion tubing, closures of antibiotic containers, etc. The cold curing elastomers are suitable *for* sealing, caulking and encapsulation.

Silicone resins are commercially prepared by batch hydrolysis of a suitable blend of chlorosilanes giving an average R/Si ratio ranging between 1.2 : 1 and 1.6 : 1. The blend of chlorosilanes is dissolved in a suitable solvent and then hydrolyzed with water under controlled conditions avoiding overheating. After the required hydrolysis, the solvent layer containing the polymer is separated from the aqueous layer and neutralized with mild alkali wash. Molecular weight of the polymer is usually allowed *to* advance further without effective cross-linking by heating or "bodying" the solution in presence of a metallic soap *to* a desired viscosity *for* a given solids content. Cross-linking of the resin is achieved in *situ* in the finished product. The silicone resins find special applications in electrical insulation in the *form* of glass cloth laminates and insulating varnishes. The resin is applied by brushing the solution on the substrate and allowing solvent evaporation or by dipping the substrate in resin solution and draining or scrapping the excess resin and allowing the solvent *to* evaporate; cross-linking is accomplished by heating. The resins also find use in special purpose industrial paints and as encapsulating agents.

24

Additives for Plastics

A major aim and objective relating *to* polymer processing is *to* "get a shape and set the shape". In general, polymers of any class, particularly those meant *for* plastics and rubber applications are seldom used in the pure *form.* In *most* cases, they are mixed or compounded with a host of additives called mixing or compounding ingredients before moulding, forming, coating, etc. The processing itself and its controlling features are dependent in a large measure on the rheological behaviour of the mix or the compound.

The additives are incorporated in the polymer keeping one or *more* of the following advantages in view: (a) reduction of material *cost,* (b) improvements in properties, performance and service life of the end product, (c) achieving ease of processing and reduction of processing *cost,* and (d) minimizing degradation during processing and use. Functionally, the additives may be categorized under the following heads and the figures in the parentheses indicate part by weight of the ingredient used per 100 parts of polymer in general:

(a) Fillers (30-100)

(b) Plasticizers (30-100)

(c) Stabilizers (0.02-10)

(d) Colouring matters (2-5)

(e) Lubricants (1-2) and flow promoters

(f) Cross-linking agents (1-5)

(g) Others (1-5)

The most important constituent of the mix or the compound is the polymer itself. The polymer plays the role of a binding material that forms the matrix which finally cements the various ingredients of the mix into a cohesive mass and holds the shape or form given to the finished article.

Fillers

Fillers are usually solid additives. They may simply be used as loading agents (inert fillers) with the objective of lowering the material cost; but very often filler incorporation brings about much desired improvements in physical properties such as tensile strength, modulus, abrasion resistance and tear strength (reinforcing fillers). Different types of fillers are in use, viz. particulate, rubbery, resinous or fibrous fillers. For particulate fillers such as carbon black and precipitated silica, the average particle size and particle shape have profound influence on the properties of the end product. Mineral fillers are often treated with specific chemicals to improve wetting or attachment of polymers to fillers; "tearic acid-treated calcium carbonate or amine- or glycol-treated clays may be cited as examples of treated fillers. Use of coupling agents, such as specific silanes, is of more recent development whereby more effective wetting or affinity of the filler to the main polymer is achieved via the coupling agent. Rubbery fillers are incorporated to improve toughness and impact resistance. Fibrous fillers such as wood flour, wood pulp, cotton flock, glass fibre and synthetic organic fibres (rayons, nylons and polyesters) are used as reinforcing agents. For improved heat resistance, glass fibre, mica and asbestos are useful as fillers.

Plasticizers

Plasticizers are usually high boiling nonvolatile liquids. They are used in a variety of polymers such as the cellulosics, acrylics and poly(vinyl chloride). Plasticization is manifested essentially through solvent action. To be effective, a plasticizer is required to have a solubility parameter close to that of the substrate polymer, such that two would be largely compatible. Both polar interaction and interactions through hydrogen bonding between the plasticizer molecules and polymer segments are considered to explain the plasticization effect. Common plasticizers used are high boiling organic esters of some organic acids and phosphoric acid such as dioctyl phthalate (DOP) diisooctyl phthalate (DIOP), dibutyl phthalate (DBP), dioctyl sebacate (DOS) and tricresyl phosphate (TCP). Substances such as hydrocarbon oils and resins which are used to make the polymer soft, and easy processing only by spacing effect without any meaningful interactions with the polymer are commonly known as *softeners.* Sometimes, chlorinated paraffins and refinery oils of lower solubility parameter than the true plasticizers are used to partly replace the plasticizer giving a comparable plasticization effect. Such replacement additives used with plasticizers are known as *extenders.* Extenders are effective only in the presence of a *true plasticizer,* and they fail to impart any plasticization in the absence of a true plasticizer.

Stabilizers

Different kinds of stabilizers are used as additives in polymers to protect them from degradation during storage and processing and under performing conditions. The most common stabilizers are: (i) antioxidants, which protect the polymer against degradation by oxygen attack, and (ii) UV absorbers, which protect the polymer against degradation by ultra violet light.

Oxygen attack or oxidative degradation becomes very critical under processing conditions when oxygen is absorbed at a high rate resulting in peroxidation or hydroperoxidation and subsequent degradation of the polymer by a radical chain mechanism follows. Antioxidants are primarily of two types: (1) *preventive antioxidants* which prevent generation of radicals, and (2) *chain breaking antioxidants* which function effectively by interrupting the propagation of the oxidative chain degradation. Most common chain breaking antioxidants are phenols, such as styrenated phenols, and amines, such as phenyl naphthylamines. Phenols are usually preferred because of their being less prone to staining, discolouration, blooming and bleeding. Amines are, however, sometimes more effective than phenols and are advantageous on cost considerations too. Among the preventive antioxidants, those more commonly used are: (i) peroxide decomposers such as dilauryl thiopropionate and p-substituted phenyl phosphites, and (ii) metal deactivators in the form of selected chelating agents which form complexes with metal ion contaminants that may otherwise initiate oxidation. Antiozonants are more relevant to diene rubbers and related polymers having unsaturations. Wax additives that form an inpervious layer of wax by blooming to the surface protect such polymers under conditions of static applications, but they turn out to be much less effective to prevent ozone attack under dynamic conditions. Selected p-phenylene diamine derivatives are more effective and useful in this regard.

Chlorine-containing polymers such as poly(vinyl chloride) and related copolymers are thermally unstable and require stabilization and protection against thermal degradation, the stabilizers commonly used being basic lead salts and selected cadmium and barium compounds and organo-tin compounds (*See* Sec. 8.10.4).

Stabilization of polymers prone to UV degradation is usually achieved by incorporation of special additives commonly known as UV-absorbers. UV-absorbers commonly in use are benzophenone and its derivatives, phenyl salicylates and benzotriazoles. Carbon black (1-5%) also gives protection against UV degradation.

Colouring Matters

Various types and shades of pigments and dyes and also carbon black are used as colour ants in polymer compounding. The colourants show different degrees of solubility in the polymer matrix. Low solubility may lead to blooming. To be efficient and effective, the colour ants should have high covering power and they should be stable under processing conditions. It is often convenient to use masterbatches or colour concentrates in appropriate proportions with the white/ colourless granules to produce coloured end-products.

Lubricants and Flow Promoters

Lubricants used to the extent of 1-2 wt % of the polymer allow quick mould release and prevent the moulded object from sticking to the mould. There are lubricants such as silicone fluids, graphite, etc., which when rubbed against the mould surface reduce friction at the interface and hence permit easy release of the moulded articles. Stearic acid and stearates of Ca, Zn, Pb, Cd and Ba blended into the polymer mix tend to exude from the composition to the polymer-metal interface during processing at high temperatures and in this manner prevent finished object from sticking to the mould. Incorporation of certain low molecular weight materials such as glyceryl stearates and cetyl palmitate impart better flow properties to the polymer mix under processing (melt) conditions without really affecting the bulk properties under service conditions. They essentially function as flow promoters. Polymeric flow promoters are also known. Polymers exhibiting very low melt viscosity at processing temperatures and having solubility parameters close to the solubility parameters of the base polymer are suitable as flow promoters. Polymeric flow promoters such as low molecular weight PVc, chlorinated polyethylenes, acrylate copolymers and ethylene-vinyl acetate (EVA) copolymers are often used in the compounding of unplasticized and transparent PVC compositions.

Cross-linking Agents

Cross-linking or curing agents are important and essential ingredients for all crosslinkable or curable compositions leading to the production of thermoset plastics and vulcanized rubbers. Nowadays, almost any polymer-linear or branched and having reactive sites in its structure or otherwise-can be cross-linked using selected chemical cross-linking agents under heat and pressure or using high energy radiations such as y-rays, X-rays and high-speed electrons. In many curing systems, suitable catalysts or accelerators in presence or absence of an activator system are used to speed up the curing process and to achieve optimum cross-link density. Peroxides, such as benzoyl peroxide and dicumyl peroxide are widely 'Used as the curing agents for many of thermoplastics and rubbers. Other curing agents in widespread use are sulphur, selenium and sulphur monochloride for diene rubbers, diisocyanates for polymers having reactive functional groups, amines and polyamines for expoxides, formaldehyde for novolacs and polyvinyl alcohols, etc.

Other Additives

Among the additives other than those mentioned above, and deserving special mention are flame retardants, antistatic agents and blowing agents (for cellular or expanded products). Plastics used in building industry, transport vehicles, mining and related industries, etc., should have prominent flame retardant characteristics. Antimony compounds such as antimony oxide, antimony oxychloride, etc., are commonly used to impart enhanced flame retardancy in plastics. Chlorinated paraffins, selected bromo compounds such as tribromotoluene and phosphate plasticizers such as tritolyl phosphate and trixylyl phosphate are useful additives which enhance the fire retarding properties of plastics. The chloro- or bromocompounds derive their effectiveness through the diluting effects of Hel, HBr or bromine formed during their thermal cracking. Flame retardants may otherwise decompose endothermically absorbing much of the heat, form impervious fire resistant layer on the surface thus preventing access of oxygen to the inner polymer layers or chemically interfere with the flame propagation process.

Selected amines and quaternary ammonium compounds are used as antistatic agents. Blowing agents of different types are in use. One type known as the chemical blowing agents, incorporated in the polymer in the compounding stage, decomposes to yield in part a gas or a volatile substance at an appropriate stage of the processing, which gets entrapped in the polymer matrix to give the expanded or blown product. Sometimes, low boiling liquids are blended and allowed to volatilize out at the most appropriate stage of processing producing the expanded product. Gases, such as air, CO_2 or N_2, are also used to produce foams or expanded items. Chemical blowing agents which are commonly used are $NaHC0_3$, azonitriles, azodicarbonamide, dinitroso pentamethylene tetramine, etc.

25

Polybutylene Terephthalate

1. *Common name* : Polybutylene terephthalate or terephthalate.
2. *Abbreviation :* PBT also known as PTMT and/pr PBTD
3. *Systematic chemical name* : Poly (oxytetremethylene oxyterephthalate).
4. *Material properties* : The reaction between acids and alcohols (to produce esters) is commonly used to make high polymers. If terephthalic acid is reacted with 1.4-butanediol then a polyester is produced-polybutylene terephthalate (PBT). This is also known as polytetramethylene terephthalate (PTMT). It is a partially crystalline thermoplastic polyester and is classed as an engineering plastic. The material has a fairly high heat distortion temperature, is stiff, tough and hard. This material also has good abration resistance, resists failure by fatigue and creep and displays good electrical properties (over a wide range of temperatures and humidities). The combustion behaviour is similar to that of polyamides. Compared to other materials, which also contain p-phenylene groups (e.g. PC). PBT has a lower heat distotion temperature and low water absorption. The key features this material are good resistance to chemical stress-cracking coupled with excellent dimensional stability. Rapid cycles are possible because of the fast set-up rate. Mouldings have very low coefficients of frictio and a hard surface.
5. *Material detection or identification* : With a density of 1.31 g cm-3 this material sinks in water and has a high, sharp melting point, e.g., 225°C; above this temperature the viscosity of the material is low. It is attacked

by sodium hydroxide and ethylene dichloride. Moulding have a hard, scratch resistant surface with a very low coefficient of friction; it is not available in clear grades.

6. *Colouring* : A range of compounded colours is available ranging from cream to black; as properties are dependent on the colouring system it is important to evaluate a product using mouldings made from the intended formulation. Masterbatches are used for small mouldings but not for large (may get colour streaking).

Gloss has been improved by blending small amounts of polyethylene terephthalate (PET) in with PBT. Addition of elastomers ia also being used to improve gloss and impact resistance, e.g., for mineral filled grades.

PET is suffer, tougher and glossier than PBT but PBT has better electrical properties,is easier to process and cycles faster.

26

Polyethersulphone

1. *Common name* : Polyethersulphone
2. *Abbreviation :* PES.
3. *Systematic chemical name* : Poly (oxy-1,4-phenylene-sulphoney 1-1,4-phenylene).

   These materials differ chemically and have, for example, differing high temperature properties; the upper use temperature increases in the order Udel; Victrex; Astrel.

4. *Material properties* : These materials all contain aromatic groups (*p*-phenylene), sulphone groups (SO_2) and ether groups (—O—); other groups (diphenyl) may also be incorporated to the polymer chain. Any plastic which contains *p*-phenylene groups (e.g. PC) has a high heat distortion temperature. PES materials are tough and have a wide temperature range of use (e.g. from -100 to +150°C). Because of these chemical structure the materials are resistant to chemical changes.
5. *Material detection or identification* : This material has a high density (e.g. 1.37 gm-3) and moulding therefore sink when placed a water. Being an amorphous material it can be obtained as transparent mouldings, e.g. pale-straw order colour. The moulding are tough and have a very high softening point, e.g., a Vicat softening point of greater than 200°C. When placed in a flame the mouldings do not burn very easily but when they burn they do so with a white flame and give off an odour of sulphur. When the mouldings are struck with a boject they can give off a metallic sound or ring.

6. *Colouring* : The natural colour is a transparent amber shade and so a wide colour range is possible. It can be dyed or pigmented; dyes give transparent colours and pigments give opaque colours. Dyes can be incorporated, in some grades by the moulder but in general the addition of pigments is not recommended as agglomerated may form. Such inclusion could act as stress-raisers and cause failure during impact.

7. *Material and component handing* : the material contains absorbed water and should be dried at 150°C for at least 3h before any attempt is made to mould. Use a heated hopper if possible.

8. *Reprocessing* : Up to 30% regrind may be blended in with virgin material. As moisture does not cause chemical degradaton, scrap mouldings (made from wet material) may be ground, dried and used again. Because of the material's excellent thermal regrind can be used several times before the physical properties change.

9. Typical components : Because these materials are expensive they are not large tonnage materials. They are used when a thermoplastics is required which has good long-term thermal stability, dimensional stability, toughness and resistance to burning. These properties together with their good electrical insulation properties have promoted their use in the microwave cooling field, e.g, for grills, dishes etc. These materials have extended the range of use of thermoplastics as, for certain applications, they may replace thermosets and metals, e.g. in cameras.

PES is used in dishwasher and automotive components, the electrical and elctronics industry (e.g. for printed circut boards, television components, etc.) hair dryer parts, oven, projector and fan heater components are also moulded. That, is the material is used when other cheaper thermoplastics (such as PC) are not suitable.

With this family of materials there is a significant difference in the maximum upper end use temperature of approximately 100°C (the highest upper end use temperature is approximately 250°C). some electrical components are required to perform satisfactorily after extensive oven egeing tests, e.g. 10,000 h at 200°C.

27

Nylon

1. *Common name* : Nylon.
2. *Abbreviation :* PA6 or PA66
3. *Systematic chemical name* : PA6 is poly (imino-l-oxohexamethylene)
4. *Material properties* : Nylon is a generic term used to describe thermoplstics which contain the amide group—CONH—: as the polymers contain many such groups they are also known as 'polyamides'. Such materials are tough, resist fatigue, impact and solvents, have low friction and absorb some water (reversibly). Many different types are possible e.g., 6; 7; 9; 11; 12 and 6 6; 6 10; 6 12, etc. Where one number is used it indicates the number of carbon atoms in the raw material (e.g., a lactam); where two numbers are used (e.g. 6 6) then the first number indicates the number of carbon atoms in the parent diamine and the second indicates the number of carbon atoms in the parent acid. Nylon 66 and nylon 6 are the best known members of the groups and as the amide groups are separated by sections based on methylene groups, they are also known as aliphatic polyamides.

   Such materials compete against each other and with the acetals; nylons have superior abrasion resistance and toughness then the acetals. Nylon 66 is probably the most widely used nylon mouling material. It is slightly stronger and stiffer than nylon 6; it has a higher heat distortion temperature, absorbs less water and has a higher flexural strength. The material is made by reacting hexamethylene diamine and adipic acid.

Nylon 6 is made caprolactam and in many respects it is similar to type 66. It is marginally lighter in colour and with a slightly lower density (1.13 g cm^{-3} as compared to 1.15 g cm^{-3}). the material has a lower melting point and can therefore be processed at a lower temperature, the shaping temperature range is also wider and processing can therefore be considered easier. Nylon 6 is slightly cheaper than type 66 (in the UK), more flexible, has a higher impact strength and slightly better low temperature properties. In general it has better solvent, grease and detergent resistence than PA66 but its resistance to dilute mineral acids is poorer.

5. *Resistant to the following* : In general these material are resistant to alkalis, dilute acids (but not nitric acids, detergets, fuels, greases, oils, chlorinated hydrocarbons, aromatic hydrocarbons, ketones and easters. Some of these materials may cause polyamide mouldings to swell, e.g. chlorinated hydrocarbons.

6. *Not resistant to* : Strong acids, bleaching agents (e.g. hydrogen peroxide). Sunlight can cause embrittlement unless the polymer is stabilised (e.g. with carbon black). Soluble in phenol, cresol, formic acid and glacial acetic acid, Water and, for example, some alcohols may cause swelling. Water acts as a platiciser and makes the material softer and tougher but worsens the electrical insulation properties.

7. *Material detection or identification* : The density of type is slightly lower than type 66 (e.g. 1.13 compared to 1.15 g cm^{-3}) therefore both will sink in water. Both the opaque, stiff, hard tough materials which are easily cut so as to yield cuts with smooth edges. Difficult to ignite but once alight they are not self extinguisihing. The polymers melts to a free flowing liquid (which can be pulled into stings) which drips and carries the flame with it as it falls. The flame burns blue, has a yellow edge and emits a smell of burning hair. The easiest way to distinguish 6 from 66 is to measure the melting point; 66 will melt sharply but at a higher temperature, e.g. 265°C. Type 66 is also more resistant to chloroform, benzyl alcohol and trichloroethylene. When type 66 is heated in boiling N, N-dimethylformamide it does not dissolve—PA66 does. Nylon is also soluble in 4N hydrochloric acid whereas 66 is insoluble.

8. *Colouring*: The fully compounded material is preferred; it is found that the addition of pigment can dramatically affect properties (e.g. impact strength) and this can cause problems if trail are performed with natural polymer. A limited amount of colour masterbatch is used and liquid

colour is being actively developed. Many of the grades now being moulded are fully colour compounded materials which are also lubricated and nucleated so as to get good colour, ease to flow and fast cycling.

9. *Material and component handling*: These materials absorb water (type 6 more than 66. e.g. 2.5% as opposed to 1.5%) and must therefore be stored in a clean, dry space. A fist-in-first-out system should be adopted and after they have reached the workshop temperature. If the moisture content is greater then about 0.2% problems will occur. Dry if possible in a vaccum drying oven at 80°C for up to 18 h; the absence of air will help to prevent oxidation.

10. *Reprocessing* : Nylon is noted for its toughness; however it is only tough when it has absorbed a certain amount of water. When it comes from the mould it will be dry and will therefore be more brittle. Regranulate immediately if possible. Use up to 30% of regrind but do not regrind contaminated material or damaged material (e.g. overheated) predry regrind if required.

11. Typical components : Polyamides have a useful combination of properties which makes them attractive for many applications. 'Under the bonnot' applications (fuel pipes, fuel filter components, etc.) take advantage of nylon's resistance to hydrocarbons and heat. Gears, cams, levers, door furniture, etc. Utilise the material's toughness, abrasion resistance, low friction and fatique resistance. Other applications are appliances housings, fans, impellers, door handles, safety belt components, bathroom fittings etc.

Glass-reinforced polyamides are used where the components must have a higher heat distortion temperature, greater rigidity and dimensional stability than that offered by the unreinforced material. A typical application that takes good advantage of this material's properties, is a power tool outer case or housing; a novel application is a bicycle flame.

These materials need higher injection speeds, and barrel and mould temperatures, than the unfilled grades. Cycles maybe shorter as the parts can be ejected at higher temperatures; it is sometimes discolouration which limits ejection temperature. Mould shrinkage is reduced but density is increased by glass addition. For example, for PA66 with 20% glass fibre, the shrinkage is approximately 0.005 in/in and the desnity is 1.28 g cm^{-3}.

28

Polyvinylidene Fluoride

1. *Common name* : Polyvinylidene fluoride
2. *Abbreviation :* PVDF or $PVF_{2.}$
3. *Systematic chemical name* : poly(1,1-difluoroethylene) as been suggested.
4. *Material properties* : There are several fluoropolymers that can be processed by injection moulding and the group includes fluorinated ethylene-propylene (FEP); ethylene tetrafluoroethylene (ETFE, ethylene chlorotrifluoroethylene (ECTFE), chlorotrifluoroethylene (CTFE), perfluoroalkoxy tetrafluoroethylene (PFA) and polyvinlyidene fluoride (PVDF). In general these materials have excellent chemical and heat resistance, they are good elecrical insulators and have high impact strengths. PVDF has the highest dielectric constant heat deflection temperature, flexural strength and modulus; its yeild strength and creep resistance resistance is high for a fluorinated thermoplastic. The abrasion resistance of this material is similar to that of polyamides. As the thermal and light stability is very good no heat stabilisers or UV stabilisers are necessary and this means that the material can benontoxic.

   By keeping the molecular weight relatively low or PVDF material can be produced which is highly crystalline-this material is used to moulding as product are still and strong PVDF is relatively easy to process for a fluoroplastic.
5. *Resistant to the following* : PVDF has excellent resistance to a wide range of chemicals, e.g., halogens, salt solutions, inorganic acids and

basis, aliphatic and aromatic hydrocarbons, carboxylic acids and acid chlorides, mercaptanes and chlorinated hydrocarbons. Resists degradation by ultra-violet light, χ and β radition.

6. *Not resistant to* : Hot concentrated sulphuric acid, strongly basic amines, hot concentrated bases and alkali metals. Swollen by polar solvents such as acetone and ethylacetate. Dissolve with difficulty in solvents such as dimethylformamide, dimethylsulphoxide and tetramethylurea. Some stress cracking is strong alkalis.

7. *Material detention or identification* : The natural colour of this material is a transluscent milky white and as it is a crystalline material it is not possible to produce transparent mouldings. It has a high density (1.78 g cm^{-3}) and will produce transparent mouldings. It has a high density (1.78 g cm^{-3}) and will therefore sink readily in water. The Vicat softening point is approximately 130°C and the crystalline melting point (as measured by differential thermal analysis (DTA)) is approximately 170°CC. Relatively easy to cut and/or machine. The material has good first resistance and will not proporate a flame. Pungent Fumes of hydrofluric acid are liberated at (about) 320°C.

8. *Colouring* : Some pigments (e.g. titanium dioxide) and some other inorganic materials (boron oxide) may cause rapid decomposition of PVDF. Before adding any compounding ingredients check with the supplier. Do not add glass fillers, e.g. glass fibre, as such fillers may cause rapid decomposition. Before processing PVDF ensure that the machine does not contain anything which could cause decomposition, e.g, a glass reinforced polymer, Use the PVDF in ready compounded form or only use masterbatchs or dry colours by the suppliers.

9. *Reprocessing* : Material can be reprocessed in many cause without obvious impairment of properties. If dust is generated during the regrinding operation than smoking should not be permitted as the PVDF dust falling on to the cigrette end can generate fluorinated compounds. Keep grinders, etc. scrupulously clean.

29

Polyphenylene Sulphide

1. *Common name* : Polyphenylene sulphide.
2. *Abbreviation :* PPS
3. *Systematic chemical name* : Poly (thio-1,4,-phenylene)
4. *Material properties* : Crystalline, thermoplatics material based on benzene groups linked with sulphur atoms. Usually sold already compounded with glass fibres (e.g. 40%) or with mixtures of glass fibres and mineral fillers. As a result of these additions and because of its chemical structure, it is classed as an engineering polymer. It retains its strength at high temperatures and/or in aggressive environments. Some grades can have high impact strengths but most have low elongations at break. The materials are excellent electrical insulators which are unaffected by humid environments.
5. *Resistant to the following* : Can withstand high temperatures without deformation. Cambines chemical resistance with hydrolytic and dimensional stability at high temperatures. Absorbs only small amounts of water e.g. 0.05%.
6. *Not resistant to* : Some chemical at high temperatures (e.g. 90°C) have some slight affect, e.g., aromatic and chlorinated solvents. Strong oxidising acids, e.g. concentrated sulphuric acid, will attack the material.
7. *Material detention or identification* : With a density greater than 1 gm cm^{-3} (e.g. 1.5-2.1 g cm^{-3}) mouldings sink quickly in water. High density materials contain mineral fillers in addition to glass fibres. Mouldings

are stiff and hard and do not cut easily with a knife. They have outstanding inherent nonflammability and can therefore only by burnt with difficulty. To set to a moulding a temperature. PPS chars and blisters with a smelt a sulphur when heated in a strong flame.

8. *Colouring* : The base colour is dark brown and therefore the colour is comparatively limited. Mouldings made from this material must be capable of performing under ardous conditions (e.g. high temperatures) and these conditions of service also restrict the colours available. Solid already compounded in pellet form.

9. *Reprocessing* : Keep material that it is to be reground in sealed containers as this will minimise moisture pick-up and contamination. Assume that regrind must be dried and keep level as low as possible, e.g. <25%. Many polymers will degrade at the melt temperature required for PPS; purge before and after PPS moulding run with a stiff flow (low MFI) HDPE.

10. *Typical components* : The ability of this material to withstand high temperatures without deformation has allowed this material to be used in connectors, terminal blocks, sockets, coil farmers, bobbins and relay components. Are resistant grades are available which are used to mould relay bases, motor housings, lamp holers and switch components. Used as a metal replacement in the automotive industry, e.g, caburettor parts. Ignition plates, lamp sockets and flow dontrol valves (for heating systems). Because of the increasing use of quartz-halogen lamps, components may reach temperatures above 200°C—PPS replaces ceramics in such applications.

30

Rubber Reinforced Polypropylene

1. *Common name*: Rubber reinforced polypropylene.
2. *Abbreviation :* EMT or PP/EP/(D)M or OTE.
3. *Systematic chemical name* : Blend of poly(polypropylene) and poly-(methylene-*co*-propylene)
4. *Material properties* : When ethylene is copolymerised with propylene (e.g. the ratio of ethylene to propylene is 70:30) an amorphous rubbery material results called EPM. If a third monomer is used then the product is called EPDM—an abbreviation that covers both of them is EP(D)M. Both are compatible with PP and if the ratio of rubber is less than 50% the blend is called an elastomer modifed thermoplastic (EMT). Rubber contents from 10 to 40% are commonly used for injection moulding compounds. By using different grades of the base polymers and/or by altering the ratios used a wide range of properties can be offered. All of these blends can be processed on conventional thermoplastics equipment and vulcanisation is not required. The blends have good resistance to impact (even at low temperature), can still have high Vicat softening points (e.g. >100°C), good agening and weathering resistance (when protected), a neutral colour (a wide colour range is therefore possible), good electrical insulation properties and a low density (0.86-0.9 g cm^{-3} when unfilled).
5. *Resistant to the following*: Oils, fats, alcohols and glycols. Because of the amorphous nature of the rubber, the blends have good resistance of EP(D)M is good and as the chemical resistance of PP is excellent, the chemical of the blends of very good.

6. *Not resistant to* : Relatively limited resistance to petrol and other hydrocarbon solvents; as the rubber content increases the solvents resistance decreases. However, as the general chemical resistance of EP(D)M is good and as the chemical resistance of PP is excellent, the chemical resistance of the blends is very good.

7. *Material detention or identification* : When unfilled these materials float in water as they have a density of 0.9 g cm^{-3}. Transparent mouldings are not possible and such mouldings can be cut fairly easily with a knife. If the materials are not well mixed together then on blending or flexing the mouldings may easily break. The blends burn readily and have no distinctive odour. As with most rubber like materials, infra-red analysis provides a convenient method of identification. As the rubber concentration in the blend increases then the hardness, moulds and softening point decreases. Such blends can be easily scratches or marked, e.g. with a thumbnail.

8. *Colouring* : A wide range of colours is possible using masterbatches or dry colours. Masterbatches may be based on PE or PP; if possible use a masterbatch which has a higher MFI than the EMT as this will give better dispersion. Compounded material gives the best colours.

   For outdoor use, use grades which contain carbon black (e.g. 2%). Light colours may be stabilised using sterically hundred amines.

9. *Reprocessing* : When reprocessing be careful as slight colour changes can occur if the material has been overheated. As exposure to shear at high temperature affects dispersion then reprocessed material may have different properties.

31

Thermoplastic Polyetherester

1. *Common name* : Thermoplastic polyurethane; thermoplastic urethane elastomer.

2. *Abbreviation :* TPU

3. *Systematic chemical name* : Not known

4. *Material properties* : Thermoplastic polyurethane are thermoplastic materials which exhibit rubbery properties. They have obtain by reacting a hydroxyl-terminated polyester or polyether with a diisocyanate so as to give linear polymers which contains the urethane group — NHCOO. Such polymers are noted for their resistance to wear and abrasion; they have high strength, resilience and flexibility. The materials are suitable for use over a wide temperature range, e.g. —40 to 140°C, and can be transparent. High compressive strength and low compression set are other desirable attributes. Both polyester TPU and polyether TPU are available in a number of grades, the hardness of which can be varied over a wide range.

   However, at the same hardness as polyester TPU, polyether TPU will have better low temperature flexibility, hydrolytic stability, fungus resistance and the highest resilience. It is not as tood polyester TPU for abrasion and oil resistance not as tough at the same hardness polyether TPU has the lower specific gravity.

5. *Resistant to the following* : Both classes of material have good resistance to oil, petrol, grease and aromatic hydrocarbon and excellent resistance to aliphatic hydrocarbon. They have good stress-crack resistance.

6. *Not resistant to* : Acids, alkalis, alcohols, ketones, chlorinated hydrocarbon and synthetic lubricants. As TPU materials contain aromatic disocyanates, discolouration will occur after a short-term exposure to weathering unless they are adequately protecting, e.g. by carbon black incorporation. Polyester TPUs have the best resistance to oils and weathering and the best physical properties.
7. *Material detention or identification* : As the specific gravity is greater than 1 (e.g. 1.11-1.22) these materials sink readily in water. Natural colour varies from milky white to clear depending on the source but is usually translucent. Being thermoplastic these materials soften on heating, e.g, above 140°C. The material will burn if placed in a flame but the flame is not self supporting. Attacked by a wide variety of reagents e.g, dilute alkalis. Mouldings are strong, resilient and have good cut resistance. High elongations are possible e.g. 500%.
8. *Colouring* :A range of standard colours is available and manufacturers will, for large lots, colourmatch to requirements. The natural state may range from colourless to amber and so a wide colour range is possible which may be achieved by using masterbatch, e.g, at 2% concentration. Universal masterbatches arc not so good.
9. *Reprocessing* : Up to 50% regrind has been used but a more realistic figure is probably around 20-25%. Regrind immediatly after moulding and then dry, e.g. 3 h at 80°C. If the material is 'wet' then bubbles may appear in the melt and/or the material properties will deteriorate even at low (e.g., 0.1%) moisture content.
10. *Other comments* : Do not use components until they have been conditioned or annealed. For example, by being heated at 100° C for 24h or by being stroed at room temperature for one month. Room temperature storage is not as good as high temperature conditioning as this permits stress relaxation and allows crystalline regions to stabilise—annealed components have a higher maximum service temperature, better creep resistance and lower compression set. Annealing is sometimes referred to as postcuring, it is not always necessary. If the colour of the components is not uniform this may be masked by adding a small amount of colour.
11. Typical components : Compared to tradition rubber these materials are expensive but as they can be handled like thermoplastics, fast production on standard matches is possible. A very wide range of grades is available so that, for example, the hardness can range from 75 short A to 70

Shore D. The 'A' scale is used for rubbers and the D for plastics (the higher) the number the harder a material will be). Linear TPU can bridge the hardness gap between rubbers and plastics as PE has a hardness of approximately 60 Shore D; PP of 75; and PS of 100. These thermoplastics elastometers are used where a flexible, durable material with good oil resistance, is required. They are used in the form of grommets, seals, washers, wheels, rollers, etc. and in industries such as automotive, mechanical handling and mining. The relatively poor resistance of some grades to synthetic lubricants (phosphates and diesters) should not be forgotton. On outdoor exposure, fading (particularly of pale colours) may occurs use ultraviolet stabilised grades for outdoor use, e.g. for animal ear tags. Fibre modified grades are under active development, e.g, for car components.

32

Fibre Reinforced Thermoplastics

1. *Common name* : Fibre reinforced thermoplastics.
2. *Abbreviation :* FRTP
3. *Systematic chemical name* : Not commonly used, materials are usually referred to a glass-reinforced nylon etc. Major materials reinforced are the engineering plastics such as nylon, acetals, polycarbonates and polymers containing *p*-phenylene groups, e.g., PBT.
4. *Material properties* : Depends on the base polymer and on the type and concentration of the fibrous filler. Glass is very popular and is used over the range 5-50% (glass content by weight), 20-40% being most common, as below 20% there may be little reinforcement whereas above 40% processing is difficult. Because of the affect of processing, final fibre length is of the order of 0.5 mm (0.02 in) and the effect on strength (or reinforcement) is not as great as it is for thermosets (where the fibre length is greater). This means that although the final mouldings may be a lot stiffer than the unreinforced material they may not necessarily be stronger.

   Materials are stiffere than the base polymer, have lower coefficients of thermal expansions, higher heat distortion temperatures and higher densities. FRTPs are available as precompounded materials and in masterbatch form, some inhouse compounding polymer and fibrous filler is done although is not easy to do well. Coupling agents can improve properties, with glass fibre reinforcement, but unfortunately there is no universal coupling agent i.e. one suitable for all polymers FRTPs may also contain inorganic mineral fillers.

5. *Resistant to the following* : The stress cracking tendency of materials such as PS, SAN and PC is reduced; the creep resistance of FRTPs is better than that of the parent polymer. Low temperature impact resistance is sometimes better than that of the parent plastics material.

6. *Not resistant to* : Those substances which attach the base polymer. The interface between resin and glass can be attacked by alkalis. Use correct moulding conditions so that attack is not glass at the surface which will help to 'wick' alkali into the moulding.

7. Material detection or identification : The presence of inorganic fibres (such as glass and asbestos) may be shown by burning off the base thermoplastic. By weighing a know sample (before and after burning) the fibre concentration may be calculated. As the glass content increases surface gloss decreases but stiffness and heat distortion temperature (HDT) increases.

8. Colouring : The presence of the fibre can result in a colour difference between the reinforced and the unreinforced material even though they have the same colourants. A matt finish is unusual on FRTP mouldings and this can affect colour.

9. Reprocessing : Regrind concentration should be kept low, e.g. below 25% as reprocessing reduces filler size which can (i) increase wear on the screw and barrel and (ii) product properties. Regranulated scrap may also require drying.

33

Polyurethane Plastics

Introduction

The polyurethanes (PU) offer the widest choice of properties of any group of plastics materials, and the opportunity to incorporate specific chemical structures into a PU chain allows the polymer chemist to trailor many specific properties into the polymer. Therefore thermoplastic, thermoset resinous and elastomeric PUs are available, many of them in cellular forms. Specific PU properties include abrasion resistance and general ease of processing.

The choice of properties stems from the vast number of monomeric and ligomeric ingredients that can be reacted together to produce polymers linkage results from the reaction between isocyanate and hydroxyl-containing compounds; catalysts and/or heat accelerate the reaction :

$$\sim R'.N{=}C{=}O + \sim R^*.O\text{-}H \longrightarrow$$

$$\sim R' - \underset{\substack{| \\ H}}{N} - \underset{\substack{\| \\ O}}{C} - O - R'' \sim$$

The reactivity of many isocyanates is exploited by promoting side reactions, either within the polymer chain or at chain ends, with reactive additives such as chain extenders or cross linking agents. The ease with which many monomeric ingredients are converted into polymer during the shaping operation permits relatively simple and cheap processes to be employed, often with low expenditure of energy.

PUs find use virtually in any field of application; product can be shaped by traditional thermoplastics processes, and by coating or calendering on to substrates. However, the major manufacturing techniques involve *dual component processing* of the liquid 'monomeric' ingredients. Products made by such methods include slabstock and moulded foams; self skinned foamed elastomers and resins, and non-foamed mouldings made by reaction injection moulding; surface coatings, sealants, encapsulants and adhesives. Foamed PUs are used in a wide range of products from cushioning materials for furnitures and automotive seating, to thermal insulation, structural stiffening for building panels or refrigerators. High quality mouldings include automotive panels (glass-fibre reinforced), head restraints, steering wheels, car trim and covers for electronic equipment. References listed at the end of the this chaper give comprehensive details of the properties of PU materials.

Molecular structure-property relationships

A polyisocyanate and a polyyol (a polyhydroxyl material) are the asic ingredients that react to form a polyurethane; polyols with functionalities from 2 to 6 are commonly used. Low molecular weight polyols (functionality 2 and higher) or chain extending diols, will tend to impart rigidity into a PU. High molecular- weight polyols, (functionality 3 or less) will tend to give softer, low moduls PUs. It follows that the ratio of polyol to isocyanate (the stoichiometry that will allow a reaction to form a full urethane polymer) is high for high-molecular-weight polyols. In addition, the amount the theoretical stoichiometry, that is, by changing the isocyanate index. A low *isocyanate index may* tend to encourage platicization of the PU because of the presence of excess polyol, and a high isocyanate index will promote stiffening through cross linking side reactions. However, to produce thermoplastics PUs, reactants with a functionality of 2 mixed of precise stoichiometric proportions must be used. Cellular PUs are relatively cheap to manufacture, and dominate the market-place, even although the cost of raw materials may be at least twice that for foamed commodity thermoplastics.

Typical reactions

Isocyanate under suitable conditions will readily react with active hydrogen containing compounds.

The side reactions (iii-v) lead to cross linking, and will readily occur with the polyol/aromatic isocyanate reactants of ambient conditions, if both the appropriate catalysts and slight excess isocyanate are used, even though the isocyanate may be difunctional urethane cross links also readily occur with polyols or isocyanates of functionality 3 or higher.

$$\sim R'.N{=}C{=}O + H_2O \longrightarrow \sim R'.NH_2 + CO_2 \uparrow$$

(i) Isocyanate /water

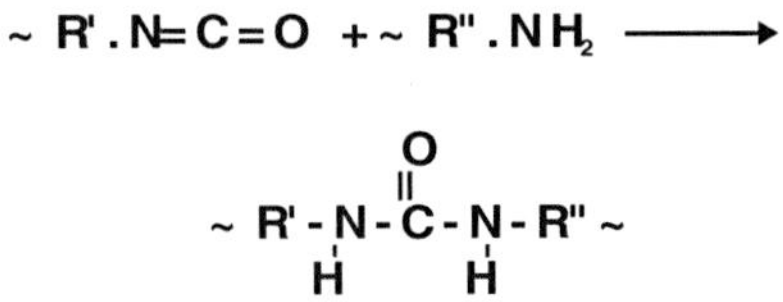

(ii) Isocyanate/amine (polyurea formation)

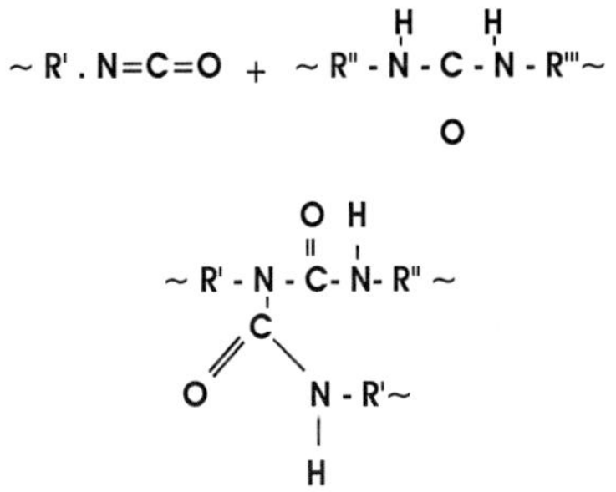

(iii) Isocyanate / urea (polybluret formation)

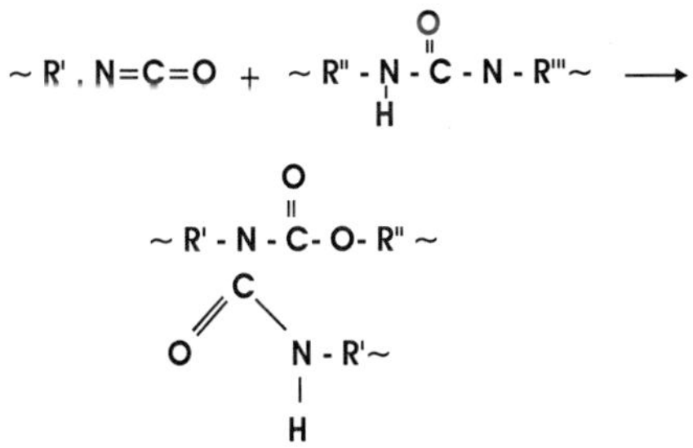

(iv) Isocyanate/urethane (polyallophanate formation)

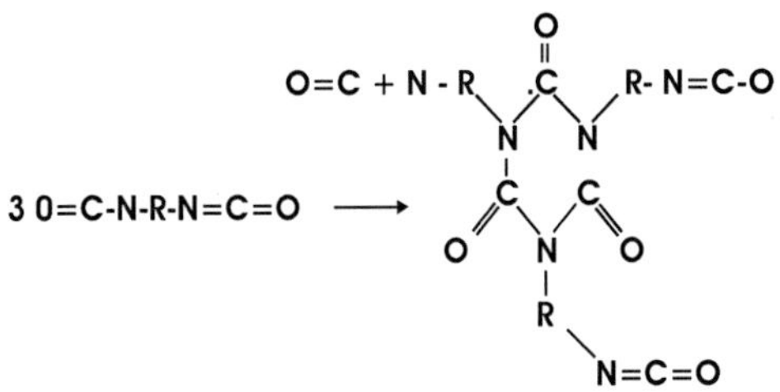

(v) Isocyanate/isocyanate (e.g. isocyanurate formation)

Monomeric components

(i) *Polyols.* Typically these are oligomers derived from several classes of hydroxyl-containing material. Polyether polyols are typically made by reacting ethylene or propylene oxides with water in the presence of alkaline catalysts.

Polyethers are used in the manufacture of flexible foams, giving good resilience and hydrolytic stability, and are basis of many PU.RIM system, although they have limited thermal stability (to a maximum of 70°C). Speciality polyesters are made from the reactions of e-caprolactone with low-molecular-weight diols (e.g. ethylene glycol) or triols (e.g. glycerol).

$$nH_2C\overset{\;O\;}{\frown}C.H.R + nH_2O \longrightarrow$$

$$HO \left[CH2\,.\,\overset{\displaystyle R}{\overset{|}{C}}.\;H\text{-}O \right]_n H$$

$$(R = H_2CH_3)$$

Polyester polyols imparts better mechanical properties and thermal stability to the PU, but have poorer hydrolytic resistance than the polyethers. Polyestes are used in the large tonnages for shoe soling, same flexible foams and many elastomer formulations. Polyols with functionality greater than two are produced from a wide number of sources, such as propylene oxide racted with glycerol or sugars (for polyols of functionality 3 and 6, respectively), and other naturally occurring materials. Sugar based polyols are used to give high rigidity in low-density structural foams, although higher molecular-weight polyether polyols may be included in a polyol blend to reduce brittleess. The easy with which many other compounds can be further hydoxylated broadens the variety of starting monomers; polybutadiene, for example, is polyhydroxylated to permit isocyanate vulcanization. Polyethers are largely low -viscosity liquids at 15°C, permitting easy processing; polyesters tend to either viscous liquids or waxy solids and need to be heated to effect processing. Polyols are characterized by hydroxyl value, water content and molecular weight.

(ii) Isocyanates. The choice of polyisocyanates is more limited. Of the aromatic isocyanates, toluene diisocyanate (TDI), and 4.4'-diphenylmethane (MDI) are commonly used.

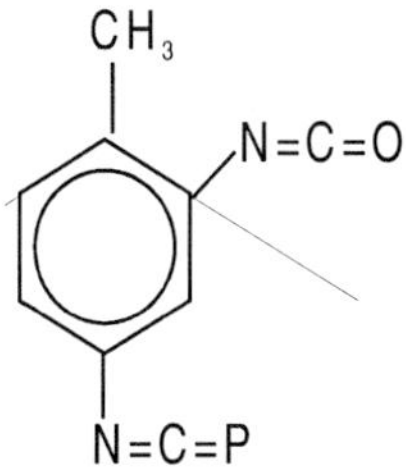

TDI

TDI is made by nitration of toluene, to give dinitro derivatives, which are hydrogenated to the diamines and these in turn are phosgenated to the disssocyanates. Typically, a 80:20 mixture of the 2, and 2,6 isomers of various purities is employed; they are low-viscosity liquids down to 0°C. MDI is made by the phosgenation of diamino-diphenylmethane, itself formed by the condensation of aniline and formaldehyde. Pure MDI is an unstable solid (melting point 42°C), readily forming diamers and trimers.

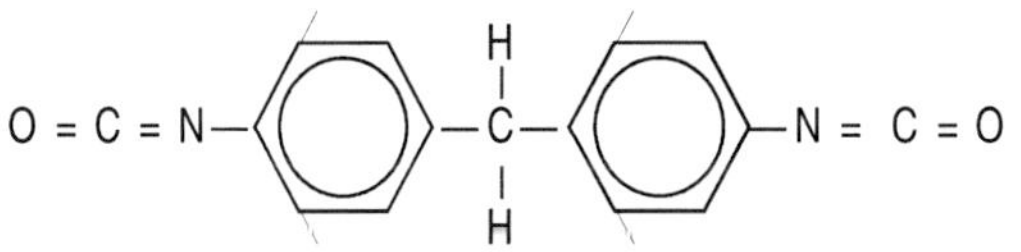

MDI

'Polymeric' or 'crude' MDIs are fractions distilled from the reaction products, having functionalities of 2 to 3. The so called commercial 'pure' MDIs are eutectic mixtures of pure MDI and products derived from the reaction of excess pure MDI with diol (e.g. butane-1, 4-diol); these have a melting point' of 10-20°C and a functionality of 2. Aromatic isocyanates are relatively expensive (1000 to 1500 per tonne). Isocyanates are characterized by isocynate content and chloride content.

Unfortunately, the aromatic isocyanate component in a PU chain may contribute to poor oxidative resistance, particularly under UV-radiation. Employing mixtures of stabilizers has limited success in eliminating embrittlement or yellowing. Alicyclic and aliphatic isocyanates give good resistance to UV, (e.g. isophorone diisocyanate), finding use in products in exterior application (e.g. surface coating) but are more than five times as expensive and tend to be less rective than the aromatic types.

The high reactivity of isocyanates together with their volatility gives rise to health and safety problems. A solution to volatility is to produce isocyanate tipped PU pre-polymers, by reacting excess isocyanate with polyol under controlled conditions; the oligomer can react with active hydrogen species some time later. This will also permit controlled development of the structure of a PU, especially when using mixture of polyols.

(iii) *Other additives. Chain extenders* are normally low-molecular-weight diols which impart limited rigidity into the PU chain. Di- and triethylene glycols, mono- and di-propylene glycols and butane-1, 4-diol are most commonly used. *Cross-linking agents* include high functional polyols, and diamines (functionality 4). Polyurea-polyurethane copolymers with superior properties are produced from 3,3'-dichloro-4,4'-diaminodiphenylmethane (MOCA) although it is a suspected carcinogen. Polyamines derived from propylene oxide are used in the high-speed polyurea/polyurethane reaction injection moulding process in the manufacture of automotive panels.

Most PU processes involve the simultaneous making and shaping of the polymer at room temperature and employ catalysts. The urethane reaction is catalysed by organic metal compounds, typically tin salts and teritiary amines. The water/isocyanate reaction is catalysed by amines; again the tertiary amines are preferred over primary or secondary amines, since they have little odour and do not react with isocyanate. Many side reactions are promoted by heat (e.g. from reaction exotherm) and by catalysts, for instance in the formation fo the allophanate cross-link. Residual catalyst in PU products will accelerate degradation in adverse conditions. The water-isocyanate reaction forming caron dioxide is commonly used to form open-cell flexible foams. Trichlorofluoromethane (TCFM) is a physical blowing agent relying on heat from the urethane reaction exotherm to boil; this is used to form rigid closed-cell foams and most self-skinned moulded products. There is considerable concern over the effect of fluorocarbonss on the Earth's ozone layer, and suitable replacements are actively being sought.

The effect of glass fibre on the properties of high-modulus polyurethane elastomers

Property	Orientation	Glass Content (% wt.) 0	10	20	30
Density (kg m-3)		1100	1150	1200	1300
Flexural modulus	par	350	600	1000	1500
@ 23°C (MPa)	RA	—	400	550	700
Coeff of thermal	Par	180	70	40	25
expansion (x 10^{-6}/°C)	RA	—	165	140	130
Heat sag. 1h at 160°C	Par	15	8	5	3
(mm)	RA	—	11	10	8
Elongation at break	Par	320	250	180	5
(%)	RA	—	250	200	140

Surfactants acting as nucleating agents are used to control foam cell size and distribution; amterials including modified silicone oils are dissolved into the polyol ingredient stream. Rigid foamed PUs which have to be painted following moulding will include dissolved air-in-polyols as a nucleaing agents, to ensure subsequent paint adhesion. Pigments are used to give solid colour to products, although surface coatings for the moulded product are now used, because MDIs are dark and contribute to poor UV stability of the PUs.Fillers are used in reaction injection moulded (RIM) products reinforced with glass fibre, used to reduce high coefficient of thermal expansion and creep. The glass is in the form of short hammer-milled or chopped-strand fibre (0.2-3.0 mm in length), long enough to give reinforcement (aspect ratio greater than 10), but short enogh to be pumped through dispensing machinery without attrition of fibres of abrasive wear of the equipment.The glass fibre used in reinforced flexible PUs does not have to surface-treated, since some fibre slippage is desirable in the flexible PU matrix.

Properties and applications of polyurethanes

Flexible polyurethane foams

The major use of PUs is in flexible foams, for upholstery, mattresses and vehicle seat cusioning. Semi-flexible grades are used as in-fill materials, for instance as an energy-absorbing composite backing plasticized PVC skins on car crahpads (part of the dashboard).

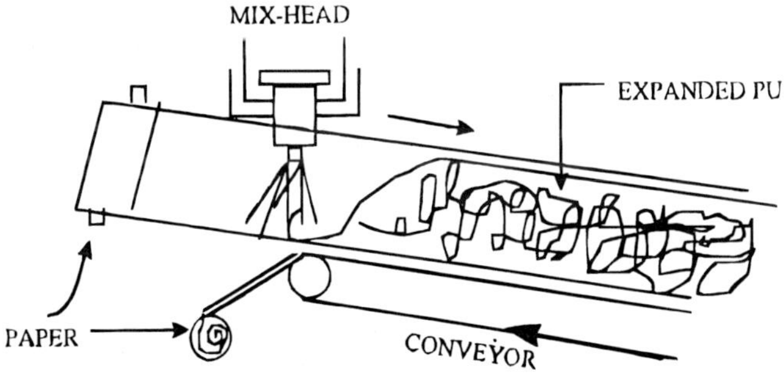

Diagram of continuous foam slab stock production

Cushion foams are made by both slabstock and moulding techniques. In large-volume slabstock production, the *one-shot* process is used; polyol, isocyanate, catalysts, blowing agents (such as water) and surfactants are metered separately and pumped to a mechanical mix-head, where the ingredients are mixed rapidly together and poured either into a moving 'tough' or a large box mould, making slabstock *loaves* or *buns* respectively. The ingredients react and expand to fill the trough or box, the foam will be fully expanded and the surface of the foam dry to the touch in less than 10 minutes, although complete cure will take longer. The freshly-made locks are stored in warm rooms to speed complete cure and allow voalites to evaporate. The blocks are cut by bandshaw to the required shapes; waste PU foam can be reconstituted by gluing foam crumble together, and this can be used as a stiff infill for seating. The cut foam can then be covered with fabric to make seating or mattresses. The inherently poor fire retardancy of the PU can be improved by incorporating halogenated phosphorous compounds, or by covering with fire-retardant fabric or interliners.

Moulded cushions tend to have slightly better fire retardancy and better resilience properties than slab-stock products. Hot-cure and, more recently, cold-cure moulding techniques have allowed better control of the side reaction (such as formation of isocyanurate and allophanate cross-links). One-short processing with low-pressure dual-compound dispensing equipment is used, the polyol being pre-blended with all the other ingredients except the isocyanate. For better control of the reaction and residual by products like unreaced isocyanate, isocyanate-tipped prepolymers are used, in the so-called two-shot process; the prepolymer is reacted with water and polyol in the foaming reaction. The mixed ingredients are poured from the mix-head into a heated mould coated with release agent, the lid of which is closed as the reaction starts. Heating will ensure, and accelerate, important side-reactions. Demould is within ten minutes. Changing the stoichiometry of the ingredients by closed-loop control of pumps allows the manufacture of products such as up-market car seats with foamed sections of different moduli to be made in a single moulding operation. The density of the open-cell PU foams ranges from 20-100 kgm^{-3}. Until the late1970s, TDI was the dominant isocyanate used, but as a result of increasing concern over the health risks, and TDI/MDI blends are now more popular.

Rigid polyurethane and polyisocyanurate foams

Rigid PU resins can be readily foamed to low densities, giving excellent insulation and imparting stiffness to many product such as panel walls and refrigerators. Again, the problem of poor fire resistance had led to the use of halogenated phosphorous compounds as fire-retardants and also to be development of PU/polyisocyanurate foams. Slabstock techniques are used, where the cut closed-cell foam can later be adhersively laminated with any of a number of facing materials such as plasterboard, paper, or metal foils. A popular manufacturing technique involves pouring the mixed liquid ingredients directly on to a continuous band of facing material, allowing partial expansion of the foam before applying an upper facing; full expansion and cur of the PU will then be accelerated by heat. Rigid foam can be injected easily into any cavity formed in a product; between the two skins of a domestic refrigerator, or into the void formed by the two sheet-steel skins of factory door and wall panels. Although the mixed liquid ingredients are mobile, the rapid reaction and increase in viscosity mean that the placement of the material has to be facilitated by optimum mould orientation, or by placing an extended nozzle of the mix-head into the cavity, then gradually withdrawing it is local filling is achieved.

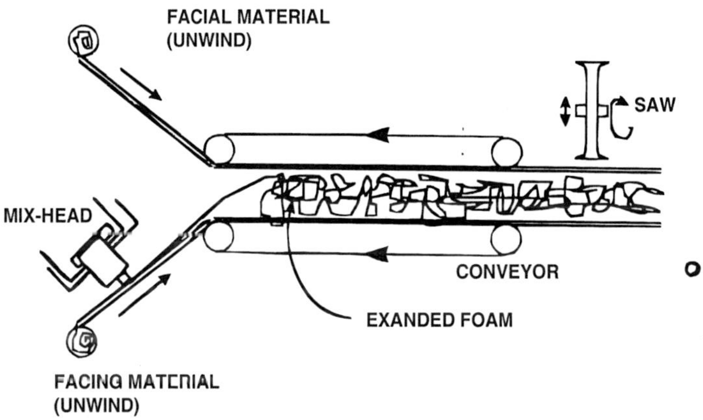

Diagram of the Continuous production of rigid foam-filled panels

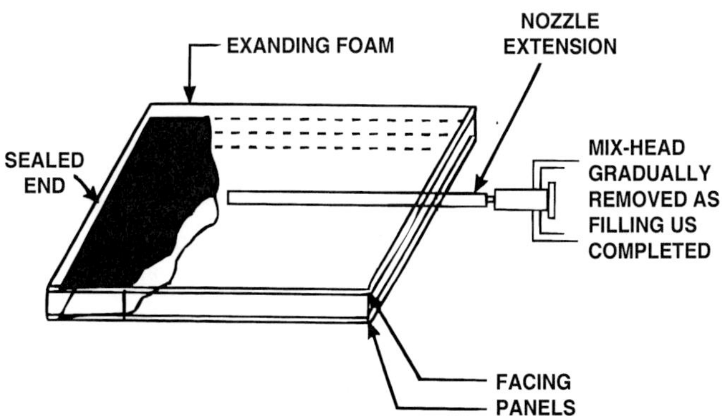

Diagram of batch production of rigid foam-filled panels

The ease with which PU ingredients can be processed permits their application away from the controlled factory enviornment, using in-situ dispense equipment, such as on a building site for cavity wall-fill or storage tank insulation. A diesel generator runs high-pressure pumps and heaters which are used to ispense materials through an inpingement mis-head; ingredients can be pumped a distance of upto 100 m. Mix- heads can be fitted with nozzles for either spraying (to cover a large surface area) or pouring (for cavity fill). Ingredients are pre-heated to ease pumping, overcome low ambient temperatures and give very high reaction rates (less than 10 seconds), preventing slump on vertical walls. Damp conditions have to be avoided. Thick elastomeric coatings or sheet are used to protect the cured PU foam from direct sunlight.

Moulded high-density rigid foamed PU products (200-750 kg m^{-3}) are finding increasing use, for example in energy absorbing blocks for car bumpers, decorative panelling, orsoles for clogs. Because of the initial low viscosity and wetting properties of the mixed ingredients, a PU will accurately reproduce the detail of a mould surface. This is particularly exploited in flexible mould techniques. Usually a wooden carving is made, and a silicone rubber *pull* cast from it, which is used as the liner of an eposide mould. To increase the life of the silicone mould (up to 100 mouldings), an *in-mould barrier* release surface coating has to be used. The coating also means that a component out of the mould will process in the same way as a primer-coated piece of timber; it can be finished product has all the appearance of the original master. Use of flexible silicone or PU elastomeric liners permits a high degree of three-dimensional relief in the product. Kitchen cabinet doors, decorative panels and beams, and ornate picture frames are made by this technique.

Reaction injection moulded polyurethane products

The advent of high-pressure metering and impingement mixing of PU ingredients through *self-cleaning* mix heads has provided a process method which allows PUs to compete with high quality thermoplastic injection moulding, for example for large automotive panels and electronic component housings. Although some products can be made using high-pressure open pour moulding techniques, reaction injection moulding (RIM) involves closed moulding processing of flexible or rigid self-skinned foams, or high modulus elastomeric products. Modified RIM equipment is used to process reinforcing fibre filled PU/polyurea system (RRIM).

RIM cycle times range from 45 seconds to 10 minutes, although the application and drying time of release agent may take upto 60 seconds. In the mass production of smaller mouldigns, if is not prohibitively expensive to employ a number of identical moulding tools (based on epoxide liners in aluminium for example) loaded on to a carousel moulding unit. The carousel can hold up to 50 moulds; these progress past lightweight IM mix head, which can be readily attached to the detached from each mould for filling. This allows the manufacturer a high outpur, although unit cycle time may be about 10 minutes. In PU-RIM systems having longer mould cycles, the high pressure dispense unit can be used to feed several mix head bolted on to separate moulds in ther own clamping process, via ring-main/mainifold units.

Mixed ingredients leave the mix-head nozzle at velocities up to $2ms^{-1}$, and gating into the mould cavity must be carefully designed to prevent turbulent flow with the associated problem of air antrapment. As PU systems may react within a few seconds, filling of larger mould cavities becomes particularly critical to prevent underfilling or weld lines, which will give structural weakness in the product. Liquid PU ingredients will readily flow into the mould cavity, but the low pressure involved means that mould orientation, the filling point and split-line locations must be chosen with care, to ensure that air is fully expelled by the moving front of liquid ingredients entering the cavity. Possible moulding faults include underfilling, air-traps and density gradients in cellular products (in vertical in inclined sections).

PU-RIM systems are normally microcellular, high-modulus elastomers, based on polyether polyols 'pure' MDI systems, although better high-temperature performance is achieved using polyamine-polyether polyol systems. Foam formation and self skinning is promoted by trichlorofluoromethane (TCFM) or methylene chloride blowing agents. The ingredients injected into the mould cavity react and exotherm, boiling the TCFM and starting the foam formtion. A little of the TCFM will escape into the air space of the mould cavity, rapidly condensing on the walls of the mould under pressure. The combination of the foam collapsing as it expands into the mould walls, due to the surfactant action of the liquid TCFM and overpacking of the foam in the mould cavity, produces a high-density skin on the surface of the moulding. Automotive steering wheels and heat restraints are produced in this way.

Both products are made in similar manner. Release agent is applied to the clean mould surface and allowed to dry. To overcome the problem of poor UV stability and to reduce production costs, a surface coating is sprayed on the mould surface and allowed to dry. Mould temperature is 40-90°C to speed paint drying and, subsequently, the foam reaction (Figure 33.1). A metal insert, intended to give regidity to the poduct is placed in the mould, which is then closed. A high pressure mixing head is clamped to the inlet port of the mould and a short of mixed ingredients fired into the cavity. The head is swung away and the expanding foam is allowed to just spill out of the mold before its linlet is plugged. The mould is heated to speed to reaction, either by internal water channeling or by transferring it to an overn, in the case of a number of small moulds on a carousel line. The product can be demoulded in a few minutes, and reflashing removes a thin line of oversprayed paint. The *inmould PU* paint appears to give near-perfect adhesion with the substrate. Shoe-soles are made from plyest-'pure' MDI systems using similar techniques' again, dual-density foams can be made in a one step process by an index change of the reactants.

(i) *Self-skinned semi flexible polyurethanes*, These give a soft and comfortable feed, with excellent abrasion and stain resistance. The foam will act as a shock absorber, for instance if a car driver is thrown against a steering wheel or head restraint. The poor resistance to UV exposure and the limited range of colours of PU has led to the successful use of barrier coats based on non-aromatic isocyanate-based PU surface coatings. The acuracy with which PU reproduces the detail of the mould surface allows the stylist to use subtle texture PU currently dominates the steering-wheel market (approximately 80% in Europe); polypropylene has the only other significant share. Although subject to fashion changes, the PU head restraints are used in many down market vehicle. Shot weights of ingredients will be under 750g with less than 5% wastage (from runners, etc.). Integral-skin components made in the production step have replaced components fabricated from stitched fabric or rotational moulded splasticized PVC, reinforced with a steel frame and filled with PU foam in a second process operation.

(ii) Self skinned rigid polyurethane. These are used for office and kitchen furniture and housings for electronic components such as television cabinets in the range of 4-15 kg moulded weight, and are made by using dedicated mix-head/mould combinations. Many of these formed products have to be surface coated. From the moulded, the product is allowed to post-cure of room temperature before solvent-degreasing to remove release agent from its surface. Degreasing is aided by sanding using emery cloth, which will also eliminate the flashline scar while creating fine scratches in the surface to enhance paint adhesion. Any small holes in the moulding's surface have to be filled at this stage using unsaturated polyester or cellulosic putty. The moulding is normally primer-coated, then lightly resanded before a topcoat paint is spray-applied. Generally the post moulding operations are the time-consuming and labour intensive steps in the production; because of this, rigid integral skinned PUs face severe competition from self-coloured foamed thermoplastics like ABS and polycarbonate. Compared with non-foamed plastics such as modified PP, foamed PU is particular offers the designer the opportunity to use thicker sections (10-20 mm) giving 'body' and elegance to the shape of a piece of furniture.

(iii) *Solid and micro-cellular elastomeric polyurethane RIM products.* These are used largely in the production of exterior automotive components; wheel arches, bumpers, panels and many add-on units employed to enhance the appearance and cost of up-market versions of cars. Legislation to improve fuel consumption by weight reduction and to reduce collision impact damage has led to the acceptance of plastics as car bumpers, replacing chromed steel.

Elastomeric and resinous thermosetting polyurethanes.

Good abrasion and chemical resistance in many environments, combined with ease of application at room temperature, has led to wide use of PU elastomers. Products ragne from covers from printing press rollers, abrasion-resistant lining materials, to low speed tyre filling and vehicle floor mats. Synthesis can be either by one-shot (polyol reacted with isocyanate) or two-shot process (a prepolymer is first made, normally with isocynate-tipping, which can later be reacted with a curing agent, e.g. diols as chain extenders or polyamines or triols as cross-linking agents), or with atmospheric moistre if applied a thin film. Diamine-cured prepolymers give excellent products; an example is the sound proofing covers for pneumatic drills used in mining and quarrying where good environmental and abrasion resistance to a prerequisite. Polyether-MDI systems can be sprayed in factory or in-situ applications, to provide abrasion and corrosion resistant coatings (in quarry conveyor buckets, hovecraft propeller blades, water-inlet ducts for power stations and in many civil contructions such as oil rigs; in these applications the PU may need to be applied in 'films' up to 50 mm thick.

Thermoplastic polyurethanes

In comparison to other types of PUs, thermoplastic polyurethanes (TPPU) are of limited availability and end-use, although they were amongst te first PUs to be developed in the early 1940s, as competition to polyamide fibres. Again they are exploited for their abrasion resistance, over a range of hardnesses from 50 Shore A to 80 Shore D. Basic thermoplastic injection moulding and extrusion equipment can be used to process. TPPU, although the polymer granules should be dried before melt processing to prevent degradation. Uses include the exotic-TPPU replaces goose feathers as flights for archery arrows, because the snapback characteristics are similar. It has also been used for combined sleeping policeman/cable protectors for geophone cables used in built-up areas. TPPUs can be blended into plasticized PVC and elastomer formulations, to improve stiffness and modulus without loss of low temperature properties for instanc in shoe soles. Recently a range of alicylic isocyanate/caprolactone polyester TPPUs has been developed for UV-resistant, water white safety materials such as faceshields. These have superior abrasion resistance to polycarbonate, more commonly found in this application.

Polyurethanes as surface coatings, adhesives and sealants

A wide range of starting materials can be used to form PU with virtually any selected properties. This is nowhere better exploited than in the surface coatings and adhesives industries. The chemistry and surface-tension properties of PUs allow wetting and excellent physical interfacial bonding with a wide range of substrate materials, and this is enhanced either by allowing PU reactants to react directly on the substrate's surface, where isocyanate will tend to form strong covalent bonds, or by dispersing reactants in suitable solvent carriers.

Adhesives can be based on either reactive or fully reacted PU systems. Large quantities of PU are used in contact adhesives in the construction industry. PU sealants normally rely on moisture curing, for instance sealants used for wooden frame constructions in domestic housing.

34

Speciality Thermoplastics

A number of thermoplastics produced in small quantities worldwide have already been described earlier, for example polyamides and polyimides. The present chapter accommodates the more important members of the thermoplastics groups not included in other sections. These include fluoroplastics, polysulphones and sulphide polymers.

Fluoroplastics

Poly(tetrafluoroethylene) (PTFE) is the oldest member of this family, having been available since the early 1950s, yet worldwide production is only a few thousand tonnes per year. Even so. PTFE is the most commonly used fluoropolymer, widely used in specialist applications by engineers. This is primarily because of its unusual properties, notably high melting temperature extreme chemical inertness and an extremely low coefficient of friction for either PTFE-metal or PTFE-PTFE contact. On the debit side, PTFE has an inherently high price and is very difficult to process, which is primarily associated with the extremely high viscosity of the molten polymer. Many attempts have been to improve the processing behaviour, mostly by copolymerization, without sacrificing too many of its desirable characteristics. A limiting compromise is to substitute other fluorine-containing homopolymers such as poly(vinylidene fluoride), into part of the PTFE molecular structure, these do not present processing problems, but unfortunately they do not have the very desirable properties of PTFE.

Poly(vinyl fluoride) is included, although it shows greater similarities of poly(vinyl chloride) than to the other fluoropolymers. It also should be mentioned that a wide variety of fluoropolymer elastomers is used under extreme conditions of temperature and chemical environment.

Fluoride-free polymers find particulars use in high temperature and corrosion resistance environments, and some consideration will be given to them in this chapter.

Poly(tetrafluoroethylene)

There is a large number of companies manufacturing PTFE; this is surprising when the difficulties and hazards associated with the industrial preparation of the monomer and its polymerization are taken into account. Suspension and emulsion polymerization are employed to give materials suited to particulars processing methods. Further, to obtain optimum properties in the final product, work-up operations for the polymer must be carried out under rigourously dust free conditions.

Experimental and theoretical evidence indicates that suspension polymerized (granular) PTFE is a linear and unbranded polymer, with a molecular weight exceeding half a million. PTFE has the comparatively high specific gravity of 2.28 and the virgin polymer has very high crystallinity, 90-95% and a melting point of 340°C. However, after melt processing the crystallinity is not fully regained, dropping to between 50-70% with a melting temperature of 328°C. A reversible volume increase of about 30% takes place between 15°C and the melting point. Above the crystalline melting point, the 'melt' has a very high viscosity, typically, typically a million times greater than for most thermoplastics; this precludes normal thermoplastics processing methods.

Lower crystallinity, and consequently density, are associated with higher -molecular-weight polymer. This is a useful relationship, since the normal solution methods of molecular weight determination are precluded by the insolubility of PTFE in all solvents excepts at temperatures above 300°C, which property is exploited in many applications. PTFE is chemically inert, attack being limited to materials such as molten sodium. It may be dissolved by highly fluorinated liquids near its melting point. It has excellent weathering resistance and is suitable in air to at least 250°C for continuous service.

Very low coefficients of friction are obtained for PTFE-PTFE or PTFE with most metal systems; as a corollary, nothing will stick to PFTE is preheated (e.g. by plasma or sodium xanthate etching). Dielectric losses are very small, particuarly for unsintered material, and volume resistivity is very high. Mechanically PTFE is touch and moderately flexible with a high elongation to break. Toughness is retained at very high and very low temperature; PTFE is one of the few materials which does not embrittle at liquid helium temperature. On the other hand, PTFE creeps under moderate stress, a design consideration and possible limitation on the engineering use of the material.

Although PTFE is a linear-chain polymer and a thermoplastic, its extremely high melt viscosity does not permit the usual thermoplastic processing technology. Instead the methods of powder metallurgy are adopted pressure performs are sintered at temperatures above the crystalline melting point, typically 380°C. Complicated shapes are obtained by maching, making products very expensive. Powder processing in a compromise between powder flow and good strength, particle shape, size, size distribution, external topography and internal structure are all important. Some highly toxic cyclic fluoro-compounds are liberated by heating PTFE to sintering temperatures, so good ventilation is essential. Extrusion, particularly of thin sections, is accomplished by lubricating dispersion PTFE powder with petroleum by lubricating dispersion PTFE powder with petroleum ether, and subsequently drying and sintering the extrudate (tube for example). Unsintered tape is obtained by calendering.

Applications cover nearly all property regions, PTFE is exploited for nonstick coatings in a variety of applications, including cookware, bread processing, toffee making and coating on skins. Bearing, particuarly composite systems, frequently involve PTFE. An extracting application is in suspension bushes used in some rally cars, which have been spectacularly successful. Chemical inertness in the presence of biological fluids is one basis for the many medical application of PTFE; a typcial use is in the catheters used in dialysis equipment employed in the treatment of renal failure. PTFE is widely used for critical electrical insulation, but polimides and polyketones are now preferred for wire coating applications. The unsintered, extended material is used by plumbers, as tape for sealing threads. Valves, gaskets expansion bellows are typical uses for PTFE.

Many of the properties of PTFE depend on the characteristics of the particle (which can be affected by polymerization technique) and on the processing conditions, including moulding pressure, sintering temperature and time, and heating and cooling rates. Crystallinity and porosity are affected, which in turn influence properties such as strength, modulus, hardness and permeability. Fillers are used in PTFE to give particuar technical effects rather than, as might be expected, to reduce the cost. Creep behaviour is improved by inclusion of short glass fibres; the excellent frictional characteristics are further enhanced by incorporating graphite or molybdenum disulphide, or both; metal powders increase thermal condudctivity thus reducing overheating and consequent failure in bearings.

Poly(vinylidene fluoride)

Poly(vinylidene fluoride) (PVDF) is a fluoropolymer which shares some properties, including high cost, with PTFE. It contains the repeat unit —CH_2—CF_2—,explaining its chemical intertness, but it will degrade at high temperature (380—400°C), liberating HF. It has a crystalline melting point of 170—171°C. The various grades of PVDF homopolymer are available for most thermoplastics processing methods without significant degradation at 200—240°C. PVDF is incompatible with other polymers (except acrylics) and the melt may be degraded by impurities. Therefore process equipment must be scrupulously clean and care must be exercised in the selection of pigment, although PVDF may be recycled at normal melt temperature.

The properties of PVDF are influenced by its molecular weight, which also strongly affects processing and the crystallinity level achieved. Generally, the properties are not strongly dependent on operating temperature in the range 60—150°C this leads to applications as pipes, pumps and fittings, poly(vinylidene fluoride) is resistant to halogens, oxidants, strong bases and acids (except at high temperatures); it is less resistant to polar organic solvents. On of its main application areas is in chemical processing plant, PVDF having good strength and impact resistance and outstanding resistance to abrasion/erosion. This exceptional property has led to the satisfactory use of PVDF as a coting on propellers for high-performance water craft. Representative creep data are given in figure.

Filled compositions are available, but it must be remembered that fillers can reduce the stability of the polymer or introduce instability in their own right, glass beads reduce stability in the presence of hydrogen fluoride, for instance. Filled compounds show markedly lower shrinkage and higher regidity; toughness is generally decreased.

Copolymers of vinylidene fluoride and tetrafluoroethylene are available, characterized by lower crystallinity and melting point, with greater flexibility, extensibility and toughness. Otherwide they are generally similar to the hompolymers.

Other fluoropolymers

Polyvinyl fluoride (PVF) is generally similar to PVC, but is transparent to UV radiation and therefore has excellent weathering resistance. It is used in laminates because of this property. Its brittle temperature is very low,-165°C.

Polychlorotrifluoroethylene, (PCTFE) is less crystalline and less inert than PTFE; it can be shaped by normal thermoplastic melt procesing methods. Because of its relative transparency, it finds limited use as observation windows (in sheet form), or as specialist tube material.

Other fluoropolymers are produced in small quantities and for specific application, including copolymers of ethylene with chlorotrifluoroethylene and TFE.

Polysulphones

These plastics are characterized by having the sulphone group—SO2— as a constituent in a polymer structure consisting largely of aromatic groups, generally linked in the *para*-position (p= phenylene). Thermal stability in air, high softening temperature and good mechanical properties are attributes leading to an increasing interest in a variety of applications, in spite of their high cost. Polysulphones can be readily processed by conventional thermoplastic techniques although their softening temperatures exceed 200°C.

Polysulphones may be formally expected to have regular and linear structures, but in fact most types contain a 'kink' or 'dog leg' which inhibites crystallization. This similarly exists in the polycarbonates, and it is persumed that the reductance to crystallize is related to similar structural features.

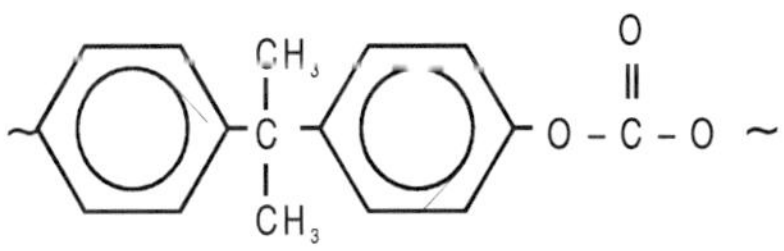

(i) Polycarbonate

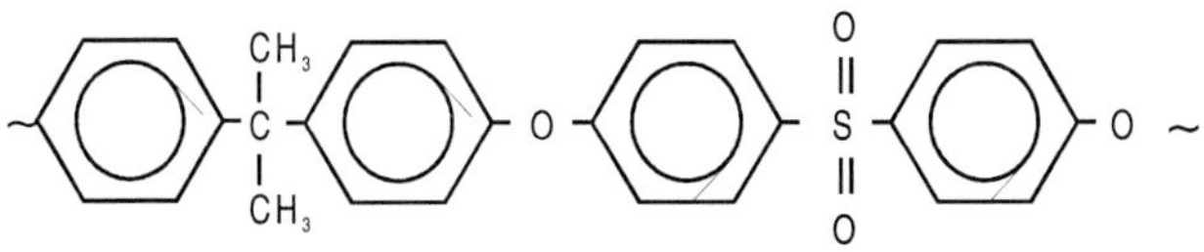

(ii) Polysulphone, e.g. Udel™ polysulfone (Union Carbide), Softening point 190°C

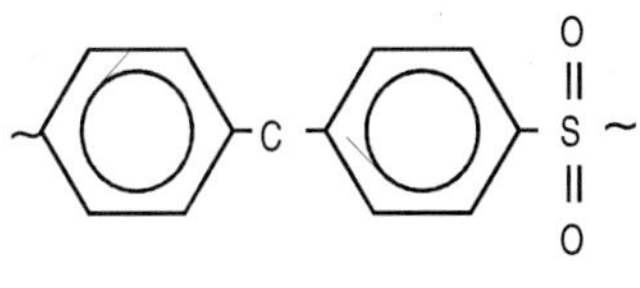

(iii) Polyethersulphone (softening point 220°C)

Therefore, most commercial polysulphones are available as amorphous materials, which consequently are transparent after melt processing. There is an exception in the family, which does not possess the 'kinked' feature (iv); this is a crystalline polymer having a melting point exceeding 500°C, at which temperature it will be also starting to degrade:

Crystallinity is not a characteristic of the commercially significant polysulphones, which consist of the homoplymers (ii) and (iii), together with a copolymers based on (iii) and (iv). The inclusion of increasing amounts of the latter increased the softening point of the polyethersulphone.

Polyuethersulphones can be used for tens of thousands of hours at 200°C without significant loss in strength, a property which is the basis for a number of applications, including internally illuminated push-button switches and indicator lights for cookers. This excellent stability at high temperatures is not matched by ultraviolet resistance in weathering, which is poor. However resistance to ionizing radiations, (ß-, γ and X-ray) is good in the temperature range 20-200°C. Polyethersulphone is a highly polar aromatic, polymer, thus as expected, it is resistant to aqueous acids, bases and most salts and to hydrocarbons, including petrol, oils and greases, even at high temperatures, where glass-filled grades are recommended. A typical application is in the inlet manifold between curbrettor and cylinder in a petrol engined power chain saw. Polar solvents, particularly of an aromatic type, are liable to dissolve polyethersulphone partially or completely. In the prescence of residual or extenally applied stresses, polar solvents will also give rise to crazing.

Polyethersulphone is used in the heater element holder of a high speed hand drier. This unit has to endure a working temperature of 100°C, with peaking temperature under fault conditions of 200°C, or even higher. Polyethersulphone is eminently suitable for these temperature conditions and, since it is unlikenly to encounter solvents in this application, it would be expected to have a very long service life. The part can be manufactured by injection moulding on conventional equipment and has in fact, proved successful in service. The non flammability of the polymer is relevant in this application, a characteristic leading to its use in aerospace applications where cost considerations are minor compared to safety factors. A further attribute of polyethersulphone is its ability to be shaped to fine tolerances, which is also dependent on its inherent dimentsional stability. An application ilustrative of this property is a base fitting or integrated circuits.

Poly(phenylene sulphide, (PPS)

Poly (phenylene sulphide) has a symmertrical repeat unit consisting alternately of sulphide links and para phenylene groups so it is not surprising that this is a crystallizable plastic.

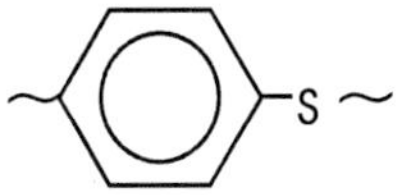

The melting point, 277°C is not particularly high, considering the predominance of the aromatic groups in the structure (compared with polyamide 6.6 and T_m=265°C). The T_g of the polymer (88°C)is marginally higher than that of poly(ethylene terephthalate,) 70°C, suggesting that some problems might arise in processing if rapid chilling is imposed. Quenching does indeed affet the crystallinity significantly.

Processing is usually by injection moulding for which the melt temperature is 315-360°C. Mould temperatures of 50-160°C have been used, although temperatures above 130°C are preferred, giving increased crystallinity, better dimensional stability at elevated temperatures, and improved gloss. High filler content gives rise to low mould shrinkage (0.2-0.6%) for a crystallizable polymer.

PPS has been called 'the poor man's polysulphone' because of its relative cheapness; this refers to some similarity in properties between the polymers, particularly temperature resistance. There is a significant change in the mechanical properties of PPS, associated with a glass transition temperature below 100°C, a phenomenon which does not occur with polysulphones. The resistance of PPS to high-energy ionizing radiations is excellent, probably, surpassing that of polysulphones. However, its poor resistance to UV radiation encountered in weathering is similar to that of polysulphones; fortunately this behaviour can be markedly improved by the addition of stabilizers. On the other hand, the chemical resistance of PPS is a crystalline plastic. It may be inferred that the sulphide linkage, (—S—) is not as chemically inert as is the sulphone group (—SO_2—).

An outstanding characteristic of PPS is its resistance to fire. It is self-extinguishing (having a critical oxygen index of 50), although if a flame is present PPS will burn, charring without dripping or fire-spread. At the same tine, some smoke may be formed, but the concentration of potentially toxic gases (e.g. carbon monoxide and mercaptans) is low.

These two materials differ considerably in mechanical properties, however the cheaper phenolics have much lower tensile strength, along with low tensile elongation (0.5%). Both have good electrical properties and will withstand direct contact with metal at 250°C. The main reason behind the choice of specific materials for these application is the design of each part. The design with the open end will have to withstand large flexural stresses at its corners. Also, if any impact loads on the cantilever end will induce large stresses in the component. Poly(phenylene sulphide) is therefore suited for this application because of its excellent mechanical properties and its suitability for operation at high temperature (up to 250°C; by contrast, phenol-formaldehyde lacks the strength. Another features in favour of the PPS is its high impact strength, which could be significant for equipment designed for industrial use. Furthermore the 'integrity' of the design means that it is inherently much stronger. Threfore both materials could be used in this application; however, the much cheaper phenolic is chosen since it will operate adequately under the applied stresses. The designer's task is to produce an attractive and useful products at an economical price. In designing the irons, one designer has tried to change the concept of the iron by adopting a cantilever shape, which should be technically more satisfactory in use. By doing so, employing a higher-cost material has resulted in a more expansive product. Nevertheless, the manufacturer has decided that a more attractive product with a price disadvantage would be more marketable than an iron with a more traditional design.

Properties of poly(phenylene sulphide) and cross-linked phenolics)

	PPS Phenolics	
Cost	High	Low
Tensile strength	140 MPa at 100°C	50
MPa at 20°C		
	20 MPa at 240°C	20
MPa at 250°C		
Flexural modulus at 20°C	12 GPa at 100°C	21 GPa
	3GPa at 250°C	
Impact strength at 20°C	80J,m^{-1}at 210°C	20j,m^{-1}
Deflection temperature	260°C	182°C

35

Styrene Plastics

Polystyrene

During the 1939-45 war, supplies of natural rubber were denied to the Western Allies by the Japanese occupation of Malaysia and other areas producing natural rubber in the Far East. As a substitute, butadiene-styrene synthetic rubber was urgently manufactured on a large scale, requiring the manufacture of styrene on a considerable scale. At the end of the war, with natural rubber freely available, the demand for synthetic rubber was reduced, and the styrene plants were sold cheaply to the chemical industry. Styrene is prepared by the Friedel-Crafts reaction between benzene and ethylene to yield ethylbenzene, which is dehydrogenated to the monomer. It is not an important chemical, except as a constituent of polymers, which are produced by mass, solution or suspension polymerization, usually the last; emulsion polymerization gives polystyrene latex. The quality of the polymer is monitored by softening point, solution viscosity of a 2% solution in toluene, and the proportion of methanol-soluble material. The softening point is particularly affected by residual monomer, as is odour and the acceptability for food contact applications.

Although polystyrene (PS) is commodity plastic, must of the recent growth has been in the modified grades; however, crystal polystyrene, is available in a number of variants of different molecular weight. These include *general-purpose*— a compromise between high molecular weight for good mechanical properties and low molecular weight for adequate flow; *high molecular weight*— for better impact performance; low *valatiles*— increased softening temperature by up to 7°C; and *easy* flow polymer of lower molecular weight, plus internal lubricant.

The commercial plastic is non-crystalline, with a softening point of approximately 100°C. The low softening temperature and the amorphous nature of the plastic mean that PS is one of the easiest plastics to mould, since temperature may be used to reduce the viscosity to acceptable levels. However PS tends to degrade by depolymeriztion at temperature above 150°C, so that long dwell times in the melt should be avoided. Further, due to its ready mouldability, there is a temptation to use long flow paths, and low mould temperatures, for economy in cycle time, resulting in high residual strain in the mouldings, with disastrous consequnces on the strength. Other processing advantages accuring from the non-crystalline nature are lower mould shrinkage than for crystalline platics, and a low heat content to the processing temperature, again compared with crystalline plastics.

Since polystyrene is amorphous, it is transparent unless unsoluble additives are used, and for the same reason it is soluble in aromatic solvents and chlorinated hydrocarbons, and has a strong tendency to stress-solvent crazing. As expected for a hydrocarbon polymer PS has low water absorption and excellent electrical properties. The specific gravity is 1.07 and the plastic is hard and brittle; the strength is not exceptional, with pronounced stress-crazing prior to fracture. Polystyrene is susceptible to degradation by UV radiation (weathering); it is also flammable, burning with a yellow, sooty flame.

The properties militate against the use of this plastic in critical engineering applications, but PS is widely used in decorative and commodity packaging; examples are cosmetics and foodstuffs. An engineering use is approached in lighting fittings, where evenness and intensity of illumination are important, for instance in bookshops. There have been many trivial and transient applications resulting from the easy processing rigidity, transparency and relatively low price.

Polystyrene has suitable rigidity and high-temperature performance to enable it to be formed into attractive light fittings, expecially covers for strip lighting. However, the designer should be aware of the limited resistance of the material to UV radiation, which may limit its use with high-intensity fluorescent tubes,. Furthermore, when PS is stressed, there is a tendency for the material to craze at stress considerably lower than that for failure; crazing is the lower stres involved and the minimal impact abuse; nevertheless, sharp corners should be avoided and generous radii given to reduce the risk of premature failure.

For the highly competitive lower price cosmetics market, the packaging is often used to sell the product; thus it has to look attractive without increasing the selling price significantly. For an attractive product, the essential requirements are a good surface finish and colourants, whilst only a small amount of post-moulding distoration is acceptable; with the added property of transparency, PS is a reasonable choice. These same qualities are involved in the marketing of confectionery, but here it is the higher-quality end of the market which has adopted plastics packaging. This is preferred to the paperboard used at the lower end of the market. For economic reasons the melt temperature and the mould temperature are sometimes kept at low melts to obtain short cycle times; this leads, however, to stresses frozen into the moulding. These are detrimental to the mechanical properties and could result in premature failure. It is desirable, therefore, to mould with higher mould and melt temperatures, with consequently increased cycle times to reduce the moulded-in stress; a balance must be reached between cost and performance.

High-Impact polystyrene (HIPS)

The main deficiency of polystyrene is its brittleness; this may be improved by a number of techniques, which are generally applicable in polymer technology;

(i) Increasing the molecular weight; this inevitable increases the melt viscosity which, in turn, may result in higher residual orientation in mouldings and extrudates, with consequent deterioration in impact strength

(ii) Planner orientation; this is applicable only to films, and, more recently, pipes and bottles.

(iii) Addition of plasticizer; only a limited improvement in toughness is obtained, and there are significant losses in softening temperature, rigidity and strength.

(iv) Copolymerization

(v) Polymer blending : a variety of blends is possible homogenous blends with other plastics of good impact strength, composites involving filters, and blends with rubbers.

Although there is limited scope for improving impact performance by increasing the molecular weight, (iv) and (v) provide the main methods by which the toughness of polystyrene is improved.

The addition of rubbers to PS is widely practised; the secret of obtaining good impact behaviour without compromising rigidity is that the blend should be heterogenous. Butadiene styrene rubber (SBR) may be blended with PS, but this can lead to molecular mixing, resulting in plasticization and little improvement in toughness. Better results are obtained if the rubber is dissolved in styrene. The greatest improvement toughness is obtained if rubber latex (polybutadiene is preferred for good low-temperature properties) of particle size 0.1-1.0 µm is reacted to give a grafted coating, and the product then added to styrene monomer which is polymerized. Usually 10-20% rubber is involved. The structure of this consists of a PS matrix, with the inclusions of discrete rubber particle, some of which themselves contain smaller particle of polystyrene. The rubber phase is rendered visible in the electron microscope by staining with osmium tetroxide or iodine; the particle are too small to be seen by light microscopy, although they scatter light, leading to opacity.

The easy processing characteristics of polystyrene are retained in HIPS; indeed for pre-gelled rubber particles, injection moulding is fasciliated, but if they are larger than 10 µm, surface finish deteriorates. Thermoforming, especially vaccum forming of extruded sheet, is a favoured way of shaping simple objects, e.g. disposable beakers for drinks, and more complex engineering structures, such as refrigerator linears.

The modification of PS with rubber results in a considerable increase in impact toughness, by an order of magnitude, but with deterioration in other properties; 5-15°C in softening temperature and 20-40% in rigidity and strength. The agening behaviour is also worsened by inclusion of rubber; but incorporation of antioxidant largely restores the situation.

Properties of PS, HIPS and SAN

	PS	HIPS	SAN
Tensile strength (MPs)	34-51	27-43	65
Elongation (%)	4	20-50	2.5
Impact strength (J/m)	10-20	45-65	10.5
Vicat Softening Temperature (°C)	90	85	102

These properties allow the use of HIPS in many applications, especially where impact abuse is encountered; however, the low softening temperature offers some limitation. Applications include refrigerator linears and fittings, toys, games and sports equipment, and ratio and electrical equipment housings. As with PS design with HIPS has been largely empirical, as in the following case study.

There have been several examples of the unsatisfactory use of PS, because of the brittle nature of the material; the application in toys is typical. Children frequently abuse their toys and thus a good impact performance is essential. General-purpose polystyrene (GPPS breaks and exposes a shapr edge as an additional hazard. The advent of HIPS allowed the good features of PS to be retained, with the additional benefit of toughness at room temperature (the toughness falls dramatically below-20°C), for only a small increase in material cost. Several material could be considered for the manufacture of toys; impact modified PP and HDPE are durable and appear superior to HIPS. However, HIPS is frequently preferred for the following reasons :

(i) PS can be easily joined using solvent adhesives

(ii) Amorphous materials have less shrinkage, and take more detail from the mould surface.

(iii) Painting and planting are much easier for HIPS

Refrigerator liners are simple open-section parts which could be made by a variety of shaping methods. However, the comparatively small numbers required for any one design precludes techniques such as injection moulding. Thermoforming is more favoured, but his restricts material choice; further, the material must stand abuse at 4°C, and withstand thermal cycling between this temperature and ambient conditions. Crystalline polymers are more difficult to handle since their melt stregnth is low. PVC thermoforms satisfactorily but has generally less suitable low-temperature properties.

The linear is manufacture in sheet of 3 mm thickness which is heated on both sides and blown with compressed air. The art is subsequently shaped on a male former by vaccum. A minimum thickness of 1 mm is retained after moulding to ensure robustness, with the overall thickness 1.5-2 mm. When the liner is in position in the body of the refrigerator, the space is injected with polyurethane foam, giving rigidity in the protruding features of the linear and thermal insulation.

The low temperature impact performance of HIPS is unsuitable for deep freeze applications, where ABS is preferred.

Styrene copolymers

Although styrene has been copolymerized with a wide variety of comonomers, only the systems involving butadiene and acrylonitrile are of commerical importance; the former are employed as rubbers and, at higher styrene contents, as coating resins and rubber reinforcing agents. They will not be considered further. In the styrene-acrylonitrile system, one particular copolymer is unique, that containing 65-70% styrene (SAN), which is a preferred composition is respect of properties, and especially since it is easily manufactured. The reader is referred to other texts for details of copolymerization mechanisms, but it should be mentioned that it is rare to find copolymers formed at the same ratio as the comonomer feed; the copolymer quoted is such a case. Compositions containing more than 80% acrylonitrile have also seen development as barrier resins; they are melt processed but there progress is retarded by fear of the toxidity of residual acrylonitrile monomer.

Incorporation of acrylonitrile into a styrene polymer increases softening point and toughness, presumbly by increasing the interchain attraction. For the same reason, resistance to non-polar solvents; such as fats and oils, is improved. Some data are given in table. To summarise its properties, SAN has a softening point some 10°C higher than that of PS; is transparent, but with a tendency to yellowing, particularly on weathering; and is somewhat tougher and stronger than polystyrene, SAN is used for drinking tumblers, jugs and other transparent domestic ware, and for transparent and reasonably tough covers for domestic, electrical and automotive equipment, as shown in the following case study.

Recently, a new family of styrene copolymers has been marketed, combining a high transparency (although marginally inferior to PS) with good impact properties and rigidity. They are block copolymers of styrene and butadiene, containing a preponderance of the former (70-80%); this constitutes the transparent matrix in which submicroscopic demains of (block) poly-butadiene are dispersed. Thse provide energy-dissipative mechanisms during impact, but are sufficiently small not to scatter light appreciably, although a 'blue haze' can be discerned. As with other block copolymers, processing subsequent behaviour may not be straightforward. An example, a transparent component for a toy.

ABS plastics

The availability of SAN, of greater toughness and higher softening temperature than PS, gives an opportunity for composites analgous to HIPS. The polar copolymer allows the use of polar butadiene- acrylonitrile rubber which, pre-gelled in a blend at 20 content, gives a composition of very high impact strength. A product with superior low temperature performance is obtained from polybutadiene latex, grafted with a SAN-compatible coating on to which the SAN is polymerized. Following much development work by the manufacturers a wide selection of grades of ABS is marketed, sharing very great resistance to impact abuse, with a softening temperature similar to that of PS, ABS plastics are usually opaque, although a tranparent version can be made by matching the refractive indices of the resin and rubber phase. This is , however, inferior to ABS and more expensive, so is not widely used.

The dominant property of ABS plastics is the very impact strength, which is coupled with less desirable features, such as a softening point similar to that of PS, and comparatively low stiffness and strength for structural use. They retain, however, the excellent injection moulding behaviour of styrene plastics, particularly good melt flow, low mould shrinkage and excellent sufrace finish. Properties relevant to design are given in figure. The rigidity can be improved by reinforcing fillers; glass fibre composites appear to be the most popular, although the sufrace finish and toughness are compromised. Attention is drawn in figure. Which records that the fatique behaviour is not comparable with the excellent impact property.

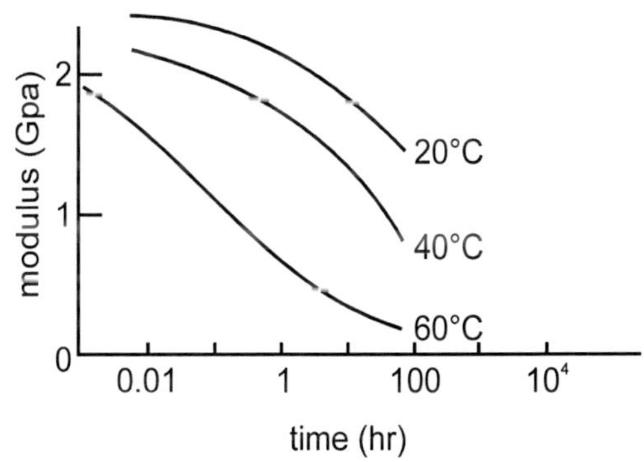

Tensile creep modulus of ABS

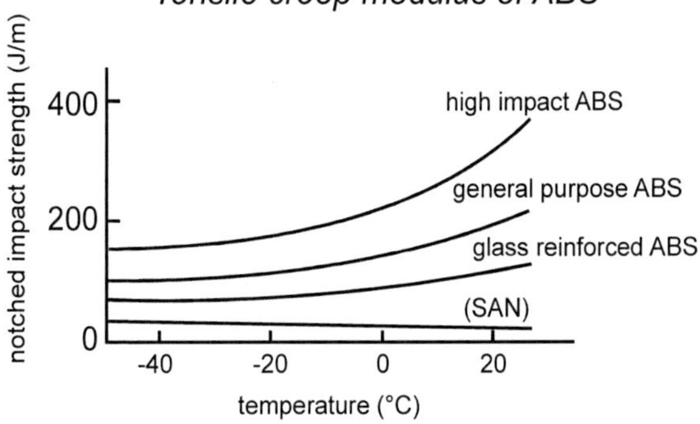

Impact properties of ABS

Application of ABS plastics reflect the processing behaviour and the high impact strength; vaccum cleaner covers, carpet sweeper housings, lawn mower housings, telephone handsets (repalcing PMMA which in turn replaced PF), and hair dryer housings of higher softening temperature than HIPS. They also find application where good dimensional tolerance, coupled with good surface finish and adequate mechanism properties, is required, car instrument clusters, car fascias and trim.

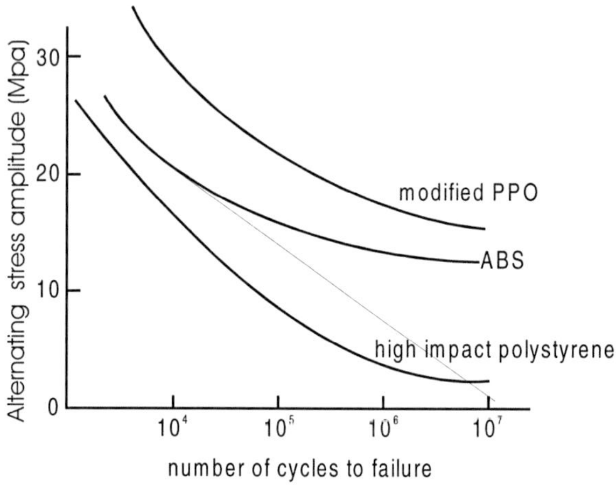

Fatigue properties of some styrene plastics

Polystyrene-poly (phenylene oxide) blends

A product range of incresing commercial importance is based on blends of PS with poly (phenylene oxide) (PPO). The latter is in fact the dimethyl homologue, which is used to restrict linkages in the polymer chain to the *para*-position. PPO hompolymer is a high strength, reasonably tough,non-crystalline thermoplastics which is very difficult to process. It is also comparatively expensive. Somewhat surprisingly, PPO is miscible with PS on a moleculr scale, and the blends are also capable of being further toughned by technique analogous to those used in HIPS and ABS, Design data are given in figures. Typically, grades with softening point some 30-40°C higher than polystyrene are available, with rigidity and strength approximately 50% higher than high impact ABS, and with similarly enhanced long term behaviour. The processing characteristics are inferior to those of ABS, particularly the melt flow, which is restricted; in consequence, it is usual to work at very high temperature (280-300°C), and to use mulitple gating. A property unusual is styrene plastics but exhibited by these blends is that they are self extinguishing when ignited.

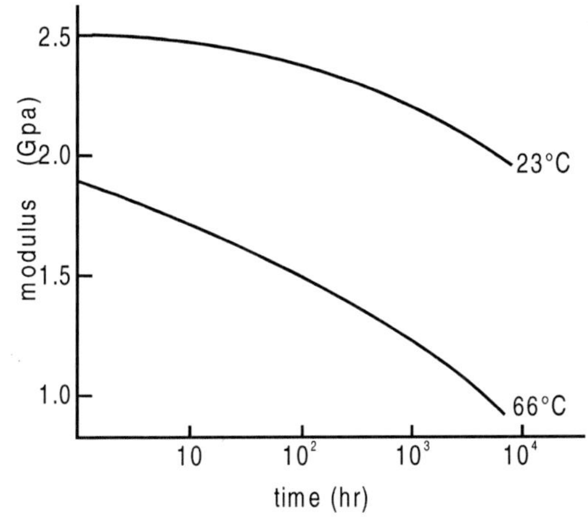

Tensile creep modulus of modified PPO

The blend have the good dimensional tolerance of amorphous plastics in general and of styrene-based plastics in particular, and are finding increase in care components, television set packplates, transforms cases, electrical equipment housings, etc. They can be made in structural foam grades, and as glass-fibre and mineral-filled composites. Further, the foam may be reinforced, giving a diverse family of materials, with many actual and potential uses.

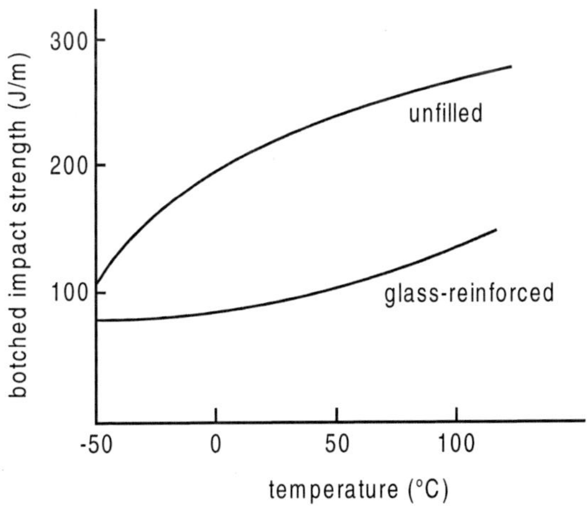

Impact properties of modified PPO

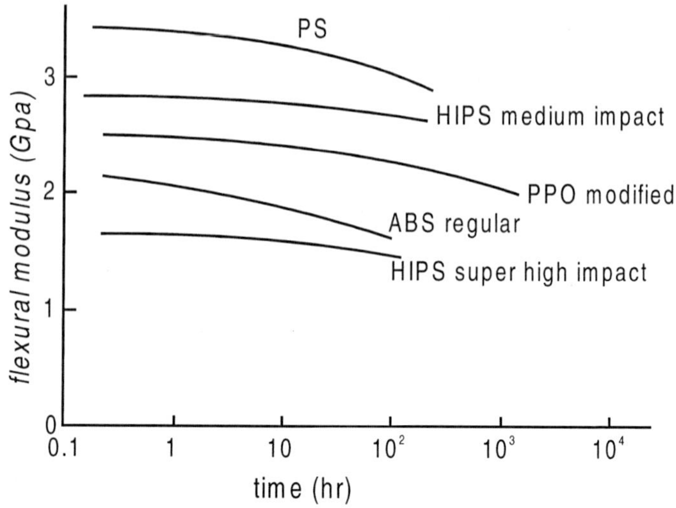

Flexural creep modulus data at 20°C for some styrene plastics

Foamed modified PPO business machine components are large mouldings which need rigidity to retain several parts of the equipment (such as the keyboard), good dimensional stability and very good tolerances. Other performance requirements are good impact resistance, pleasing appearance and cost effectiveness. A structural foam based on a PPO-PS blend has been found very satisfactory at a density of 900 kg m^{-3} with an integral skin.

As a concluding comment it must be pointed out that considering styrene based plastics for particular applications, the poor solvent resistance might be a limitation. Simultanous application of stress, in the presence of a solvent, may give premature failure due to environmental stress cracking. These comment apply equally to PS, HIPS, and the PPO-PS blend.

36

Polyolefin Plastics

(1) Polyethylene

(i) High density (HDPE), produced by comparatively low-pressure routes with Ziegler or complex oxide catalyst.

(ii) Low-density (LDPE), traditionally made by a high pressure route.

(iii) Linear low-density (LLDPE), comparable in structure and general properties with LDPE and manufactured by copolymerizing ethylene with butene, hexane, oxtene or 4-methyle pentene at low pressure

(iv) Very low-density (VLDPE) is an extreme version of LLDPE

(v) Ethylene copolymers, typically with polar monomers such vinyl acetate, are made by LDPE technology

(vi) Blends of various types of ethylene polymers are now widely used; sometimes their use in deliberate, sometimes incidental.

(2) Polybutene

This is an isotactic polymer, produced by Ziegler-Natta catalyst by a process analogous to that used to manufacture polypropylene.

(3) Poly (4-methyl pentene)

Another isotactic polymer produced by Ziegler-Natta catalyst

Polyethylene

Chronologically, the manufacture of LDPE preceded that of HDPE, but since the latter has the simpler structure it will be considered first. The monomer, ethylene, was originally obtained from sugar by fermentation and dehydration.

molasses→ethyl→ethylene

Ethylene is now obtained from oil, or preferably light naptha, but cracking.

High-density polyethylene

Two distinct process were developed almost simultaneously in the mid 1950s, based on Ziegler catalyst and on mixed oxide catalysts; the Phillips is the most widely employed of the latter.

Ziegler and Phillips HDPEs can be virtually unbranched hydrocarbon chains, leading to densities in the range 0.945-0.956 Mgm^{-3}, although commercial Ziegler polyethylene can have a few ethyl side-groups (5-7 per 1000 chain atoms), Oxide catalysts polymers generally have the highest densities of the polyethylene series.

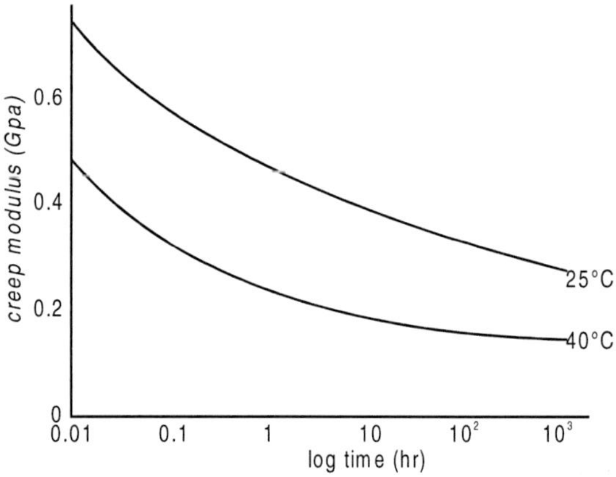

Flexural creep modulus as a function of time for HDPE (density 0.953 Mg/m^3) for stress of 4. Mpa

Processing is dominated by the linearity of the chains, leading to pronounced flow orientation and a rapid crystallization rate with only little supercooling compared with polypropylene. The attainable crystallinity in standard processing operation is somewhat higher than for PP, resulting in generally higher shrinkage. For reasons concerned with processing, HDPE is sometimes problem, or where it can be tolerated (margarine tubes), and for very large blow-moulidngs, where the stability of the parison is helped by the orientation induced during extrusion, and by the pronounced non-Newtonian behaviour of the melt.

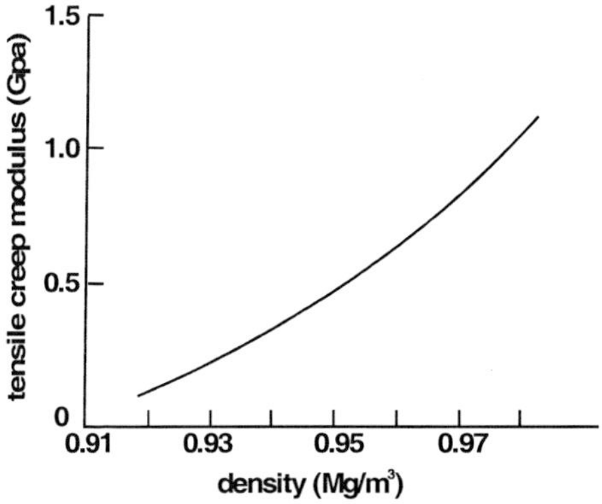

Dependence of 100-see tensile creep modulus at 1% strain on density of polyethyelebe

The properties of HDPE include a crystalline melting point lower than that of PP, 130-135°C, with very little supercooling wand a rapid crystallization rate, HDPE, is comparable in rigidity with PP, but with inferior creep behaviour and scratch resistance figure shows flexural creep moulds as a function of time and the considerable effect of temperature on the deformation behaviour. The effect of density is seen in figure, which embraces data covering a density range including LDPE and HDPE. Low density grades of HDPE are brittle if pronounced stress concentrations are present, but high molecular weight materials are tough, even at low temperatures. Low molecular-weight polymers may stress crack in the presence of some chemicals. Density of some 5% greater than PP, with implications for volume cost. HDPE is flammable, although flame retardants improve the polymer in this respect.

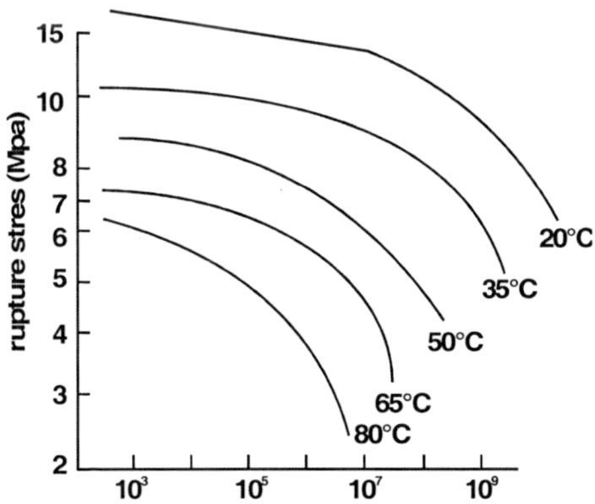

Rupture stress v. Time for HDPE pipe at various temperature

As noted above, HDPE, is very important for blow moulding especially large capacity containers, such as 220-litre barrels; dustbins are shaped in this way, two at a time. HDPE is also important for bleach and detergent bottles where the higher rigidity compared with DLPE leads to a cheaper package. Blow-moulding technology is exemplified by a prestigious application of growing importance-fuel tanks for road vehicles. HDPE, because of its high crystallinity, meets the need for an effective barrier at a mean thickness of 5.5 mm, while the impact requirement specified by the EEC is satisfied by the grades of HDPE developed for this application. As the thickness is 5.5 mm, the moulding cycle is dominated by the cooling time. An increase in productivity can be achieved most readily by reducing the cooling time. An inrease in productivity can be achieved most readily by reducing the cooling time by providing internal cooling in addition to the normal heat transfer coefficient, plastic to air, by circulating the air and provision of sufficient capacity to extract the heat energy. The later again comprises two factors, the volume of coolant and the temperature at which it is introduced.

Reference has been made to injection moulding, which is a fair market for HDPE. Extruded pipe from HDPE and a tougher varient of lower density is widely used for natural gas distribution, particularly in cold climates where some failures of PVC have been encountered. HDPE has also been formed into mudguards for commercial vehicles, where the non-corroding polymer withstands and arduous service conditions. Very thin film, made by the tubular process, finds applications as a tissue-paper replacement and for point-of sale wrapping, especially of wet foodstuffs, such as meat and fish. HDPE has been preferred over PP in mold-bottle crates, since creep is less important than for beer crates and the incidence of impact abuse at low-temperature is likely to be greater, but the trend is to PP because of its more tolerant moulding characteristics.

HDPE, and more recently, modified polyethylene of lower density, are used in gas distribution systems for many important reasons, including economic shaping, ability to withstand both the internal and external loads, good low-temperature impact properties and relative impermeability to the gases carried. Gas pipes are required to have many years of maintenence free life, so it is important for the design of the system to be correct. A typical installation requires the pipe to operate for up to 50 years at 20°C at an internal pressure of 0.25 MPa, with a mean diameter of 250 mm. For thin walled pipes and the wall thickness can be calculated, based on a failure stress after 50 years of 6.5 MPa.

As with polypropylene, reinforcement of HDPE with short glassfibres is practiced; compounds with loading of glass up to 20% are available, giving much improved rigidity and reduced thermal expansion compared with the unreinforced material. The modulus is increased by a factor of 3 for 20% glass fibre but, in the presumed absence of coupling of the glass to the matrix HDPE, the stress at yield is unchanged and may even be reduced in some circumstances.

Low-density polyethylene

Low-density polyethylene, generally considered to have a specifice gravity in the range 0.915-0.930, is manufactured at high pressure and high temperature usually 1500-3000 bars at 150-250°C, in a process which is usually continuous in stirred reactors or tubes. The reaction conditions invite free radical attack on polymer, leading to long chain branching and to pendant C_1 and C_4 chains, and to other irregularities, including unsaturation. Molecular weight, molecular-weight distribution and branching are controlled in the reaction by modifiers, by temperatures and pressure, and by the type and concentration of initiator.

The structure of LDPE is generally similar to that of HDPE but the crystallinity is limited by branches which cannot fit into the crystalline lattice. Crystallinity is frequently 50-65%, is also dependent on molecular weight, the higher molecular-eight grades achieving lower crystallinity. Branching is specified as the number of CH_3 per 1000 carbon atoms, generally 25-30 for high pressure polymers. Specific gravity of the crystalline and amorphous states are very different, 1.01 and 0.84 respectively, giving a method for assessing crystallinity; X-ray methods are also used. Melt Flow Index (MFI), is still widely used as a monitor of processability; the higher the MFI the greater the fluidity (the lower the viscosity), of the melt. Grades of LDPE suitable for all processing methods, including rotational moulding, are generally available. Notes on the processing methods employed are given in the survey of application below.

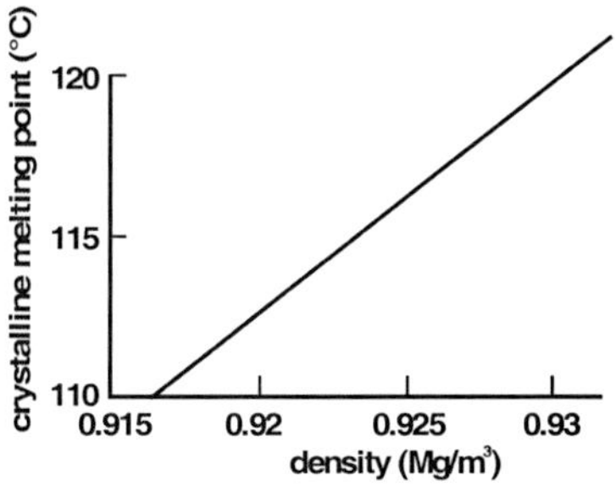

Dependence of crystalline melting point of LDPE on density

The properties of LDPE are those expected of a lower crystallinity variant of HDPE; the melting point is lower approximately 115°C, varying with density, with a more gradual melting process. It is almost a factor of 10 less rigid than HDPE or polypropylene and the yield stres is much lower. Both modulus and yield stress depend on density (crystallinity) and on MFI. At moderate and high molecular weights the polymer is very tough, but low-molecular-weight grades are susceptible to environmental stress cracking. Long-chain branching affect molecular weight vs. processing behaviour favourably. Elecrical properties can be excellent, but depend on impurities and additives. Additives are frequently incorporated in LDPE to modify the properties for particular applications for film antioxidants, UV stabilizers, pigments and occassionally prodegradants.

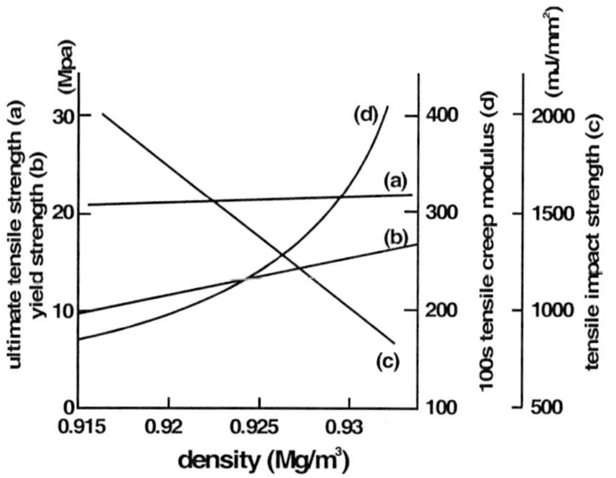

Effect of density of LPDE (MFI=0.25g/10 min) on some mechanical properties

Applications include film for packaging manufactured by the tube-blowing process, which consumes some 70°C of LDPE production; a miscellany of uses takes the remaining 30% including.

Bottles	Extrusion blow moulding
Mustard jars	Injection blow moulding
Bowls, buckets	Injection moulding
Cold water tanks	Rotational moulding
Paper Coating	Extrusion

For many years, wheelborrows have been made from wood or metal, both of which have to be protected from the degrading effect of weathering.

Unfortunataly, the conventional protective coatings are not durable and the substrate is quickly exposed to the elements. The idea of using a plastic moulded bin as a part of a wheelbarrow was novel, and allowed changes in the general design. The bin injection-moulded, so that there is little hindrance to introducing more complex shapes; the design of the barrow was changed to that it was much deeper, with a less acute tipping angle, enabling a larger volume of material to be carried. The feet were connected to the base and the handles placed wide apart to make the wheelbarrow more stable inuse. The main performance requirement was that it should withstand the impact of objects such as bricks being thrown into from a short distance. Assuming a maximum load of 150 kg, the approximate stress assuming a wall thickness of 3 mm, is less than 1 MPa, a stress level which could be tolerated by all thermoplastics; the choice depended, therefore, on impart performance and price.

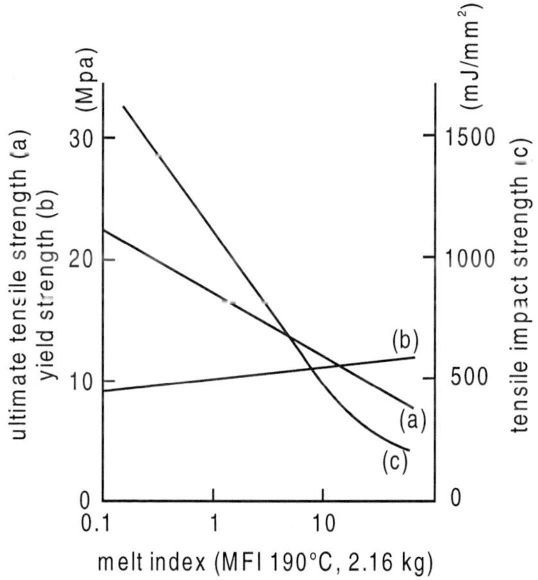

Effect of Melt Flow Index of LDPE (density 0.918 Mg/m³) on some mechanical properties

Low-density polyethylene is still one of the cheapest thermoplastics, possesses excellent impact importance, but is very flexible. A grade of LDPE was selected to give the best overall properties, viz., density of 0.92 Mgm^{-3} and MFI of 12 -14 g per 10 min (2.16 kg at 190°C).

Linear low-density polyethylene

The structure and propertes of LLDPE are comparable with those of LDPE, with the notable different that LLDPE does not have long chain branching. the practical consequence is that LLDPE has much superior strain accommodation, which allows far greater draw-dawn, but in the melt and in the solid state. It is interesting to compare the tensile stress vs. strain curves for HDPE, LDPE, and LLDPE.

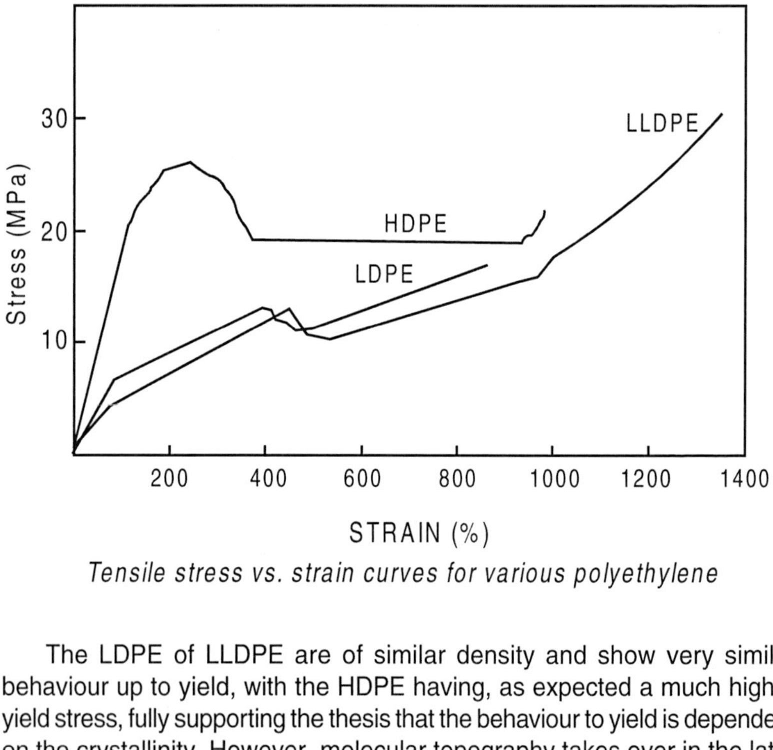

Tensile stress vs. strain curves for various polyethylene

The LDPE of LLDPE are of similar density and show very similar behaviour up to yield, with the HDPE having, as expected a much higher yield stress, fully supporting the thesis that the behaviour to yield is dependent on the crystallinity. However, molecular topography takes over in the later stages of the test. The elongation of LDPE is limited by long-chain branching, and that of HDPE by shortage of amourphous polymer. Not being limited by these two factors, LLDPE can extend to very high elongation.

The melt rheology of LLDPE differs from that of LDPE, so that processing equipment for the later cannot be used without modification. consequently, much interest in blends has been generated.

Film appears to be the main application area at present.

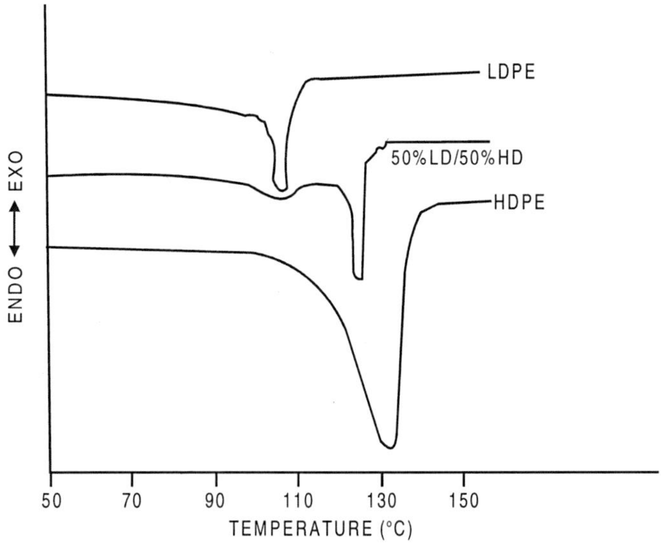

Thermograms of LDPE, HDPE and a 50/50 blend of the two

Very-low-density polyethylene

This material, with a density down to 0.88 Mgm^{-3}, is believed to be a copolymer of ethylene with a higher olefin. No pattern of application seems to have been established.

Blends of ethylene polymers

It might seem axiomatic that the various polymers of ethylene discussed above should be miscible; indeed, recently it was recommended that blends of HDPE and LDPE be used to obtain properties intermediate between those of the homopolymers. However work in several centres has shown that miscibility is the exception rather than the rule; even blends of LDPE and LLDPE tend to become 'unmixed' into separate crystallinity phases. This sound a warning concerning masterbatch carrier polymers; it is not prudent to use LDPE or, worse, an EVAC copolymer as carrier in a masterbatch introduced into matrices of HDPE and LDPE, or , worse polypropylene. It my apparently be tolerated in a large number of cases, but critical applications may fail. The separation is shows in differential scanning calorimetry thermograms, blends of LDPE-HDPE are shown in figure, and LDPE-LLDPE in figure. The difference between figure (c) and (d) is that (c) was quenches from the melt, where as figure (d) refers to slower cooling Clearly, for the

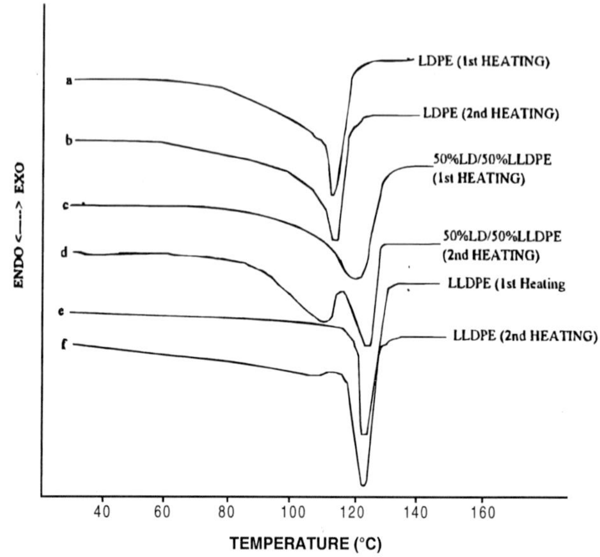

Thermograms of LLPE, LLDPE and a 50/50 blend: quenched and slow-cooled specimens

LDPE-LLDPE system the response is very dependent on the thermal history, and it is no surprise that the mechanical properties are affected.

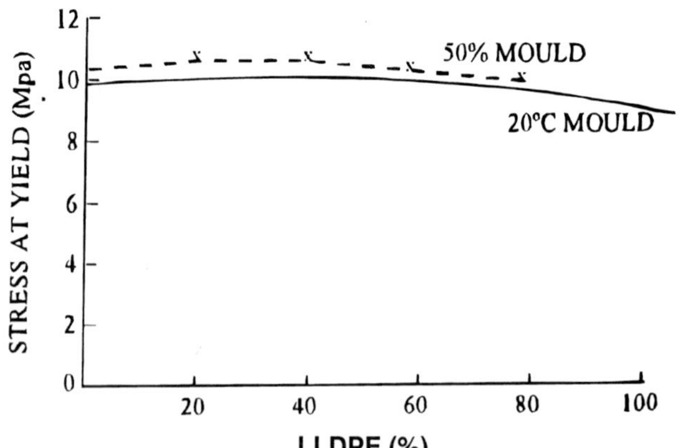

Yield stress vs. composition for LDPE-LLDPE blends. (Specimen did not reach yield in the flow direction)

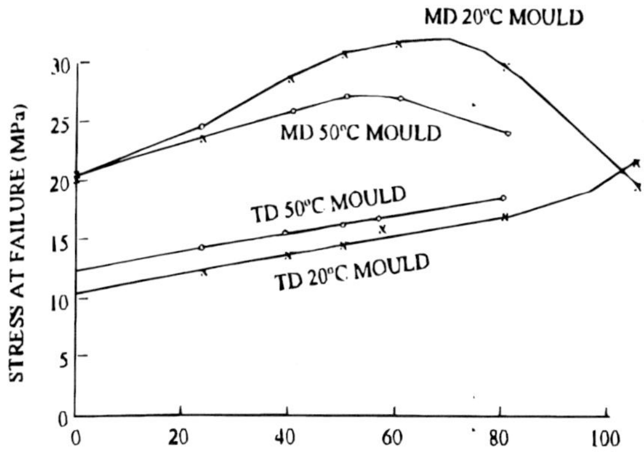

LLDPE (%)

Failure stress vs. composition for LDPE-LLDPE blends

However, the yield stress in the transverse direction seems to be little affected by the mould temperature with the data being in the order expected, i.e., the quenched samples having the lower yield stresses. A similar picture is presented for the breaking stresses in the transverse direction; however, a very different situation obtains in the flow direction, (machine direction), where we find that the considerably higher failue stress is associated with the more rapidly cooled samples. The different is appreciable, some 15%.

The mechanical properties are generally as expected, with the yield stress increasing monotonically with HDPE content, while the breaking stress is sensibly constant, although the value for HDPE seems to be a little than the reminder.

Ethylene copolymers

Ethylene copolymerized with other olefins has already been covered above. Ethylene copolymers with polymer comonomers are made by the high-pressure route; the favoured monomer is vinyl acetate (VAC) which, under the usual reaction conditions, copolymerizes with ethylene ideally. Small amounts of VAC reduce crystallinity and melting point, but increase toughness and flexibility; such copolymers (EVAC) are used for tough film, although the moisture permeability is increased by the inclusion of the polar groups.

Ionomer reins are ehtylene copolymers with an active functional groups in the comonomer, frequently carboxyl. This is 'neutralized' with metal oxide to give a tough thermoplastic rubber.

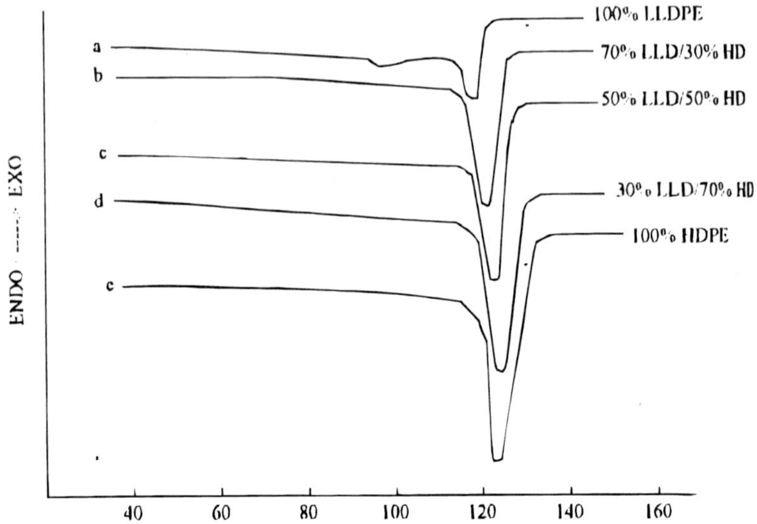

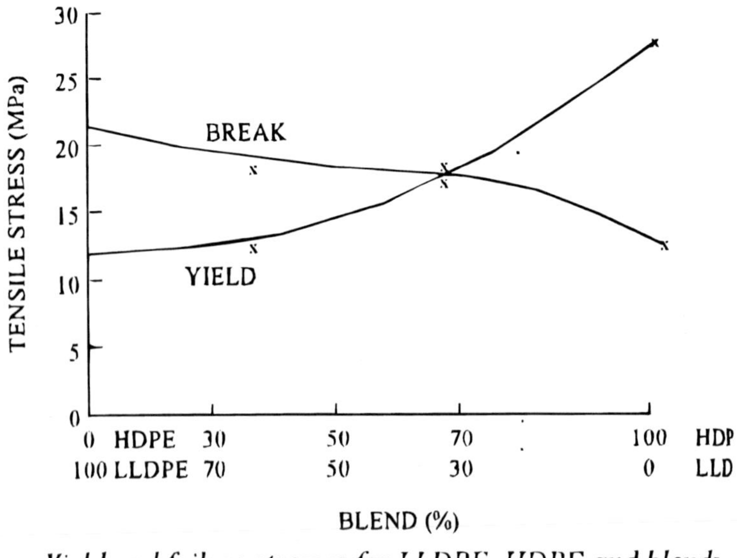

Yield and failure stresses for LLDPE, HDPE and blends

Polubut-l-ene

Up to 1957, only the non-crystallizable low-molecular-weight polymer was known, this is still used as a viscosity stabilizing additive for oils. Isotactic, crystalline polymer is generally similar to PP, but the melting point is some 40°C lower. If it manufactured by a process similar to that for polypropylene.

Polybutene is unusual in that there are two crystalline forms, I and II; the latter is metastable but is always formed from the melt during normal processing. The transition from II to I occurs at room temperature over 2-5 days, with increase in density, and consequent change in dimensions. Processing and properties are very similar to those to PP, except that the melting point is 130°C (for Type I crystallinity); similarly, the glass transition temperature is some 20°C lower than PP. Polybutene is slightly less rigid than PP, but has a significantly better creep resistance and seems to be immune to environmental stress cracking.

Application must be tolerant of the crystal transition and benefit from the creep behaviour, Pipes, especially for high pressure distribution, appears to be the only important outlet particularly for cold water and gas, and for hot water installation. They are manufactured in diameters upto 400 mm.

Poly-4-methylpent-l-ene (P4MP)

This polymer has the repeat unit :

The isotactic form is the only polymer is commercial important . An unusual feature is that bulk polymer is transparent because of the molecular chain is only very slightly birefringent. A second unusual feature is that the crystalline density and the amorphous density are very similar. The transparency is further enhanced by nucleation giving finer texture, and by balancing crystalline and amourphous densities even more closely, by copolymerization.

The principal properties of poly-4-methylpentene are a melting temperature of 230-235°C and glass transition 40-50°C. There is some tendency to brittleness, although P4MP is tougher that glass, but is very susceptible to UV attack. It is the only bulk transparent polyolefin in commercial production or development. The high melting point forces processing temperatures into the degradation range for the polymer. Melt stabilizers and lubricants are employed; even so, it is difficult to mold orientation-free products, and the presence of residual stresses increase the probability of brittle failure at low imposed stresses.

Applications include a number of small items which require polyolefin inertness, reasonable toughness compared with glass, coupled with either transparency or high softening temperature. Examples are ; spirits dispensers, automatic milking equipment, car interior light covers and 'cook-in -the-bag' trays. P4MP is an expensive mateial, but has a low specific gravity, 0.83, making it cheaper on a volume basis than its main competitor, polycrabonate, which is also more susceptible to chemical attack. P4MP can withstand up to 50 'hot hair' sterilization cycles of 1 h at 160°C.

P4MP is suitable for laboratory ware because it has good chemical resistance, transparency and high-temperature performance. For medical ware these same properties are advantageous; in addition, no toxic products are extracted under normal use. In such applications, additives, such as antioxidants must be chosen appropriately.

37

Plastic Processing Technology

Plastic Processing Technology

The plastic processing begins with the mixing or compounding process. Equipment and machinery widely used in the compounding stage are open mills or two-roll mills, internal or Banbury mixers, sigma blender, ribbon blender, low-shear extruders, pulverizers and granulators. High speed equipment, such as Henschel mixer, Buss-ko-kneader or the ZSK corotating intermeshing twin screw extruder are advantageous particularly in mass production units.

For the plastic materials, the 'plastic' deformable state, attained by thermoplastic polymers at appropriate temperatures and possessed by thermosetting polymers before being set or cured through chemical reactions, allows them to be shaped into a spectrum of finished products. The usefulness and often the essentiality of polymers and plastic products with all their profound impact on our life-style are due as much to the versatility, flexibility and sophistication of the shaping methods as to their inherent properties.

The shaping of plastics may be accomplished by the following general approaches and techniques:

(i) Shaping in the molten state (melt processing) employing compression, transfer and injection moulding, melt spinning, calendering, blow moulding, roto moulding and extrusion techniques,

(ii) Shaping in the leathery or rubbery state employing thermoforming tech niques and calendering,

(iii) Wet processing of polymers solutions employing wet spinning, spraying, spreading, brushing and dipping techniques,

(iv) Shaping of objects using polymer suspensions or emulsions (paste and latex technology), low molecular weight resin syrup (cast phenolics) or monomer polymer syrup (casting of acrylic sheets or laying up of fibre reinforced laminates and composites), and

(v) Finishing operations.

Each of the techniques other than the finishing operations involves a setting operation (freezing, cross-linking, gelling, extended polymerization, drying or precipitation and drawing) after the desired deformation has been achieved, so as to stabilize the imparted shape. The whole spectrum of processing as outlined above may also be viewed under three major categories as detailed below:

(a) Moulding—(i) Compression moulding, (ii) Transfer moulding, (iii) Injection/jet moulding and (iv) Blow moulding.

(b) Forming—(i) Extrusion, (ii) Spinning, (iii) Calendering, (iv) Thermoforming and (v) Casting, slush moulding and rotomoulding.

(c) Others—Lamination, reinforcement and coating.

Moulding Techniques

Moulding is usually defined as the process of shaping of an article from a plastic material usually by the simultaneous application of heat and pressure or pressure alone in a closed chamber called the mould.

(a) ***Compression Moulding*** This process is widely used for thermosetting polymers, even though in principle, it is also applicable to thermoplastic polymers. Compression moulding involves forcing a measured dose of polymer granules, moulding powder or the preform, preheated or otherwise, into the shape of the mould. In general, the charge is placed in the heated mould cavity and then the mould is closed and a desired degree of compression is effected by manipulating the hydraulic system attached to the compression press, resulting in intimate contact of the polymer charge with all parts of the mould surface aided by the heat applied and pressure developed and maintained. Both heat and pressure ensure good flow of the resin or the polymer, filling of all the intricate parts and comers of the cavity and good surface finish. For thermosetting systems, pressure is maintained till cross-linking to optimum level is attained. Thereafter, the mould is opened and the moulded object is ejected from the hot mould cavity. For thermoplastics, the mould has to be cooled well below the glass transition temperature or the heat distortion temperature of the polymer before the mould is opened and the moulded object is ejected.

A moulding cycle is constituted of all the steps beginning with charging the mould cavity and ending with ejection of the moulded object. The time interval covering the moulding cycle is commonly known as the cycle time. A slight excess of material is normally placed in the mould only to ensure that it is completely filled. The excess material is squeezed out between the making surfaces of the mould in the form of a thin film known as flash which can be easily removed. For many thermosetting systems, a short breathing spell is normally allowed seconds after the mould closing by reopening for a brief period to enable entrapped air, liberated steam or other volatiles to escape and subsequently closing it again. Use of preforms against moulding powders gives advantages in handling, ensuring low bulk factor or compression ratio. Breathing is helpful in minimizing or eliminating voids in the form of porosity, blisters and bubbles, and thereby improving the quality of the moulded part. The sketch of a compression moulding unit is shown in Fig 37.1

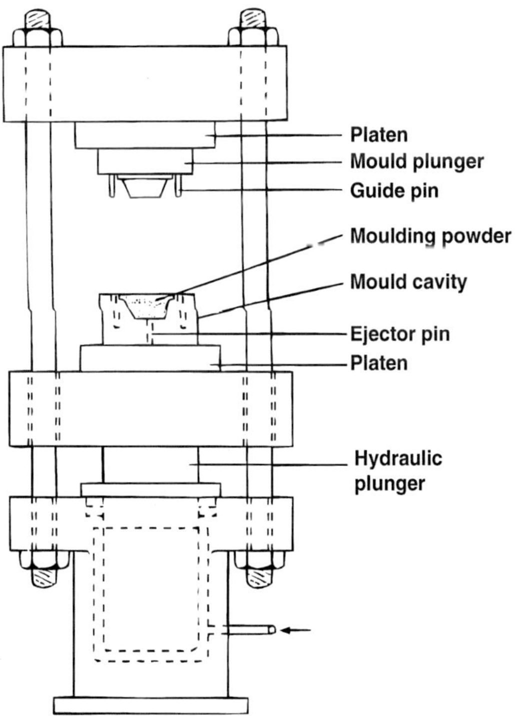

Fig. 37.1 Sketch showing a compression moulding press and the mould parts

(b) ***Transfer Moulding*** Poor heat transmission limits the compression moulding to a low rate process, and as a consequence it also suffers from limitations with respect to the parts that can be moulded. Transfer moulding was developed in an effort to overcome these limitations partly or substantially. In the transfer process, the charge is melted in a separate chamber or in a barrel called the "plasticizing pot" or the "transfer pot" which sometimes constitutes a part of the heated mould. The melt is forced into the mould cavity through narrow, heated runner / gate flow channels by ram pressure or a reciprocating screw plunger action (Fig. 37.2). The mould is kept at a temperature high enough to cause rapid heat curing of the resin system.

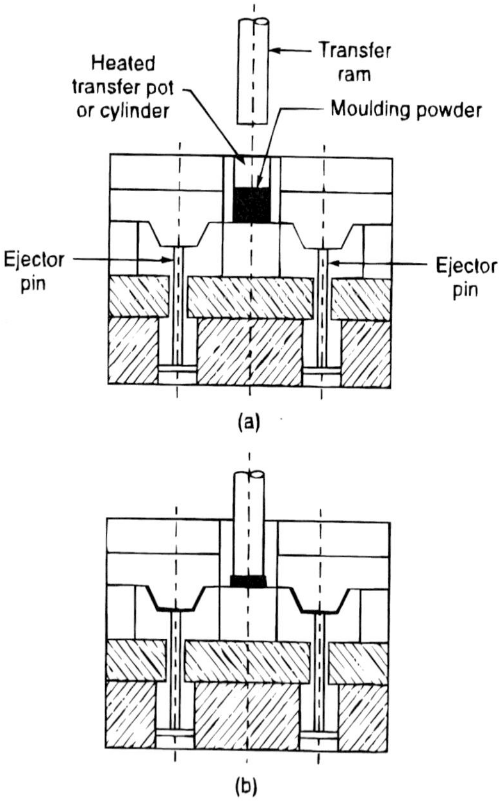

Fig. 37.2 Sketch of a transfer moulding unit : (a) before moulding begins, (b) after moulding is just completed

Transfer moulding cycles are usually shorter than those of compression moulding as moulding is done at higher temperatures and pressures in the transfer process. The premelted polymer charge flows more readily into the mould permitting moulding of large and intricate parts with sophisticated inserts which are not as readily attainable by compression moulding. Even thick pieces cure almost uniformly keeping the shrinkage at a minimum. The transfer moulding also produces moulded pieces of higher density and mechanical strength.

(c) *Injection Moulding and Jet Moulding* The technique of injection moulding of polymers was developed to achieve high-speed moulding of thermoplastics. In this process, a molten thermoplastic is injected or shot into a steel mould cavity under high pressure with the help of plunger system.

An injection moulding equipment (Fig. 37.3), consists of two units, the injection unit and the clamping unit. The polymer is melted into the injection unit from where it is injected into the mould by the plunger action.

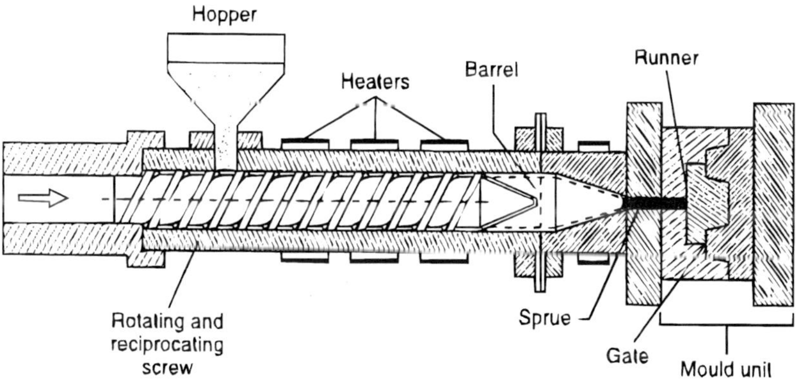

Fig. 37.3 Sketch of an injection moulding unit

The clamping unit is where the mould is attached. The mould can be closed or opened automatically or otherwise and ejector pins are used to eject the moulded object out of the mould. The injection unit consists of a barrel of appropriate length to allow melting of the polymer ot the plastic compound as it runs down its length through successive zones of higher temperatures under the pressure applied through a ram, plunger or a screw. Present injection units are almost exclusively of the inline reciprocating screw type. As the screw rotates, it pumps the molten polymer forward, the screw itself moving backwards allowing accumulation of enough material to fill the mould. The screw stops rotating as the mould is closed and then as it moves forward axially, it plays the role of an injection plunger. The two kinds of motion of the screw are controlled by a hydraulic system. The filling of the mould is accomplished by the flow of the polymer melt under high injection pressure along the nozzle, runners and gates into the cavities.

The rapidity of moulding and other advantages of injection moulding process prompted efforts toward developing similar techniques for the processing of thermosetting compounds. The process must be so designed and controlled as to prevent premature hardening of the thermosetting mass in the injection unit or the plasticating chamber as it is preheated there, but at the same time to heat it sufficiently to enable it flow rapidly and fill the mould under positive pressure. The jet moulding process solves this problem nicely by heating the moulding powder in the plasticating cylinder just enough to permit only flow under high pressure but allowing no measurable chemical reactions to take place in the plasticating cylinder. The plasticated mass at a relatively low temperature is then forced or injected at a high speed through the jet or nozzle into the mould which is kept at a much higher temperature leading to fast curing inside the mould.

Reaction injection moulding (RIM) technique is of a more recent development. It involves injection of low viscosity monomers or low polymers into the mould. The process is specially suitable for the production of polyurethane moulding by rapid injection of metered liquid streams of a diol and a diisocyanate into an impingement chamber where the two reactants get mixed intimately and wherefrom they are led into a mould at a relatively low pressure. Fast polymerization occurs inside the mould cavity under the influence of catalyst, heat and pressure employed. The speciality about RIM is that it allows production of solid moulded object from liquid monomers and low-viscous, low-polymer (reactive) intermediates.

(d) *Blow Moulding* Blow moulding is an important polymer processing technique for manufacturing hollow articles such as bottles and the like, and the technique is borrowed from the glass industry. The process involves in the first step the forming of a molten "parison" usually by extrusion. The parison is engaged between the mould halves and compressed air is used to blow the molten plastic into the configuration of the mould. The plastic mass quickly solidifies coming in contact with the cold mould. The process is schematically shown in Fig. 37.4. There are different types of blow moulding, processes such as extrusion, injection and stretch blow moulding, differing in the technique of forming the parison and also in the process of imparting orientation on the product. Stretch blow moulding is usually done in two steps. First, a test tube shaped preform is moulded which is then reheated, stretched and blown into a bottle. Stretching produces orientation and improves strength of the blow moulded object.

Forming Techniques

(a) *Extrusion* In this process, a polymer is melted and the melt is pushed ahead by a rotating screw continuously along the extruder barrel and across a metal die that shapes the melt into the desired form. End-use items of any desired length are manufactured by the extrusion process. The product range covers coated wires, cables and sheaths, rods, pipes and tubings, hoses blown films and a variety of other profiles including sheets and cast films. A sketch of an extruder with its components and sections is shown in Fig. 37.5.

The screw is divided into several zones each with a specific purpose. As the screw rotates, the feed zone picks up the polymer or the compounded granules from the. hopper and pushes them forward into the plasticating

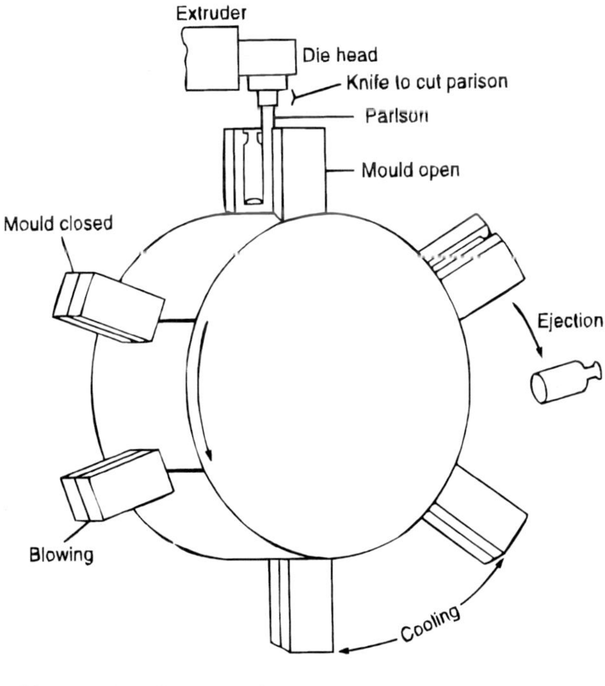

***Fig. 37.4** Diagram showing a continous extrusion below moulding operation- a vertical rotating wheel carrying the mould stets on the periphery*

zone where the granules melt under the influence of shearing action and external heat. The molten mass then passes through a compression zone to the metering zone. The metering zone helps in maintaining a uniform flow rate at the die point and build up enough pressure to force the molten mass out of the die through the screen pack and breaker plate assembly. The barrel is usually heated to different temperatures at different zones with the help of electrical heaters fixed around it or it may be cooled by passing cooling water through the cores, if necessary. The design variables of the extruder are the length to diameter (L / D) ratio, the screw geometry including its pitch, flight and their variations along its length, and the die.

In addition to single screw extruders, there are also twin screw (or multiple screw) extruders in which two or more neighbouring screws are made to work side by side rotating in opposite directions. There are also vented

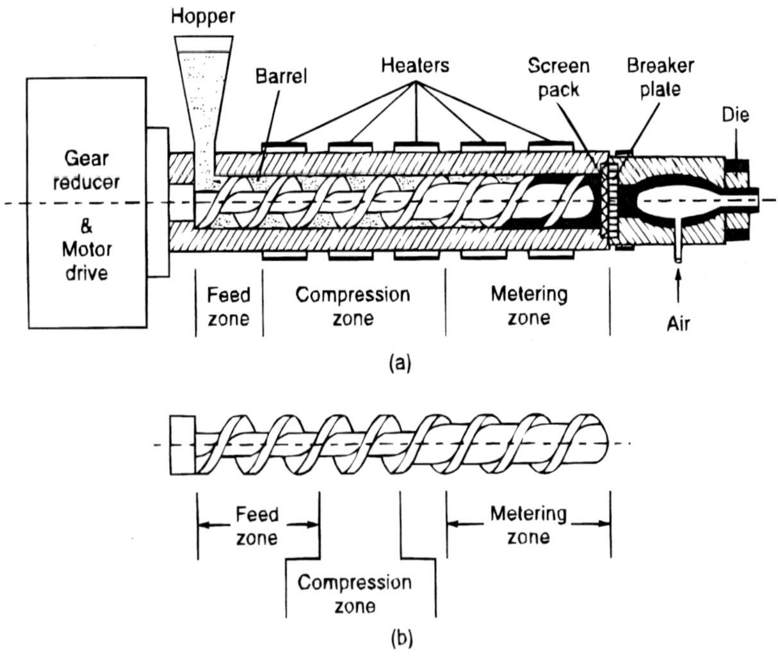

Fig. 37.6 Sketch showing : (a) an extruder with major components fitted with a screw for polyethylene extrusion (L/D = 20 : 1 to 30 : 1 ; compression ratio = 3 : 1 to 4 : 1), and (b) type of a screw for nylon extrusion (L/D = 16 : 1 ; compression ration = 4 : 1)

extruders having an opening or vent at some point along the screw or the barrel. The vent is attached to a vacuum line and is used to let off volatiles from the polymer melt. The finished product of the extrusion process is determined by the die which shapes the product and by the sizing equipment, i.e. the blowing, cooling, drawing and cutting system. Two or more extruders may be used to produce co-extruded films or other objects.

Various coated and laminated objects are formed making use of the extrusion process. A typical blown film extrusion set-up and a cross head assembly for wire coating are shown in Fig. 37.6.

(b) *Spinning* The process of converting a suitable synthetic polymer to the fibre form is done by spinning usually from its melt or from its solution in a selected solvent. Of the different spinning techniques, melt spinning is the simplest, requiring no handling of solvents or non-solvents and hence requiring no post-spinning solvent evaporation, precipitation or coagulation and drying. Solution spinning is practised when melt spinning cannot be carried out. Solution spinning may be of two kinds, (a) dry spinning, where the polymer solution is spun in a heated vertical chamber and the solvent is removed by evaporation, and (b) wet spinning, where the solvent is leached out by another liquid medium acting as a non-solvent for the fibre forming polymer or its derivative which is coagulated as soon as the spun solution impinges into the coagulating bath (non-solvent liquid medium); the chemical reaction to convert a derivative to the final polymer may take place in the coagulating bath or even later. Wet spinning is essentially done for viscose rayon and poly acrylonitrile spun from salt solution. Dry spinning is practised by spinning cellulose acetate (acetate rayon) from acetone solution and for such vinyl fibres as poly(vinyl chloride) and its copolymers and poly acrylonitrile (acrylic fibres) spun from solution in selected organic solvents. Melt spinning is common for polyamide, polyester and polyolefin (polypropylene) fibres.

As the spun polymer filaments or fibres solidify (by simply cooling, if melt spun, by solvent evaporation and cooling if dry spun and by coagulation and leaching action if wet spun), they are brought together to form a thread and subjected to drawing immediately after spinning in a continuous operation (usually for solution spinning) or in a subsequent step (usually for melt spinning).

(c) *Calendering* Calendering is a process most convenient for fast and continuous formation of sheet or film. The calender usually consists of four highly polished rolls commonly arranged in '2', '1' or inverted 'L' shape (Fig 37.7.) The soft, plasticized or dough-like plastic mass is worked and metered

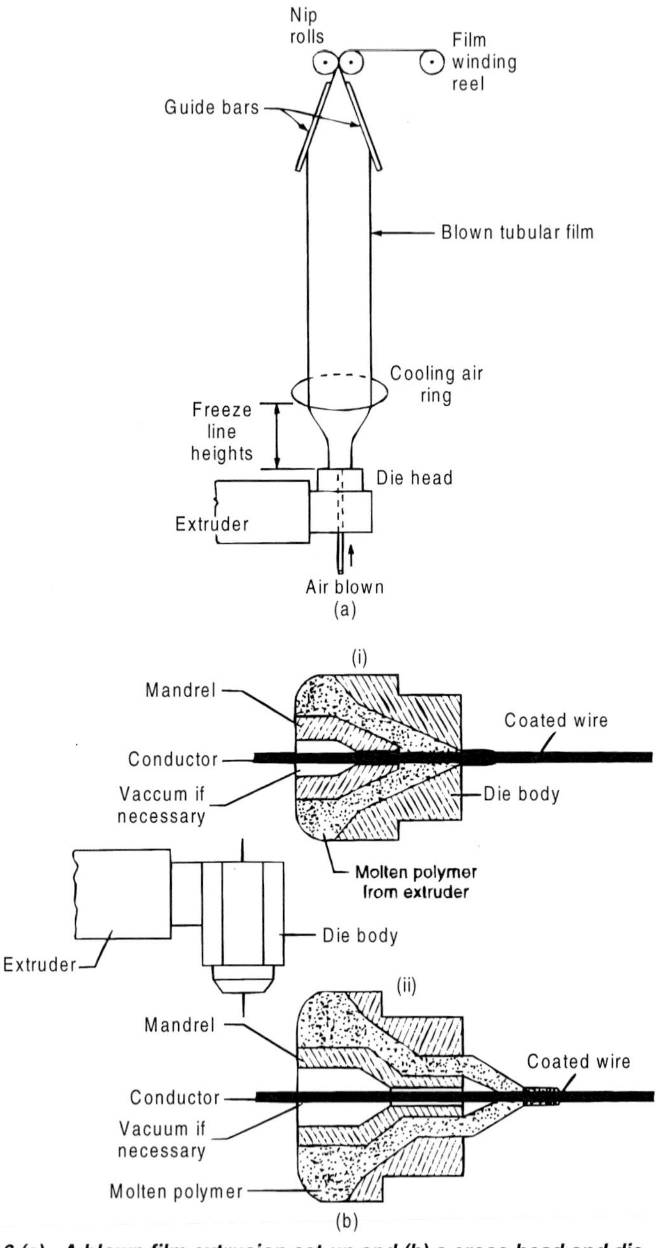

Fig. 37.6 (a) A blown film extrusion set-up and (b) a cross-head and die showing the operational principle of wire coating

through the nips between the heated rolls to give a product of uniform thickness. The first nip controls the feed rate while the second and the third control the thickness of the product. An embossing effect or surface design may be produced using an appropriately engraved calender roll. One may also have a three-roll assembly.

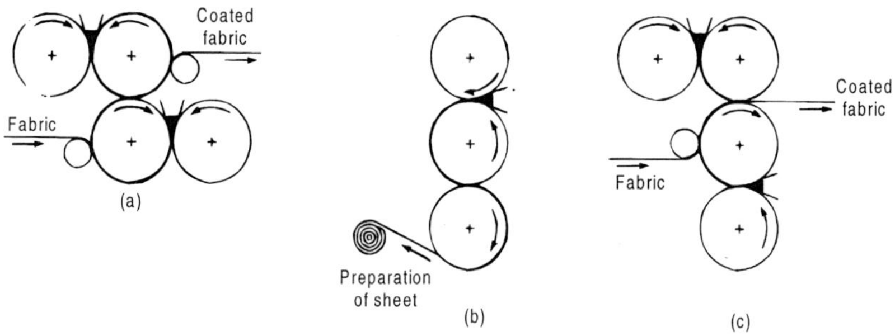

Fig. 37.7 Typical roll assemblies for calendering

(d) ***Thermoforming*** Thermoforming is a process for converting a piece of a thermoplastic sheet into a fairly deep drawn container, e.g. tray for packaging meat, hot or cold drink cups, ice cream cups, refrigerator door liners, etc., employing vacuum or air pressure from a compressor. When vacuum is used, the process is called vacuum forming. The sheet is clamped in a frame and brought close to a radiant electric heater. As it softens to a deformable state, it is placed down over a mould and the soft sagging sheet is sucked against the mould by applying vacuum and then cooled.

For deep moulds with big surface area, stretching the heat-softened web to fill the mould employing only vacuum or air pressure is often difficult or inadequately accomplished. However, the stretching of the heat-softened sheet in part may be effected using a simple mechanical aid or assist, such as a plug assist, prior to application of vacuum or air pressure to allow forming to the desired shape by contact with the mould. One such method is shown schematically in Fig. 37.8. The main advantage of the thermoforming processes is low cost for the equipment, moulds and the processing itself.

(e) ***Casting, Slush Moulding and Rotomoulding*** High viscosity melts or fluids cannot be conveniently cast in a mould, but they are moulded into a shape by employing injection, compression or transfer moulding techniques. But we can otherwise readily process a monomer system, a prepolymer (monomer-polymer syrup) or a polymer dispersed in excess plasticizer. All these are low viscosity systems, convenient for casting operations. Thus,

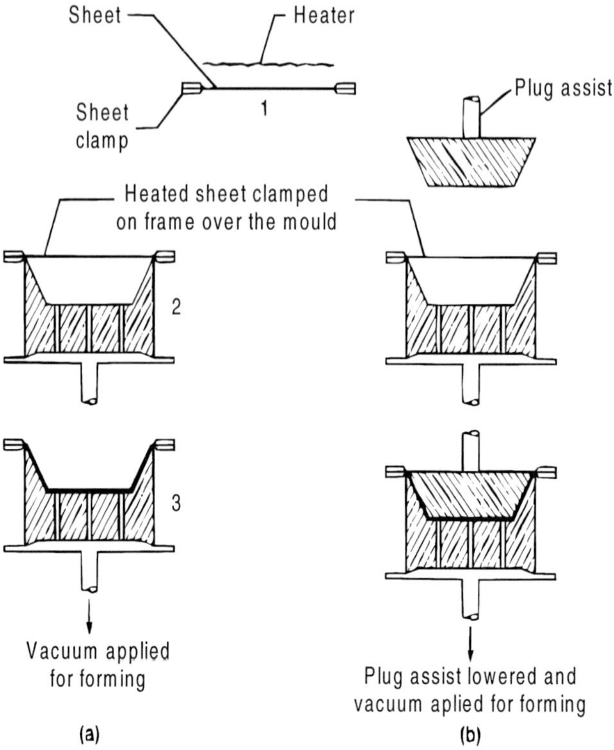

Fig. 37.8 Sketch showing thermoforming operations : (a) simple vacuum forming ; (b) vacuum forming with a plug assist

polyester and epoxy resins are sometimes cast into moulds and heated to cross-linked products. Acrylic prepolymers are frequently processed into finished products (acrylic sheets) by casting. A common method of processing largely plasticized PVC is casting of plastisols which are low viscosity dispersions of PVC in a liquid plasticizer. On heating, the PVC sol swells and gels into a rubbery product.

A significant variation of straight casting of plastisols is "slush moulding". The material is poured inside the hollow heated mould which is rotated to ensure formation of a thick and uniform casting along the inner walls and the excess material is poured out. The product is gelled on heating before taking out of the mould.

Rotational moulding is a unique technique of making large, hollow objects, even of complex shapes, usually from polyethylene and related polymers in the form of fine powder. A measured quantity of powder is placed inside an aluminium/ sheet metal mould which is then heated and rotated at a low speed. The polymer melts and coats the inside of the mould. When the melting is thoroughly achieved and the melt uniformly spread by rotation, the mould is cooled and the polymer coat solidifies duplicating the inside of the mould. Common rota-moulded objects are drums, large storage tanks, big containers, toys and dolls, etc: Crystalline sharpmelting polymers such as nylon or 'Terylene' or PET polyester are suited for the production of film by melt-casting techniques as outlined in Figs 37.9 and 37.10.

Other Techniques

(a) *Lamination and Reinforcement* Laminates, as the term suggests, consist of layers or laminae, held together by a suitable binder. The base of the layers is made of such materials as paper, woven fabric from cellulose, glass fibre, etc. which act as the reinforcing agent. The binders are usually synthetic resins used in solution or emulsion form for impregnation into the base laminae. The resins most commonly used are phenolic and amino resins, epoxy resins, polyesters, silicones, etc. The essential steps in the lamination process as outlined in Fig. 37.11 are: (a) impregnation of the base with the resin solution or emulsion, (b) drying of the impregnated web and (c) finally, cutting into size, plying them up as required and then pressing under heat to a permanently bonded (infusible) unitary mass of the desired finish. Major applications of the thermosetting laminates include components of electrical and electronic equipment, parts and components used in mechanical engineering and for storage and handling of chemicals. Decorative laminates are used in building and furniture industries. Fibre reinforced plastics are made by hand lay-up, die moulding and filament winding techniques.

(b) *Coating* The application of polymers or plastics as coatings is quite important. The coating item or formulation based on a resin or polymer may be used in the form of a solution, emulsion, powder, melt or film. Coating by impregnation in a solution or emulsion for lamination has already been discussed. Solution or emulsion formulations are often formed into a protective coating by brushing or spraying, and then drying into a hard finish.

Dip coating is often accomplished by dipping hot or cold metal parts into an emulsion, a plastisol or a polymer powder bed (fluidized or otherwise). Powder coating is practised using polyolefins, PVC, polyesters, nylons, epoxies and acrylics. A good and efficient technique is the electrostatic coating and spraying where the polymer particles are given an electric charge of one kind and the surface to be coated is given the opposite charge. Dielectric coating is also gaining prominence because of efficiency and uniformity.

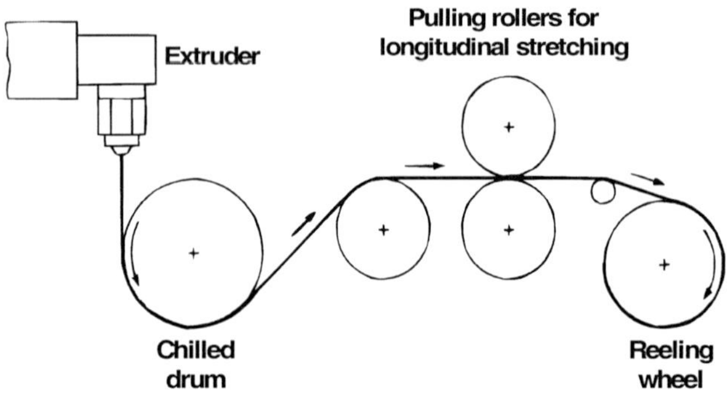

Fig. 37.9 Melt-casting of a nylon (polyamide) film

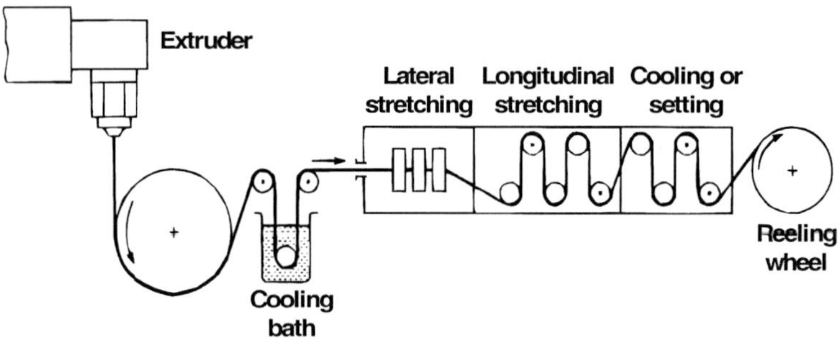

Fig. 37.10 Melt-casting and biaxial orientation of polyester (PET) film

Extrusion-coating is another coating technique of widespread use. Coated sheets and laminates produced by this technique find extensive use in various fields including packaging of food, pharmaceuticals and chemicals. Coating using polymer melts or solutions is also extensively done by what is commonly known as the spreading or roller-coating technique. "Skim coating" or "topping" and "frictioning" techniques are employed for coating of fabrics. In the topping method, the compound is fed around a calender roll from a nip and the sheet formed is applied to the fabric at a second nip. The sheeting usually but not necessarily travels at the same speed as the fabric at the point where it is laid onto the fabric. When the operation demands coating on both sides of the fabric, a four-roll calender is used.

Sheeting is produced in the two terminal nips (first and the third nips) and they are brought together and laid on both sides of the fabric simultaneously in the middle nip (second nip) (Fig. 37.7). The second and the third rolls which lay the sheets on the fabric must have even speed while the

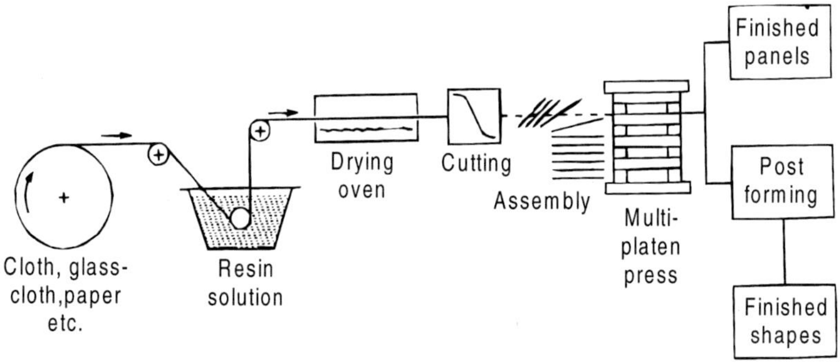

Fig. 37.11 Sketch showing layout of a high pressure lamination unit

first and the fourth may have even or odd speed. In case there is an appreciable difference in the speed of the fabric and the compound (sheeting) at the nip of the calender, the compound is forced into the fabric weave. If the compound is tacky so that a part sticks to the bowl and returns to the first nip, the process is commonly called "frictioning". On the other hand, if all the compound is laid on the fabric, it is known as "friction coating" or "layering". (c) *Finishing* Finishing operations consist of numerous processes after moulding or forming, and they may include cutting, trimming, polishing, mechanical fastening, bonding, sealing, welding, dyeing, painting, electroplating, vacuum metallizing, printing, engraving, etc. Each of these processes involves use of a specific type of equipment and operational approach or technique.

(d) ***Microencapsulation*** Microencapsulation is the process of coating any solid or liquid material to form tiny particles of size ranging from several tenths of a micron to several thousands of micron. Depending on the nature of the core and coating materials, the thickness of the coating and the size of the microcapsules formed, microencapsulation allows: a) formation of solid entities from oil, b) protection of drugs from moisture, light and oxidation, c) delayed or retarded escape of core substrates by rapid volatilization, d) masking of disagreeable taste and odour of the core substrate, thus making drug administration easy and comfortable, and e) control and sustained release of fertilizer, pesticides and herbicides and also similar release of drugs and pharmaceuticals, making continuous chemical and drug delivery at controlled, desired rates into the environment or within body of patients possible and to achieve prolonged therapeutic effect after administration of a single, measured dose, thus making the endeavor in each case not only much more costeffective and less dose sensitive but also in many cases free from possible adverse side effects.

The coating (polymeric) materials may be water soluble, such as gelatin, gum arabic, poly(vinyl pyrrolidone), carboxymethyl cellulose (CMC), methyl cellulose, poly(vinyl alcohol), poly(acrylic acid), or water insoluble, e.g. ethyl cellulose, polyamides (nylons), EVA copolymers and silicones; natural resins such as shellac or such items as paraffin, beewax, stearic acid, stearyl alcohol or glyceryl stearates may also be used for coating of powders of clay, $CaC0_3$ etc. used as activated fillers in polymer compounding. Biodegradable polymers such as microbial poly (3-hydroxy alkanoates), poly (lactic acid), gelatin, starch etc. are useful in microencapsulation of food and medicines.

The primary objective for uses of polymers in medicines administered in tablet form are to formulate them appropriately such that the polymers serve as the binder for shape retention and strength and regulate drug dissolution rates. Microencapsulation is widely employed for dispensation of analgesics, steroids, vitamins and for administration of antidotal drugs as a "one way trap" for toxins such as for patients suffering from kidney failure and hepatic coma. Health and beauty aids are other areas where microencapsulation has helped relevant industries; such applications include many modern cosmetic items such as skin creams or lotion (base for oil-inwater emulsion) with much improved softness and smoothness,' wet-look lip-stick with oil-containing micro-capsules, encapsulated perfumes and microcapsules of flavouring oils for use in chewable gums or tablets or of dyes for making coating on paper to produce carbonless copying paper.

In a preparative method, solid, particulate core materials are dispersed in a supporting heated (if required) air stream and are coated by spraying emulsion or solution of the polymer encapsulant. Another method of microencapsulation utilizes coacervation-phase separation technique; the core material is dispersed in a solution of the coating polymer in a solvent of its own and then phase separation coacervation is effected by lowering of temperature, addition of salt or a non-solvent. Sometimes crosslinking of the polymer is effected to impart extra rigidity to the micro-capsules.

Polymer Molecular Society: A Grand Model for Human Society

Social Relevance and Perspective

Polymers constitute a diverse range of light and energy efficient materials discovered and developed in a large measure out of the sheer necessity of meeting the growing needs and demands of our high profile society. The present level of growth, sophistication and advancements of our expanding society have been made possible in a large measure through sustained,

Table 37.1 Properties of plastics

Property	ASTM	Acrylics	Cellulosic Polymers		
			Cellulose acetate	Cellulose acetate butyrate	Cellulose propionate
Burning rate (inflamability)	D635	Slow	Slow	Slow	Slow
Carity/transparency		Transparent (92% transmission)	Transparent	Transparent	Transparent
Compressive strength (psi)	D695	1200 - 20000	2200 - 36000	2100 - 22000	3100 - 22000
Dissipation (power) factor (10^3 cycles/s)	D150	0.02 - 0.04	0.01 - 0.10	0.01 - 0.04	0.01 - 0.04
Dielectric constant (10^3 cycles / s)	D149	2.2 - 3.2	3.2 - 7.0	3.2 - 6.2	3.4 - 3.6
Dielectric strength (short time. 1/8" thic. volts / mil	D149	450 - 550	260 - 365	250 - 400	300 - 450
Effect of sunlight	—	Very slight	Slight	Slight	Slight
Elongation in tensile (%)	D638	3 - 10	6 - 70	40 - 90	30 - 100
Flexural strength (psi)	D790	13000 - 17000	2000 - 16000	1800 - 9300	3900 - 11000
Hardness (Rockwell)	D785	M85 - M105	R35 - R125	R31 - R116	R20 - R120
Heat distortion temperature °F)	D648	160 - 195	110 - 209 (66 psi)	115 - 227 (66 psi)	110 - 250 (66 psi)
Impact strength (ft 1b in notch. 1zod)	D256	0.3 - 0.5	0.4 - 5.2	0.8 - 6.3	0.5 - 10.0
Low temperature resistance	—	Good	Good	Good	Good
Machining qualities	—	Good to excellent	Excellent	Excellent	Excellent
Modulus of elasticity (psi x 10^{-5})	D638	4.5	0.65 - 4.0	0.5 - 2.0	0.6 - 2.15
Mould shrinkage (in / in)					
(a) Injection	—	0.002 - 0.008	0.003 - 0.007	0.002 - 0.005	0.001 - 0.005
(b) Compression	—	0.001 - 0.004	0.003 - 0.007	0.003 - 0.009	0.003 - 0.005
Moulding qualities	—	Excellent	Excellent	Excellent	Excellent
Odour	—	None	Slight	Slight odour of rancid butter	Slight
Refractive index (nD)	D542	1.49	1.46 - 1.50	1.46 - 1.49	1.46 - 1.49
Resistance, chemical					

Table 37.1 (Cont.)

Property	ASTM	Acrylics	Cellulosic Polymers		
			Cellulose acetate	Cellulose acetate butyrate	Cellulose propionate
(a) Strong acids	D543	Attacked by oxidizing acids and H_2SO_4	Decomposes	Decomposes	Decomposes
(b) weak acids	D543	Hardly affected	Slight	Slight	Slight
(c) strong alkalis	D543	Attacked	Decomposes	Decomposes	Decomposes
(d) weak alkalis	D543	Hardly affected	Slight	Slight	Slight
Resistance, solvent	D543	Soluble in ketones, esters and chlorinated hydrocarbons Resistant to alcohols at room temperatures	Soluble in ketones and esters, softened or slightly soluble in alcohols, little affected by hydrocarbons		
Softening point [(Vicat)°C]	—	80 - 98	70	70	—
Specific gravity	D792	1.17 - 1.20	1.23 - 1.24	1.15 - 1.22	1.18 - 1.24
Specific heat (cal. °C / g)	—	0.35	03 - 0.42	03 - 0.40	03 - 0.40
Specific volume (cu. in / lb)	D792	23.7 - 23.1	22.5 - 20.6	24.5 - 22.7	23.4 - 22.5
Tensile strenght (psi)	D638 D651	7000 - 11000	1900 - 8500	2600 - 6900	2000 - 7300
Thermal conductivity (cal /s /sq.cm °C / cm x 10^4)	C177	4 - 6	4 - 8	4 - 8	4 - 8
Thermal expansion (cm/ cm/ °C x 10^4)	D696	5 - 9	8 - 16	11 - 17	11 - 17
Volume resistivity (ohm cm at 23°C and 50% R.H.)	D257	$>10^{14}$	10^{10} - 10^{13}	10^{10} - 10^{12}	10^{12} - 10^{15}
Water absorption (% 24 h, 1/8" thicness)	D570	0.3 - 0.4	1.9 - 6.5	0.9 - 2.2	1.2 - 2.8

Contd.

Table 37.1 (Contd.)

Property	ASTM	Fluorinated Plolymer			Melamine Fomaldehyede	
		Fluorinated Ethylene propylene	Polytetrafluoro ethylene	Polytetrafluoro chlorethylene	Unfilled	a -cellulose filled
Burning rate (inflammability)	D635		None	None	Self extinguishing	None
Clarity / transparency	—	Translucent	Opaque	Translucent of opaque	Opalescent	Translucent
Compressive strength (psi)	D695	1400 - 2850	700 - 1800	2000	40000 - 45000	25000 - 43000
Dissipation (power) factor (10^3 cycles / s)	D150	0.003	0.005	0.01	—	0.127 - 0.045
Dielectric constant (103 cycles / s)	D149	2.1	2.0	2.5	—	7.2 - 8.2
Dielectric strength (short-tim, 1/8" thick, volts / mill)	D149	500 - 600	400 - 500	530 - 600	—	300 - 400
Effect of sunlight	—	None	None	None	Slight colour change	Slight colour Change
Elongation in tensile (%)	D638	300 - 900	250 - 350	125 - 175	—	0.6 - 0.9
Flexural stregth (psi)	D790	95000	1600	3500	11000 - 14000	10000 - 16000
Haredness (Rockwell)	D785	D55	J75 - 95	R110 - 115	—	M110 - 115
Heat distortion temprature (°F)	D648	—	—	110 - 209 (66 psi)	298	400
Impact strength (ft, lb/in, notch, Izod)	D256	No break	2.5 - 4.0	2.5 - 3.6	—	0.24 -0.36
Low temprature resistance	—	Good	Good	Good	—	Good
Machining qualities	—	Good	Good	Good	—	Fair
Maodulus of elasticity (psi x 10^{-5})	D638	0.5 - 0.7	0.38 - 0.65	1.9 - 3.0	—	13
Mould shrinkage (in/in)			—			
(a) Injection	—	0.001 - 0.005	0.03 - 0.06	—	—	—
(b) Compression	—	0.003 - 0.005	0.03 - 0.06	—	0.005 - 0.01	0.011 - 0.012
Moulding qualities	—	Good	Fair	Fair	Good	Excellent
Odour	—	None	None	None	None	None
Refractive index (nD	D542	1.34	1.35	1.43	—	—

Contd.

Table 37.1 (Contd.)

Property	ASTM	Fluorinated Plolymer			Melamine Fomaldehyede	
		Fluorinated Ethylene propylene	Polytetrafluoro ethylene	Polytetrafluoro chlorethylene	Unfilled	a -cellulose filled
Resistance, chemical						
(a) Strong acids	D543	Unaffected	Unaffected	Unaffected	Decomposes	Decomposes
(b) Weak acids	D543	Unaffected	Unaffected	Unaffected	Unaffected	Unaffected
(c) Strong alkalis	D543	Unaffected	Unaffected	Unaffected	Attacked	Attacked
(d) Weak alkalis	D543	Unaffected	Unaffected	Unaffected	Unaffected	Unaffected
Resistance, solvent	D543	Unaffected	Unaffected	Unaffected	Unaffected	Unaffected
	—					
Softening point [(Vicat) °C]	D789	MP 285 - 295	Decomp.pt	Decomp.pt	—	—
	53		>300	>400		
Specific gravity	D792	2.14 - 2.17	2.1 - 2.3	2.10 -2.15	1.48	1.47 - 1.52
specific heat (cal/°C/g)	—	0.28	0.25	0.22	—	—
Specific volume (cu. in/lb)	D792	12.85 -12.66	13.09 - 11.95	13.09 - 12.78	18.7	18.8 -18.2
Tensile stregth (psi)	D638	2500 - 3500	2500 - -3500	4600 - 5700	—	7000 - 13000.
	D651					
Thermal conductivity (cal s sq. cm / °C x 10^4)	C177	7	6	—	—	7 - 10
Thermal ecpension (cal/ cm/ °C x 10^4)	D696	1.3 - 1.9	1.0	0.7	—	4.0
Volume resistivity (ohm cm at 23° and 50% R.H)	D257	10^{19}	19^{19}	10^{18}	—	10^{12} - 10^{14}
Water absorption (% 24h, 1/8" thichness)	D570	0.00	0.00	0.00	0.3 - 0.5	0.1 - 0.6

Table 8.1 (Contd.)

Properties	ASTM	Nylons		Phenol Formaldehyde	
		Type 6	Type 66	Unfilled	Woodflour/cotton flock filled
Burning rate (inflammability)	D635	Self-extinguishing	Self-extinguishing	Very low	Very low
Clarity / transparency		Translucent to opaque	Translucent to opaque	Translucent to translucent	Opaque
Compressive strength (psi)	D695	7000 - 14000	7000 - 16000	10000 - 30000	22000 - 40000
Dissipation (power) factor (10^3 cycles / s)	D510	0.02 - 0.13	0.0.2 -0.06	0.015 - 0.03	4.5 - 5.0
Dielectric constant (103 Cycles -/ s)	D149	3.0 - 5.0	3.6 - 6.0	4.5 -5.0	4.0 - 7.0
Dielectric strength (short-time, 1/8" thick, volts/mil)	D149	440 - 510	385 - 470	300 - 400	200 - 425
Effect of sunlight		Discolours slightly	Discolour slightly	Slight surface darkening	General darkening
Elongation in tensile (%)	D638	90 - 320	90	1.0 - 1.5	0.4 - 0.8
Flexural strength (psi)	D790	8000 - 16000	8000 - 3800	12000 -1500	8000 -12000
Hardness (Rockwell)	D785	R103 - 118	R111 - 118	M124 - 128	M100 - 120
Heat distortion temperature (°F)	D648	260 - 340(66psi)	300 - 360(66psi)	240 - 260	260 - 340
Impact strength (ft lb / in notch, Izod	D256	1.0 - 3.6	1.0	0.24 - 0.36	0.24 - 0.60
Low temperature resistance		Good	Good		Good
Machining qualities		Excellent	Excellent	Fair	Excellent
Modulus of elasticity (psi x 10^{-5})	D638	1.5 - 3.6	2.6 - 4.0	7.5 - 10	8 - 12
Mould shrinkage (in/in)					
(a) Injection		0.009	0.015		
(b) Compression				0.01 - 0.02	0.004 - 0.009
Moulding qualities		Exellent	Excellent	Fair to good	Fair to good
Ordur		None	None	None	None
Refractive index (*n*D)	D542		1.53	1.5 - 1.7	
Resistance, chemical					
(a)Strong acids	D543	Attacked	Attacked	Decomposed by oxidizing acids	

Contd.

Table 37.1 (Contd.)

Properties	*ASTM*	*Nylons*		*Phenol Formaldehyde*	
		Type 6	*Type 66*	*Unfilled*	*Woodflour/cotton flock filled*
(b) Weak acids	D543	Resistant	Resistant	Unaffected to slight	Unaffected to slight
(c) Strong alkalis	D543	Unaffected	Unaffected	Decomposes	Attacked
(d) Weak alkalis	D543	Unaffected	Unaffected	Unaffected to slight	Slight to marked
Resistance, solvent	D543	Resistant to common solvents	Resistant to common solvents	No effect	No effect
Softening point [(Vicat) °C)]	D789-53	M.P. 215 - 220	M.P. 260 - 265		
Specific gravity	D792	1.13	1.09 - 1.14	1.25 - 1.3	1.32 - 1.45
Specific heat (cal /°C /g)		0.4	0.4	0.38 - 0.42	0.35 - 0.40
Specific volume (cu.in/lb)	D792	24.5 - 24.2	25.5 - 24.2	22.2 - 21.3	20.9 - 17.8
Tensile strength (psi)	D638				
	D651	10000 - 12000	7000 - 10900	7000 - 8000	6500 - 8500
Thermal conductivity (cal/ s /sq.cm/ °C/ cmx 10)	D177		5.2 - 5.8	3 - 6	4.7
Thermal expansion (cm / cm/ °C x 10^4)	D696	8 - 13	10 - 15	2.5 -6	3.0 - 4.5
Volume resistivity (ohm cm at 23° and 50% R.H.)	D257	10^{12} - 10^{15}	(0.45 - 4) x 10^1	10 x10^{12}	10^9 - 10^{12}
Water absorption (% 24 h, 1/8" thickness)	D570	1.9 - 3.3	0.4 - 1.5	0.1 -0.2	0.3 - 1.0

Contd.

Table 37.1 (Contd.)

Properties	ASTM	polyacetals	polycarbonates	Polyethylence		
				Low density	Medium density	High density
Burning rate (inflammability)	D635	Slow	Self-extinguishing	Very slow	Very slow	Very slow
Clarity / transparency	—	Translucent to opaque	Transparent	Traslucent to opaque	Traslucent to opaque	Traslucent to opaque
Compressive strength (psi)	D695	18000	11000	Excess cold flow	—	2400
Dissipation (power) factor (10^3 cycles / s)	D150	0.005	0.010	< 0.002	< 0.005	< 0.003
Dielectric constant (10^3 cycles / s)	D149	3.7	2.6	2.25 - 2.35	2.25 - 2.35	2.25 - 2.35
Dielectric stregth (short time, 1/2" thick volts / mil)	D149	465	400	>800	>800	>800
Effect of sunlight		Chalks slight1	Yellows slightly	Good in black or specially stablished grades		
Elongation in tensile (%)	D638	15 injection 75 exrusion	60 - 100	400 - 600	50 - 600	50 - 600
Flexural stregth (psi)	D730	14100	11000 - 13000	No fractur	4800 - 7000	2000 - 3000
Haredness (Rockwell)	D785	M94 -R118	M70 - R118	D41 - 46 (shore)	D50 - 70 (Shore)	D60 70 (Shore)
	D648	338 (66 psi)	280 - 290	105 - 221 (psi)	120 - 150 (66 psi)	140 - 180 (66 psi)
Impact strength (ft, lb/in, notch, Izod)	D256	2.3 extrucsion 1.4 injection	12 - 16	>16	—	1.5 - 12
Low temprature resistance	—	Good	Excellent	Good	Good	Good
Machining qualities	—	Excellent	Excellent	Fair	Good	Excellent
Maodulus of elasticity (psi x 10^{-5})	D638		3.2	0.17 - 0.35	0.25 - 0.55	0.8 - 1.5
Mould shrinkage (in/in) (a) Injection	—		0.005 - 0.007	0.02 -0.035	0.02 -0.035	0.02 -0.035
(b) Compression	—	—	—			
Moulding qualities	—		Fair	Excellent	Good	Good

Contd.

Table 37.1 (Contd.)

Property	ASTM	Polyacetals	Plolycarbonates	Polythylenes		
				Low density	Medium density	High density
Odoure	—	None	None	None	None	None
Refractive index (*n*D)	D542	1.48	1.584	1.51	—	1.54
Resistance, chemical						
(a) Strong acids	D543	Attacked	Attacked slowly by oxidizing acids	Attacked slowly by oxidizing acids	Attacked slowly by oxidizing acids	Attacked slowly by oxidizing acids
(b) Weak acids	D543	Resistant to some	Unaffected	Resistant	Resistant	Resistant
(c) Strong alkalis	D543	Attacked	Attacked slowly	Resistant	Resistant	Resistant
(d) Weak alkalis	D543	Resistant to some	Resistant	Resistant	Resistant	Resistant
Resistance, solvent	—	Excellent resistance to practically all solvents	Soluble in aromatics and chlorinated hydrocarbons Resistant to paraffinics	Soluble in aromatics solvents above 60°C	Soluble in aromatics solvents above 60°C	Resistantbelow 80°C
Softening point [(Vicat) °C]	D789-53	175	215 - 226	85 -87	91 - 114	127
Specific gravity	D792	1.425	1.2	0.913 - 0.925	0.926 - 0.940	0.914 - 0.965
specific heat (cal/°C/g)	—	0.35	0.30	0.53 - 0.55	0.53 - 0.55	0.53 - 0.55
Specific volume (cu. in/lb)	D792	19.3	23	30.2 - 29.9	29. 8 - 29.5	29.4 - 28.7
Tensile stregth (psi)	D638 D651	10000	8500 -9500	1000 - 2300	1200 - 3500	3100 - 5500
Thermal conductivity cal s/sq. (cm / °C / cm x 10^{4})	D177	5.5	4.6	8.0	—	11 - 12.4
Thermal ecpension (cal/ cm/ °C x 10^{4})	D696	8.1	7.0	16 - 18	—	11 - 13
Volume resistivity (ohm cm at 23° and 50% R.H)	D257	6 x 10^{14}	2.1 x 10^{16}	$>10^{16}$	$>10^{16}$	$>10^{16}$
Water absorption (% 24h, 1/8" thichness)	D270	0.12	0.3	<0.015	<0.01	<0.01

Contd.

Table 37.1 (Contd.)

Properties	ASTM	Polyproylene	Polyytrenes		Styrene Copolymers	
			Conventional	Toughened	Styrene/ acrylonitrile	Acrylonitrile/ butadiene/ styrene
Machining qualities	—	Excellent	Fair to Good	Good	Good	Good to excellent
Modulus to elasticity (psi x 10-5)	D638	1.3 - 2.0	4 - 6	3 - 4.5	4 - 5.6	1.0 - 4.1
Mould shrinkage (in / in)						
(a) Injection	—	0.015 - 0.025	0.002 - 0.006	0.002 - 0.008	0.002 - 0.005	0.003 - 0.008
(b) Compression	—	—	0.001 - 0.008	—	—	—
Moulding qualities	—	Excellent	Excellent	Excellent	Good	Good
Odour	—	None	None	None	Sligaht	None
Refractive index (nD)	D542	1.49	1.59 - 1.6	—	1.57	—
Resistance, chemical						
(a) Strong acids	D543	Attacked slowly by oxidizing acids	Attacked by oxidizing acids		Attacked byoxidizing acids	
(b) Weak acids	D543	Resistant	Unaffected	Unaffected	Unaffected	Unaffected
(c) Strong alakalis	D543	Resistant	Unaffected	Unaffected	Unaffected	Unaffected
(d) Weak alkalis	D543	Resistant	Unaffected	Unaffected	Unaffected	Unaffected
Resistance, solvent	D543	Resistantbelow 80°C	Solube in aromatics and chlorinated hydrocarbons, esters ketones and higher alcohols		Soluble ifn ketones, ester, and some chlorinated hydrocarbons	
Softening point [(Vicat) °C]	—	150	82 - 103	78 - 100	85 - 103	85
Specific gravity	D792	0.90 - 0.91	1.04 -1.11	0.98 -110	1.075 - 1.10	0.99 - 1.10
Specific heat (cal/ °C/ gm)	—	0.46	0.32 - 0.35	0.32 - 0.35	0.32 - 0.34	0.33 - 0.40
Specific volume (cu. in. /lb)	D792	31 - 29	26.4 -24.8	28.1 - 25.2	25.8 - 25.2	28 - 25.2
Tensile strength (psi)	D638 D651	4300 - 5700	5000 - 12000	3500 - 6500	9500 - 12000	2500 - 900

Contd.

Table 37.1 (Contd.)

Properties	ASTM	Polyproylene	Polyytrenes		Styrene Copolymers	
			Conventional	Toughened	Styrene/ acrylonitrile	Acrylonitrile/ butadiene/ styrene
Machining qualities	—	Excellent	Fair to Good	Good	Good	Good to excellent
Modulus to elasticity (psi x 10-5)	D638	1.3 - 2.0	4 - 6	3 - 4.5	4 - 5.6	1.0 - 4.1
Mould shrinkage (in / in)						
(a) Injection	—	0.015 - 0.025	0.002 - 0.006	0.002 - 0.008	0.002 - 0.005	0.003 - 0.008
(b) Compression	—	—	0.001 - 0.008	—	—	—
Moulding qualities	—	Excellent	Excellent	Excellent	Good	Good
Odour	—	None	None	None	Sligaht	None
Refractive index (nD)	D542	1.49	1.59 - 1.6	—	1.57	—
Resistance, chemical						
(a) Strong acids	D543	Attacked slowly by oxidizing acids	Attacked by oxidizing acids		Attacked byoxidizing acids	
(b) Weak acids	D543	Resistant	Unaffected	Unaffected	Unaffected	Unaffected
(c) Strong alakalis	D543	Resistant	Unaffected	Unaffected	Unaffected	Unaffected
(d) Weak alkalis	D543	Resistant	Unaffected	Unaffected	Unaffected	Unaffected
Resistance, solvent	D543	Resistantbelow 80°C	Solube in aromatics and chlori-nated hydrocarbons, esters ketones and higher alcohols		Soluble ifn ketones, ester, and some chlorinated hydrocarbons	
Softening point [(Vicat) °C]	—	150	82 - 103	78 - 100	85 - 103	85
Specific gravity	D792	0.90 - 0.91	1.04 -1.11	0.98 -110	1.075 - 1.10	0.99 - 1.10
Specific heat (cal/ °C/ gm)	—	0.46	0.32 - 0.35	0.32 - 0.35	0.32 - 0.34	0.33 - 0.40
Specific volume (cu. in. /lb)	D792	31 - 29	26.4 -24.8	28.1 - 25.2	25.8 - 25.2	28 - 25.2
Tensile strength (psi)	D638 D651	4300 - 5700	5000 - 12000	3500 - 6500	9500 - 12000	2500 - 900

Contd.

Table 8.1 (Contd.)

Properties	*ASTM*	*Polyproylene*	*Polyytrenes*		*Styrene Copolymers*	
			Conventional	*Toughened*	*Styrene/ acrylonitrile*	*Acrylonitrile/ butadiene/ styrene*
Thermal conductivity (cal /s /sq. cm /°C / cm x 10^4)	D177	3.3	2.4 - 3.3	1.0 - 3.0	2.4	1.48 - 8.6
Thermal expansion (cm / cm/ °C x 10^4)	D696	11	6 - 8	3.4 - 21	6 - 8	6 - 13
Volume resistivity (ohm cm at 23°C and 50% R.H.)	D257	$>10^{16}$	$>10^{13}$	$>10^{13}$	$>10^{13}$	0.5 x 1013- 2.7 x 1016
Water absorption (%24 h, 1/8" thickness)	D570	<0.01	0.03 - 0.4	0.1 - 0.3	0.2 - 0.3	0.1 - 0.3

Contd.

Table 37.1 (Contd.)

Property	ASTM	Urea-Formaldehyde a - cellulose filled	Vinyl Polymers: Reigid poly(vinyl chloride	Vinyl Polymers: (Rigid) Vinyl Chloridelvinyl acetate	Vinyl Polymers: Rubber modified PVC	Vinyl Polymers: Vinylidene chloride
Burning rate (inflammability)	D635	Very low	Self-extinguishing	Self-extinguishing	Self-extinguishing	Self-extin guishing
Clarity/transparency	—	Transparent to opaque	Transparent to opaque	Transparent to opaque	Transparent to opaque	Transparent to opaque
Compressive strength (psi)	D695	25000 - 35000	8000 ←	—	→ 13000	2000 - 2700
Dissipation (power) factor (10^3 cycles/s)	D150	0.028 - 0.032	0.006 ←	—	→ 0.14	0.05 - 0.08
Dielectric constant (10^3 cycles / s)	D149	6.4 - 6.9	3.0	3.0 - 3.5	—	3.0 - 4.0
Dielectric strength (short time. 1/8" thic. thick, volts/mil)	D149	300 - 400	425	1400	1100	400 - 600
Effect of sunlight	—	None	Good in stabilized grades		Rapid fall in physical strength	Slight
Elongation in tensile (%)	D638	0.5 - 1.0	2 - 40	200 - 450	—	Up to 250
Flexural strength (psi)	D790	10000 - 16000	13500	12000	12000	4200 - 6200
Hardness (Rockwell)	D785	M115 - 120	R110	—	R105	M60 -65
Heat distortion temperature °F)	D648	270 - 280	165 (66 psi)	145 - 170 (66 psi)	160 (66 psi)	130 - 150
Impact strength (ft 1b in notch. 1zod)	D256	0.25 -0.35	0.8	0.5 - 1.0	15 (unaged)	0.3 - 1.0
Low temperature resistance	—	Good	Good	Good	Good	Good

Contd.

Table 37.1 (Cont.)

Properties	ASTM	Urea-Formaldehyde a-cellulose filled	Vinly Polymers: Reigid poly (viryl chloride)	Vinly Polymers: (Rigid) Vinyl Chloride/vinyl acetate	Vinly Polymers: Rubber modified PVC	Vinly Polymers: Vinlyidene chloride
Mechanical qualities	—	Fair	Excellent	—	—	Good
Modulus of elasticity (psi x 10^{-5})	D638	15	3.5	←——→	6	0.5 - 0.8
Mould shrinkage (in/in)						
(a) Injection	—	—	0.001	←——→	0.05	0.005 - 0.025
(b) Compression		0.006 - 0.014	—	—	—	—
Moulding qualities	—	Excellent	Fair to good	Fair to good	Fair to good	Excellent
Odour	—	None	None	None	None	None
Refractive index (n_D)	D542	1.54 - 1.56	1.52	1.55	—	1.60 - 1.63
Resistance, chemical						
(a) Strong acids	D543	Decomposes	Unaffected	Unaffected	Unaffected	Good but attacked by strong H_2SO_4 or CH_3COOH
(b) Weak acids	D543	Unaffected to sight	Unaffected	Unaffected	Unaffected	Unaffected
(c) Strong alkalis	D543	Decomposes	Unaffected	Unaffected	Unaffected	Resistant
(d) Weak alkalis	D543	Slight to marked	Unaffected	Unaffected	Unaffected	Resistant
Resistance, solvent	D543	None	Resists alcohols, aliphatic hydrocarbons, and oils; soluble in ketones and esters; swells in aromatic hydrocarbons			None to slight
Softening point [(Vicat) °C]	—	—	82	—	78	71 and above
Specific gravity	D792	1.47 - 1.52	1.38 - 1.4	1.37 - 1.45	1.35	1.65 - 1.72
Specific heat (cal/°C/g)	—	0.4	0.2 - 0.5	0.2 - 0.5	0.2 - 0.5	0.32

Cont.

Table 37.1 (Cont.)

Properties	ASTM	Urea-Formaldehyde a-cellulose filled	Vinly Polymers			
			Reigid poly (vinyl chloride)	(Rigid) Vinyl Chloride/vinyl acetate	Rubber modified PVC	Vinlyidene chloride
Specific volume (cu.in/lb)	D792	18.8 -18.2	20.1	20.4-19.1	20.5	16.8 -16.1
Specific strength (psi)	D638 D651	6000 - 13000	8500	7500-8500	6000	3000 - 5000
Thermal conductivity (cal/s/sq/ cm/°C/cm x 10^4)	C177	7 - 10	3.5	3.7 4.5	3.0	
Thermal expansion (cm/cm/°C x 10^4)	D696	2.75	7	10 19		
Volume resistivity (ohm cm at 23°C and 50% R.H.)	D257	10^{12} - 10^{13}	10^{13}		10^{16}	10^{14} - 10^{16}
Water absorption (% 24h, 1/8" thickness)	D570	0.4 - 0.8	0.05	0.08 0.10	0.10	

Table 37.2 Metals and alloys—applicable properties

Properties	ASTM	Aluminium (99% pure)	Brass (Cu-Zn, 70/30)	Carbon steel (0.4% Carbon)
Compressive strength (psi)	D695	—	—	200000
Elongation in tensile (%)	D638	50	65-70	17
Hardness (Brinell)	—	22	100	180
Impact strength (ft in /in notch,Izod)	D256	20	66	13
Melting point (°F)	—	1200	17.15	2725
Modulus of elasticity (psi x 10^5)	D638	0.21	0.59	5.27
Specific gravity	D792	2.7	8.5	7.85
Specific heat (Btu/lb°F)	—	0.23	0.09	0.11
Specific volume (cu.in./lb)	D792	10.3	3.3	3.53
Tensile strength (psi)	D638	10100	46300	89600
	D651		0.12	
Thermal conductivity			0.12	
(cal/s/sq. cm/°C/cm) C177	0.52	0.29	0.12	
Thermal expansion (cm/cm/°C x 10^4)	D696	0.240	0.199	0.112
	ASTM	**Duralumin (Al-Si-Cu-Mg)**	**Mild steel (0.06% carbon)**	**Phsophor bronze (Cu-Sn-P)**
Compressive strength (psi)	D695	—	110000—130000	—
Elongation in tensile (%)	D638	5	28	15
Hardness (Brinell)	—	82	140	110
Impact strength (ft lb/in. notch,Izod) D256	1	20	—	
Melting point (°F)	—	1100	2760	1710
Modulus of elasticity (psi x 10^5)	D638	7.16	0.61	3.88
Specific gravity	D792	2.8	7.87	8.9
Specific heat (Btu/lb/°F)	—	0.23	0.11	0.09
Specific volume (cu.in./lb)	D792	9.9	3.52	3.12
Tensile strength (psi)	D638 D651	35800	44800	58200
Thermal conductivity (cal/s/sq.cm/°C/cm) C177	0.35	0.15	0.2	
Thermal expansion (cm/cm/°C x 10^4)	D696	0.225	0.126	0.178

imaginative and creative efforts of scientists, engineers and technologists in the polymer field. The base material constituting all plastics, structural resins, rubbers, adhesives, coatings and related products is usually a polymer or a group of polymers. As a class of materials, polymers are so much distinctive that polymer education covering origin, synthesis,

Table 37.3 *Major applications of some polymers*

Acrylic	Automotive parts, control knobs, dials and handles, pens and pencils, brush-backs, hospital equipment, display material, signs, lighting fittings, inspection panel covers, skylights
Cellulosic Plastics	
Cellulose acetate	Toys, beads, cutlery handles, electrical parts, knobs, steering wheels, shoe heels, packaging, sheeting, toothbrushes, cosmetics
Cellulose acetate butyrate	Moulded or extruded parts for metallization (reflectors, etc.), outdoor signs, automobile tail light covers, tool handles, tooth-brushes, pipe inspection traps, piping
Cellulose propionate	Automotive parts, pens and pencils, telephone housings, shoe heels, toys, radio / TV parts, tooth-brushes, sunglass frames
Fluorinated polymers	
Fluornated ethylene propylene (copolymers)	Coil formers, wire insulation, electronic components, encapsulations and fluidized bed coatings, non-stick valves
Polytrifluorochlorethyelen	Gaskets, packings, valves, anti-adhesive coatings, rigid and flexible pipes, membranes, wire insulation, electronic engineering applications Extruded sheet, profile and film, electronic parts, gaskets, pump sealants, dispersion coatings, liquid level indicators of particular use where resistance to aggressive chemicals is needed
Melamine formaldehyde	
Unfilled	Noted for durability, hardness and good electrical properties, suitable for appliance housings,

	dinnerware, closures, writing equipment, clock housings, knobs, handles, lighting fixtures, appliances, instruction panels
a-cellulose filled	As for unfilled material
Nylons	
Type 6	Moulded mechanical parts, gear wheels, bushings, elevator gibs, sliding parts for storm windows, automobile and refrigeration door closures, mixer valves, switch housings, grommets, cable clamps, tubing, filaments, aerosol bottles
Type 66	As for Type 6
Phenol formaldehydes	
Unfilled	Bottle caps, electrical parts, impact resistant, heat resistant and special purpose mouldings requiring rigid durable properties. Restricted colours, close tolerance in moulding articles
Woodflour filled	As for unfilled material
Polyacetals	Instrument panel mouldings, aerosol packs, moulded zip-fasteners, wheels for lawn mowers and push carts, impeller blades, cosmetic cases, gear wheels, conveyors
Polycarbonates	Business machine parts, electrical apparatus, sterilizable ware, draughtsman's instruments, lamp covers, safety helmets, taillights, deluxe housewares, engineering and industrial components
Polyethylenes	
Low density	Housewares (bottles, bowls, buckets, containers) closures for squeeze tubes, spouts for detergent cans, carboys, shoe parts, toys, packaging film, garment bags, sheet, piping for domestic, industrial and agricultural use
Medium density	As for low density polyethylene
High density	As for low density polyethylene, materials have

	greater rigidity, specially suitable for large carrying cases, housings, closures, appliance parts, packaging film, sheet, piping, carboys, containers and bottles
Polypropylene	Domestic, hospital and laboratory ware, textile, motor, electrical and chemical industrial usages, containers and closures, shoe heels, combs and toys, blown containers, extruded sheet, pipe, film, filament and fibre
Polystyrenes	Conventional packaging (disposable and others), dishes and utensils, refrigerator parts, emblems, signs, displays, toys, novelties, combs, brush-backs, radio and TV cabinets, lighting fixtures, rigid containers, housewares, reels/spools for film/tape, appliance panels, handles and switches
Toughened	Wheels, helmets, valve parts, refrigerator parts, bobbins, radio cabinets, electric fan blades, toys, housewares, containers, battery cases, sheeting for refrigerator linings and trays
Styrene copolymers	
Styrene/acrylonitrile (SAN copolymers)	Housewares (dishes, tumblers, cutlery handles), hair curlers, cosmetic packaging, fountain pen barrels, radio cabinets, battery cases, oil dispensing devices, laboratory utensils electric razor parts, vacuum cleaner parts and casings
Acrylonitrile/butadiene/ styrene (ABS terpolymer)	Calendered sheet, electrical housings, office machinery components, industrial mouldings, luggage, automobile parts, domestic appliances
Urea formaldehyde (a-cellulose filled)	As for Melamine Formaldehyde. In laminate form surfacings for tables, etc.
Vinyl polymers	
Rigid poly (vinyl chloride) PVC	Extrusion of piping, profiles and sheet in applications requiring chemical inertness and scuff-resistance combined with light weight
(Rigid(Vinyl chloride/	Similar applications to those for PVC but widely

vinyl acetate copolymer	used in the manufacture of calendered sheet used for toys, novelties, wall coverings, displays, templates etc.
Rubber-modified PVC	Same as for PVC
Vinlyidene chloride polymers	Specialized applications including weather resistant screening: rigid pipes and fittings; in film form, uses include a variety of heat-sealing packaging applications

processing and fabrication, properties and uses and applications of polymers fast grew as a separate branch of science and technology.

In our social relevance, polymers symbolise beauty, balance, stability, creativity and growth. Hazardous volatile and highly flammable petroleum and petroleum products are turned into nonvolatile, relatively dense and stable polymer products. The first lesson in polymer education relating to polymer synthesis by polymerization of monomers or mixtures of monomers makes one realise the high if not unlimited scope for achieving strength and balance through unification. One may appreciate better the meanings of unity in diversity or diversity in unity through meaningful polymer education. A polymer material is an embodiment of a molecular society where big chain molecules of specified repeat units and of different sizes, shapes, molecular weight and molecular complexity exist in peace and harmony. As in human society, so also in the polymer society, variety is the essence of existence. Polymers come into being by different routes following different mechanistics, and taking help of different catalysts, they develop into systems showing varieties in structural features ranging from linearity and branching to cross-linking or networking with variations in molecular weight and molecular weight distributions, monomer sequence distributions (in a co-polymer), cross-link density (in a cross-linked system), tacticity, nature of end groups etc., in their growth process, environments prevailing impart a great influence. Also depending on these structural variations, polymers offer different ranges of properties under different sets of static and dynamic conditions in respect of mechanical strength, chemical and solvent resistance, photostability or photodegradability, thermal resistance, clarity or opacity, rigidity, stiffness, resilience, toughness and flexibility, fatigue resistance, rheology and morphology.

Polymer Society vis-a-vis Human Society

Peaceful polymer society may be viewed as an ideal model for the strife-torn human society. In our democratic society we try to treat individuals as equals with one man one vote principle, though disallowing the voting rights to under-18 age group people or to non-members or defaulters, thus deviating from universal franchise. In the polymer system, all molecular species, big or small, like or unlike, including impurities or foreign elements contribute equally and at par when it comes to assessment of their colligative properties in an effort to have a measure of molecular weight of the system. Unlike what may happen as violation of voting rights through perpetration of violence or intimidation or snatching of ballot papers etc. in human society, the "democracy" prevailing in the polymer system shows no such aberration and it is practically foolproof; only chain molecular species, incapacitated by insolubility refrain, of their own, from casting their votes, i.e. making thermodynamic contributions in influencing the colligative property being measured, just as unwilling or incapacitated persons may of their own refrain from casting their votes in an election. The all important unifying quality of love is manifested in the polymer molecular society in the form of molar cohesion, solution tack and melt tack. It is through the property of tack that a polymer readily accommodates a host of additives including other polymers in its body matrix.

Human body, like a state or a society, remains within its bounds and does not commonly open its system spontaneously to accommodate foreign elements. We frame our own social rules and have our own likes and dislikes; we may selectively accommodate outsiders with affection, courtesy or distrust; we may try to retain them or may even throw them out sooner or later depending on proven acceptability or on stresses and strains that may develop due to economic constraints or cultural and spiritual incompatibilities. A polymer society also tends to suffer from an inclination of nonacceptance of unlike polymers or other species. In polymer blends, incompatibility and phase separation is more a rule than the exception. Incompatibility resulting in phase separation can be lowered, minimised or even eliminated by use of a right kind of compatibilizer.

Stabilization Role of Polymerization and Polymer Stability

Polymerization is a stabilization process as polymers are much more stable than the respective monomers; the stable polymers are, however, not stable enough and we need to practice a post polymerization stabilization process for the polymers so as to make them attain much higher durability, easy pocessability and stable performance. This necessitates addition of a host of additives for deriving advantages in respect of production cost and improving (1) aging resistance and photostability, (2) solvent and chemical resistance, (3) thermal stability, and (4) mechanical property balance. Relevant additives provide shields and weapons to the polymer system to enable them protect themselves and fight the adverse effects from the attack of hostile agencies of degradation such as thermal, electrical or mechanical loading under static or dynamic conditions, exposure to light and high energy radiations, solvents and chemicals and micro-organisms. Additives may be natural or synthetic, solid or liquid, polymeric or non polymeric particulate or fibrous and they may be used in minor or major proportions, sometimes taking the help of a compatibilizer or a coupling agent for achieving uniform dispersion with stable morphology and associated property advantages. The role of compatibilizers or coupling agents in improving mutual contacts, wetting and hence in uniform stable dispersion is similar to the role of a broker, match makers or third party arbiters, who may play vital roles in negotiated deals or contracts.

Education plays an important role in character building and in improving thinking power and overall ability of a man; likewise, simple thermo-mechanical processing imparts an educative role on polymer material systems and makes them mechanically much stronger and capable of bearing substantially higher load. Equipping the polymer system with selected reinforcing agents further allows spectacular enhancements in their nerve, strength and load bearing capabilities.

Helping Hand of Polymers

Man has been successful in developing modern petrochemical industries and deploying the polymer material system as substitutes for many other materials including forest wood for the welfare of human society that has finally set the stage right for much publicized globalization and establishment of one world by breaking through' geographical, political and cultural barriers. The electronic mass-media and modern communication system and developments in information technology owe a lot to all-round developments in the polymer material system. More purposeful polymer education supported by R&D efforts is all the more necessary for development of technologies based on growing utilization of renewable resources and waste materials from industry, forestry and agriculture for environmental preservation, energy conservation and for striking an improved ecological balance.

Polymers are variously useful during their life-time. However, some of them when used in minor proportions may also have a lasting, formidable and favourable impact on being destroyed *in-situ* in certain high heat-resistant refractory material system. Most modern technology of making high performance magnesia carbon or alumina carbon refractory bricks or plates for furnaces of metal extraction and preparation of alloys utilizes the high adhesive or binding power of phenolic and related resins for development of high green strength and cure strength. However, during exposure to high firing temperatures (11000-1400°C) under inert or reducing atmosphere in the final stage of refractory making, the organic resin pyrolyses to leave a network carbon skeleton with rearrangement of valence bonds when the oxides of metals (Mg, Al, Si, Zr etc.) present find chance to react *in-situ* with the network carbon skeleton being formed to randomly form the respective metal carbides, thus significantly enhancing the durability and performance level of the refractory product. Through self sacrifice, the selected polymer, a very minor component in the formulation, allows the refractory system to become higher performing and much more durable.

Polymer Education and its All-Round Influence

Polymer education permits one to appreciate the phenomenal role of polymer materials in arts, sports and entertainment, education and literacy drive, mass media and information dissemination, green revolution, and operation food, space exploration, health care and surgery, aids for the disabled, preservation of fresh and processed food, drinks, drugs and pharmaceuticals, water treatment for municipalities and in chemical and power plants, desalination of sea water for drinking and irrigation purposes and in water management in a comprehensive sense, thereby minimising or eliminating loss or wastages of precious water and ensuring its efficient use.

Polymers as they are naturally born or synthesized are mostly inert, non-toxic and harmless. Polymers the base materials for plastics, rubbers and related products may, however, exhibit toxicities that find their origin in injudicious selection of toxic/hazardous additives and incorporation thereof into the end-use items. Allround awareness about property demands, safety requirements and environmental preservation can only ensure right selection of additives for safe formulation and compounding of plastics, rubbers, coatings, adhesives and composites and further ensure their disposal or recycle all the more safe and cost effective. Technology innovation and helping hand of biotechnology would have major roles to play in future in rendering polymer disposal and recycling still safer and cost effective.

Polymers and Environment

Growing industrialization for meeting growing social demands and needs, linked to generation of job opportunities and for achieving a better quality of life and more efficient functioning of the society, imposes some constraints and additional responsibilities on the social sector for enacting legislation and enforcing rules and laws to prevent, check or minimize environmental denigration. Packaging, particularly plastic packaging is an easily identifiable portion of solid municipal wastes. Unsystematic waste disposal and indiscriminate littering of waste items largely disturb the environmental equilibrium. There is a genuine need or imperative for evolving balanced guidelines on environmentally viable and socially acceptable approaches for dealing with the growing problem of environmental pollution as linked with use of polymers and polymer waste disposal. Harmonious guidelines are required to be evolved for national and global acceptance for comprehensive management of plastics and related wastes in order to prevent their adverse effect on the environment covering urban, rural and forest landscapes, natural and artificial drainage systems, surface and ground water reserves and air, while ensuring their steady or growing production, uses and applications; in this context it is imperative to further ensure minimum waste generation leaving maximum scope for reuse and reprocessing, and easy collection, return or recovery with efficient recycling prospects. Some progress has already been made and a lot more remains to be done to achieve this goal. Turning waste to wealth or odds to opportunities is a big challenge for modern technology.

Plastics and packaging are closely interlinked, more so, in the modern age. Plastics and related wastes constitute between 5 and 10 per cent of municipal waste, but they draw much higher share of public attention as waste items because of their resistance to biodegradation and hence long life, notable lightness, being lighter than metals and alloys, minerals, glass and ceramics, ashes and clays and even water in some cases, and because of multitude of colours in which they appear in the consumer market and from there finally find refuge in dustbins and garbage heaps.

One must not be unduly obsessed with the slogan of rendering plastics and related products biodegradable. No one would like to see the plastic furniture, file covers, luggage items, pipe lines, containers and storage bins, casings and components of calculators, TV or telephone sets and computers and other electrical or electronic gadgets and innumerable essential or useful products made of polymers to perish in no time or in a short span of time as a result of biodegradation. In fact, the rapid phenomenal growth in use and popularity of polymer materials is primarily due to their non-corrosive nature and durability, exceptional lightness and significant resistance to weathering and microbial attack. Biodegradability is desired primarily for those polymer objects which are meant for packaging and related applications and are most likely to reach the garbage heaps or waste-bins soon after one time or short-time use.

Presence of chlorinated organic wastes including chlorine-containing polymers such as PVC and related polymer additives in the waste-bins or garbage heaps make their collective disposal by incineration hazardous, because of unavoidable *in-situ* generation of highly toxic dioxines (polychlorinated oxygenated aromatics or phenols) in the outcoming volatile products or relevant condensates in harmful concentrations, commonly for incineration at relatively low temperatures ($\lesssim$; 800°C). However, the dioxine concentration level can be substantially lowered to less than hazard levels or even practically brought to zero level for incineration at significantly higher temperatures, preferably> 1000°C.

38

Amino Acid by Protein Hydrolysis

Amino acids are the main components of protein, protein are found in all living organims and play on important role inliving cells. Approximately 20 amino acids are the common constituents of protein.

The general formula of an amino acid is

$$R - CH(NH_2) - COOH$$

All of the amino acids, except glycine have two optically active isomers symbolized by D-or L-before their names.

Amino acids are the main components of the elementary nutrients of living organim. There are eight and possibly ten, amino acids that are essential for existance and must be ingested through food. The Nutriential value of protein is governed by the Quantiative and qualitative balance of individual essential amino acids.

Protein are metabolized continuously by all living organism and are the dynamic equlibriumin living cell.

MANUFACTURING PROCESS

Manufacturing process of Amino Acid by protein hydrolysis.

Outline of the process : Amino acid is easily isolated or extracted from vegetable or other Natural source by protien Hydrolysis like casein, fibrin or Blood Corpuscle paste wheat Gluten etc.

Amino acid is hydrolyzed by heating the protein mateial like casein, Fibrin, Gluten, etc. with the addition of water with acid. The hydrolysate suspends relatively large amounts of humic material formed by reaction of amino acid and carbohydrates.

The filtrate is then cooled gradually after the addition of Conc. HCl (Hydro Chloric acid), still the filter. The crude hydrochloride is dissolved in warm water and filter again to separate the humic substaince formed after the first filtrate.

The pHt of the refined filtrate (Amino Acid) is adjusted to 3.2.

The filtrate is than passed ina crystallized for the formation of Crystals. The crystal in than passed in centrifuge of the complete removal of moisture. It is than dried in a drier. It is further tested for quality store and despatch for marketing.

Process Detail : Amino Acid (Glutamic acid) is produce by Hydrolysis of protein with acdi and water. After hydrolysis glumatic acid (Amino acid) may be recovered by fractional crystallization and purified.

After treatment of the hydrolyzate to remove certain impurities, the filtered liquor is concentrated and glutamic Acid (Amino Acid) crystallized at 3.2 pH.

In a hydrolyzing tank (S.S.) a calculae amount of sulphuric Acid, wheat Gluten, water is added and after hydrolysis with sulphuric Acid is neutralized by caustic soda solution. It is then washed with water and the solution thus obtained is concentrated in tripple effect Evaporator.

After Concentration in a evaporator, the amino acid (Glutamic Acid) is crystallize out in a crystallizer. The product in than acidified by addition of Hcl (Hydrochloric Acid) and is than again crystallize and filter to form Amino Acid (Glutamic Acid).

It isthan separated by centrifugation in centrifuge machine. The Centrifugate is futher adjuste in pH to 3.2 the iso electric point of Glutamic Acid. The crystal of amino acid are further dried in a dryer. Now the product is tested for quality, store/packed and despatch for marketing.

Plant Economics of Amino Acid by Protein Hydrolysis

Rated Plant Capacity = 1.00 Ton /Day

LAND & BUILDING

(Land Area 200 Sq.mts.) =	Rs.	56,00,000.00

PLANT & MACHINERY

1. Hydrolyzing Tank
2. Neutralizer
3. Evaporator
4. Filter
5. Crystallizer
6. Centrifuge
7. Dryer
8. Boiler
9. Storage Tank for Raw Materials
10. Laboratory Testing Equipments
11. Misc. Pipe and Pipe Fittings.

FIXED CAPITAL

1.	Land and Building	Rs.	56,00,000.00
2.	Plant and Machinery	Rs.	23,00,000.00
3.	Other Fixed Assets	Rs.	3,75,000.00
	TOTAL	Rs.	82,75,000.00

RAW MATERIALS

1. Wheat Gluten
2. Sulphuric Acid
3. Packaging Materials
4. Misc. Chemicals

TOTAL CAPITAL INVESTMENT

Total Fixed Capital	Rs.	82,75,000.00
Total Working Capital for 3 Month	Rs.	73,24,260.00
TOTAL	Rs.	1,55,99,260.00

TURN OVER/ANNUM

By sale of Amino Acid 300 Mt.

TOTAL	Rs. 4,05,00,000.00

PROFIT SALES RATIO = Profit / Sales x 100 = 20.99%
RATE OF RETURN = Operating profit / T.C.I x 100 = 54.50%
BREAK EVEN POINT (B.E.P) = 33.55%

39

Epoxy Resin/Powder

The epoxy resins have steadily grown in their use in the plastics and related industries due to the variety of forms in which they may be processed. As thermosetting materials, they are cured or cross-linked by addition of a hardner to the original liquid resin. The repeating molecular structure is attached to terminal molecular groups as curing taken place.

Epoxy resins are now produced in most of the developed countries of the world. But in India, although this item was introduced in late fifties, but indigenous production starred in late sixties.

Manufacturing Process :

The first commercially developed uncured epoxy resins are the reaction products of Diplophopane (DPP), also know as Bhsphenol A and Epichlorohydrin (ECH). ECH containing the epoxy group and Bisphenol A, the plyfunctional phenol, are condensed in presence of aqueous caustic soda at atmospheric pressure and temperature upto about 150°C. The product is the simplext epoxy resin known as the Diglycidyl either of bisphenol A. Different grades of epoxy resins of low, intermediate or high molecular weight can be prepared taking varied molar ratios of ECH and DPP, also varying the reaction conditions such as temperature, pressure etc. during synthesis. When the number of repeating units 'n' is less than one epoxy resins are liquid types, but when 'n' is 2 or greater epoxy resins are solid types.

Plant Economics of Epoxy Resins

Rated Plant Capacity = 0.50 Ton /Day

LAND & BUILDING

(Land Area 500 Sq.mts.) =	Rs.	13,50,000.00

PLANT & MACHINERY

1. Reaction Kettle
2. Seperator
3. ECH (Ephcholoro-hydrin) recovery Tank
4. Decanter
5. Filter Press
6. Wet Resin Storage Tank
7. Finished kettle fittled
8. Resin storage tank
9. HEK (Methyl Ethyl Ketons) Recovery Tank (Mild steel)
10. Neat Transfer
11. Meat Transfer Area
12. ECH (EPI chloro Hydrine) Storage Tank
13. Oil Fired Boiler
14. Pumps of different

FIXED CAPITAL

1.	Land and Building	Rs.	13,50,000.00
2.	Plant and Machinery	Rs.	9,85,000.00
3.	Other Fixed Assets	Rs.	2,27,000.00
	TOTAL	Rs.	26,05,000.00

WORKING CAPITAL REQUIREMENT/MONTH

RAW MATERIALS

1. Epichlorohydrin
2. Bisphenol
3. Caustic Soda

TOTAL WORKING CAPITAL/MONTH

Raw Materials	Rs.	9,87,000.00
Salary & Wages	Rs.	49,750.00
Utilities & Overseas	Rs.	82,000.00
TOTAL	Rs.	11,19,250.00

TOTAL WORKING INVESTMENT

Total Fixed Capital	Rs.	26,05,000.00
Total Working Capital for 3 Month	Rs.	33,57,750.00
TOTAL	Rs.	69,62,750.00

TURN OVER/ANNUM

By sale of 150 tonnes of Epoxy Resins Powder

TOTAL	Rs.	1,95,00,000.00

PROFIT SALES RATIO = Profit / Sales x 100 = 22.75%
RATE OF RETURN = Operating profit / T.C.I x 100 = 74.31%
BREAK EVEN POINT (B.E.P) = 33.88%

40

Hosehold Plastic Products

Electric lights are supplied with electricity from a storage battery. When the storage battery runs down, it can be recharged from an outside source, or from a dynamo, run from the engine. The old style 'carbon' filament in the electric globe consumed so much current that it was difficult to obtain a storage battery of a reasonable size and weight which would supply current from any length of time. The carbon filament lamp used a filament chemically treated and in a vacuum. The filament in the "Tungsten mazda" globe reduces the current consumption and is not liable to break with the unusual motor car vibration. There are three methods of furnishing electric current for car lighting.

1. By independent storage battery system.
2. By generator & battery system.
3. By an independent generator system.

MANUFACTURING PROCESS

Injection moulding is a multi-step process, carried out usually in a single machine, in which a thermoplastic is melted or plastic is melted or plasticized and injected into a mold farming a cavity of the shape and size of the desired article. The mould is kept at a temperature below the solidifying point of the plastic, causing the injected plasticized mass to take the Šform of the mold cavity, and after a sufficiently long cooling time the mold is opened and the article ejected. The injection molding process comprises four stages, each of which must be closely controlled and regulated to obtain good quality moldings. These stages are (1) Plasticizing. (2) Injection (3) after filling, and (4) Cooling and mold release.

Plasticizing :- The resin is fed from the hopper of the molding machine and heated and softened to make it plastic in a heated cylinder. To achieve a suitable state of plasticization, which will ensure a good quality product, requires closer control of temperature of the cylinder . In additions, on preplasticizing machines (screw type), the speed of rotation of screw and the applied pressure also influences the state of plasticization. During this operation the resin compound is conveyed from one end to the other end of the during the operation.

Injection :- In the injection stage a correct amount of plasticized melt is injected from the plasticizing cylinder into the relatively cold mold, while closed, under controlled pressure. The amount of material injected into a mold is controlled by the machine feed mechanism. On piston or plunger type molding machines this is achieved by a volumetric measurement of unmelted granules or resing itself; on a screw pre-plasticizing machine, however, the control is by volumetric measurement of molten material- the latter method being more accurate. To minimize errors on the plunger type machines, especially in the case of difficult moldings, it is sometimes necessary to fit feed weighting devices or a vibratory feeder operating on time cycle.

After - Filling : The solidification of the plasticized melt begins in the cold mold soon after its injection in the mold from the walls of the mold. The injected material is kept under pressure for some time to ensure adequate filling of the mold and prevent the back flow of the polymer, and to compensate for the decrease in volume due to solidification. The quality of the article very much depends upon the temperature and pressure of material in the mold cavity at the moment it started solidifying in the gate. When the mold is being filled, the temperature of the plasticized melt starts falling and there are two opposing tendencies taking place- the thermal contraction tries to reduce the volume of the molding and residual pressure in the melt tries to expand it. The above two tendencies exist simultaneously and in an ideal case they must counter- balance each other.

Cooling and mold release : Some further time is allowed to delapse for cooling of the molded article in the mold until it is sufficiently rigid to be ejected without any risk of deformation taking place subsequently. Control of mold temperature control systems allow the mold temperature to be raised to its optimum value before start up, so that during the initial period of production, the manufacture of highly strained parts from a cold mold and wastage of material due to short shots is avoided.

The mold is then opened to eject the molding and is closed again to receive the plasticized melt for the next cycle of operation.

Time Cycle : The basic steps and operations of injection molding process are common in all injection molding machines, e.g.taking a quantity of plastics material, softening it in a cylinder by neating, forcing it under pressure by means of a plunger or screw into a mold, cooling the plasticized melt in the mold, and ejecting it out by opening the mold. The time cycle of the operation may be considered in terms of a clock in which the hand is rotating in a clockwise direction.

When the mold is closed, the cylinder it ready in position to enable the plasticized melt to be injected into the mold. The period during which the plunger or screw moves forward displacing the plasticized melt from the cylinder into the mold is called 'injection time'. In the case of plunger type machines the shortness of injection time is limited by the speed at which hydraulic fluid will pass through the pipelines to the hydraulic cylinder which activated the plunger.

The plunger remains in forward position for a period, known as 'dwell time' determined by the nature of material and size shape of the mold, during which the material in the mold is kept at maximum pressures. The plungers withdrawn and next charge of the material enters the cylinder; however, the mold is not opened immediately and time is allowed for the material to solidify in the mold a period called time'.

Plant Economics of House Hold Plastic Products

Rated Plant Capacity = 600.00 KG./Day

LAND & BUILDING

(Land Area 500 Sq.mts.) = Rs. 24,60,000.00

PLANT & MACHINERY

1. Horizontal Plastic Injection Moulding Machines
2. Horizontal/Plastic Injection Moulding Machine
3. High Speed Mixer
4. Scraps Grinder
5. Working tools, testing equipments, measuing instruments, fixtures etc.
6. Dies Mould Sets

FIXED CAPITAL

1.	Land and Building	Rs.	24,60,000.00
2.	Plant and Machinery	Rs.	32,77,000.00
3.	Other Fixed Assets	Rs.	6,00,000.00
	TOTAL	Rs.	63,37,000.00

WORKING CAPITAL REQUIREMENT/MONTH

RAW MATERIALS

1. HDPE granules
2. Polypropylene Granules
3. C.P. Granules
4. Master batches
5. Packing materials

TOTAL WORKING CAPITAL/MONTH

Raw Materials	Rs.	10,45,000.00
Salary & Wages	Rs.	94,430.00
Utilities & Overseas	Rs.	41,100.00
TOTAL	Rs.	11,80,530.00

TOTAL WORKING INVESTMENT

Total Fixed Capital	Rs.	63,37,000.00
Total Working Capital for 3 Month	Rs.	11,80,530.00
TOTAL	Rs.	75,17,530.00

TURN OVER/ANNUM

1. By sale of HDPE Injection Moulded house hold products
2. By sale of P.P. Injection Moulded house hold products 61920 Kgs.
3. By sale of C.P. Injection moulded house hold products 61920 Kgs.

TOTAL Rs. 1,88,85,600.00

PROFIT SALES RATIO = Profit / Sales x 100 = 15.40%

RATE OF RETURN = Operating profit / T.C.I x 100 = 38.68%

BREAK EVEN POINT (B.E.P) = 45.85%

41

Nylon Granules from Nylon Waste

Nylon is a generic name for family of polyamide polymers characterized by the presence of the amide group-CONH. By far the most important are Nylon 66 and Nylon 6. Except for slight difference in melting points the properties of the two forms are almost identical, through their chemical derivations are quite different. Other types are nylons 4,9,11 and 12.

There are many types of Nylons with a Specific gravity ranging from 1.04-1.17. All types burn with blue flames and yellow dips and give off a burnt wool or burnt hair odour. Nylon self-extinguishes on removal of the flame. Different types of nylons can be identified by the Fischer-John melting point test (ASTMD789). Solubility and specific gravity tests are also used to differentiate between the types of nylons. However, infrared spectroscopy in the best method for positive identifications.

Manufacturing Process of Nylon Granules from Nylon Waste

The process of manufacture of Nylon Granules from Nylon waste consists of the following few steps.

1. Sorting
2. Magnetic Separtor for removal of Iron & Other metallic impurities
3. Passing through cyclone Separator for the removal of glass fillings.
4. Cutting
5. Bleaching for removal of colour by bleach liquor
6. Soaking in hot water
7. Washing the pieces

8. Drying the pieces.
9. Pelletisation / Granulation

Plant Economics of Nylon Granules from Nylon Waste

Rated Plant Capacity = 1.00 MT/Day

LAND & BUILDING

(Land Area 700 Sq.mts.) =	Rs.	21,80,000.00

PLANT & MACHINERY

1. Cutting Machine
2. Magnetic Separator
3. Washing Tank Fitted
4. Reaction Vessel
5. Mixer for solvent mixing fitted
6. Activated carbon Treatment Tank
7. Filter
8. Distillation column
9. Extruder (Twin-Screw) (Allow steel screw & barrel fully nitrided & chrome plated)
10. Solvent recovery
11. Granulator
12. Dehumidifer
13. Tra Drier
14. Scrap Grinder
15. Solvent Storage Tanks
16. Weighing filling, sealing
17. Mini Boiler
18. Instruments & Process Control & Lab Testing Equipment
19. Pipes, fitting, Pump valves, pumps
20. Cyclone separator

FIXED CAPITAL

1.	Land and Building	Rs.	21,80,000.00
2.	Plant and Machinery	Rs.	36,50,000.00
3.	Other Fixed Assets	Rs.	5,26,960.00
	TOTAL	Rs.	63,56,960.00

WORKING CAPITAL REQUIREMENT/MONTH

RAW MATERIALS

1. Nylon Waste
2. Ethanol
3. Toluene
4. Xylene
5. Activated Carbon
6. Packing Charges

TOTAL WORKING CAPITAL/MONTH

Raw Materials	Rs.	6,18,800.00
Salary & Wages	Rs.	93,750.00
Utilities & Overseas	Rs.	1,16,500.00
TOTAL	Rs.	8,29,050.00

TOTAL WORKING INVESTMENT

Total Fixed Capital	Rs.	63,56,960.00
Total Working Capital for 3 Month	Rs.	24,87,150.00
TOTAL	Rs.	88,44,110.00

TURN OVER/ANNUM

1. By selling 300 MT. of Nylon Granules
2. Activated carbon for Regeneration 45 MT

TOTAL	Rs.	1,61,25,000.00

PROFIT SALES RATIO = Profit / Sales x 100 = 27.97%

RATE OF RETURN = Operating profit / T.C.I x 100 = 45.52%

BREAK EVEN POINT (B.E.P) = 43.98%

42

Poly Vinyl Acetate Emulsion

In a useful discussion of some aspects of emulsion formulation, sutheim has pointed out the wide variability existing in the definition of the term "emulsion," and has illustrated this with a series of such definitions from random sources. Adapting and expanding Sutheim's listings, the following series of definitions is worthy of study.

1. An emulsion is a very fine dispersion of one liquid in another with which it is immiscible.
2. An emulsion is a system containing two liquid phases, one of which is dispersed as globules in the other.
3. Emulsions are mechanical mixtures of liquids that are immiscible under ordinary conditions, and which may be separated into layers on standing, heating, freezing, by agitation or the addition of other chemicals.
4. An emulsion is a two-phase liquid system consisting of fairly coarse dispersions of one liquid in another with which it is it is not miscible.
5. Emulsions are intimate mixtures of two immiscible liquids, one of them being dispersed in the other in the form of fine droplets.
6. ... emulsions are finely divided liquid to semi-solid substances.
7. Emulsions ... are microscopically visible droplets of one liquid ... suspended in another.

8. Emulsions are stable and intimate mixtures of the oil or oily material with water.
9. An emulsion ... consists of a stable dispersion of one liquid in another liquid.

MANUFACTURING PROCESS

There are two types of emulsions produced today, a fine particle size (0.1-0.24) polyvinyl acetate without a protective colloid but only with anionic or nonionic surfactants and a large particle size (0.5-3.04) emulsion which is only stabilized by the protective colloids.

Protective colloids most often used are polyvinyl alcohol which is 88% hydrolyzed and hydroxy ethyl cellulose.

A typical recipe for a large particle size emulsion is as follows:-

Formulation

(For 100 kg batch) PVA Emulsion

Water	-	42.75% kg.
Vinyl Acetate	-	55.00% kg.
Hydroxyethyle cellulose	-	2.00% kg.
Tergitol NPX (non ionic surfactant)	-	0.05% kg.
Potassium Peroxy disulphate	-	0.15% kg.
Total	=	100.00% kg.

The starting step for the manufacture of polyvinyl acetate is the mixing and heating of ingredients. The cellolose, tergitol NPX and water are mixed in the proper proportion and heated to about 80°C.

The mixing and heating of the above mixture is carried out in same tank. This tank is generally made of mild steel equipped with an agitator and a steam jacket. Agitator is rotated at a speed of 50-80 rpm. For reducing the rpm. of the motor a gear reducer is used. The pressure of the steam is kept around 2 atomosphere.

This heating to 80°C is done for about one to one and half hour. After heating the solution is cooled to about 30°C by flowing cold water into the steam jacket after closing the steam valve and opening the vessel provided at the top of the jacket.

Now about 10% of the total vinyl acetate is added into the above cooled mixture and agitated. Along with vinylacetate, potassium peroxy disulphate and soldium bicarbonate are also added to the above mixture, and mixing is done in a separate vessel. This second vessel is also equipped with a steam jacket for heating purpose. The mixture of all the ingredients is now heated to about 70-75°C by using steam at one atmosphere. At this temperature i.s. 70-75°C, the remaining 90% of the total vinyl acetae is so adjusted that should take about 2 hours. During the addition period of vinyl acetate the temperature of the reaction mixture is kept arround 80°C.

When all the vinyl acetae i.e. monomer is added to the reacter, then the reaction mixture temperature is raised to 90°C. This 90°C temperature is maintained for about half hour. After keeping the mixture at 90°C for about 30 minutes, the solution is cooled to room temperature and filtered through a filter.

One completion of the polymerization of emulsion is either spray-dried or coagulated by adding an electrolyte then filterd and finally flash dried various washing process are necessary for the removal of the soap if polymer of high purity are to be obtained.

Plant Economics of Poly Vinyl Acetate Emulsion

Rated Plant Capacity = 5.00 MT/Day

LAND & BUILDING

(Land Area 2000 Sq.mts.) = Rs. 45,00,000.00

PLANT & MACHINERY

1. Reactor (5 mm - 6 mm thickness) (Stainless steel-316 made) with (mild steel jacketed), fitted with stainless steel stirrer and 3 HP motor, other accessories as temperature controller, pressure controller and other with cooling coils.
2. Condenser (heat exchanger) (Shell & tube type with S.S. tubes and M.S. body) with all accessories.
3. Raw Materials and finished products storage tanks
4. PVC water storage tank
5. High speed emulsifying unit fitted with 5 H.P. motor and starter
6. Laboratory equipment
7. Filter
8. Alpha-therm heater
9. Pipes, pumps, valves, structures and other
10. Water chilling unit

11. Instrumentations & process control equipments
12. Tools, jigs, fixtures & others

FIXED CAPITAL

1.	Land and Building	Rs.	45,00,000.00
2.	Plant and Machinery	Rs.	45,75,000.00
3.	Other Fixed Assets	Rs.	14,00,000.00
	TOTAL	Rs.	1,04,75,000.00

WORKING CAPITAL REQUIREMENT/MONTH

RAW MATERIALS

1. Distilled Water
2. Vinyl acetate monomer
3. Hydroxy ethyl cellulose
4. Tergitol NPX
5. Potassium peroxy disulphate
6. Laboratory chemicals

TOTAL WORKING CAPITAL/MONTH

Raw Materials	Rs.	49,60,200.00
Salary & Wages	Rs.	2,63,340.00
Utilities & Overseas	Rs.	3,57,500.00
TOTAL	Rs.	55,80,540.00

TOTAL WORKING INVESTMENT

Total Fixed Capital	Rs.	1,04,75,000.00
Total Working Capital for 1 Month	Rs.	55,80,540.00
TOTAL	Rs.	1,60,55,540.00

TURN OVER/ANNUM

By sale of 1500 MTs Poly Vinyl Acetate emulsion

TOTAL	Rs.	9,00,00,000.00

PROFIT SALES RATIO = Profit / Sales x 100 = 21.61%
RATE OF RETURN = Operating profit / T.C.I x 100 = 121.15%
BREAK EVEN POINT (B.E.P) = 25.22%

43

Phenolic Resin

Process of Manufacture

When a catalyzed mixture of Phenol and formaldehyde contain are of more than one mole of formaldehyde per mole of phenol is catalyzed with a Base, Resol of one-step resin resin Is formed.

Hower in commercial practice the following preparation of formaldehyde to phenol is used.

Phenol	1 mole
Formaldehyde	1.5 to 3.0 moles
i.e.	1.5-3.0

moles of formaldehyde per mole of phenol are used. Resole are physically liquid of socid brittle products depending on the catalyst and conditions of manufacture. The type of catalyst has mmcb higher influence on molecular structure and molecular weight distribution than in acidic range. Sodium hydroxide Barium hydroxides and hydroxides ammonia, testary ammines organic ammies are the most important basic catalysts themolar catalyst ratio based on phenol as applied in technical reols is very different.

Plant Economics of Phenolic Resin

Rated Plant Capacity = 1.00 MT/Day

LAND & BUILDING

(Land Area 1000 Sq.mts.) = Rs. 26,00,000.00

PLANT & MACHINERY

1. Reaction Kettle
2. Melting tank for Phenol
3. Storage tanks for formaldehyde
4. Vacuum Pump
5. Resin Cooler
6. Boiler
7. Water Tank
8. Thermostate
9. Air Draft Equipment
10. Curing chamber fitted
11. Testing & Lab Instruments
12. Instrumentation
13. Pump
14. Misc.

FIXED CAPITAL

1.	Land and Building	Rs.	26,00,000.00
2.	Plant and Machinery	Rs.	19,70,000.00
3.	Other Fixed Assets	Rs.	3,60,000.00
	TOTAL	Rs.	49,30,000.00

WORKING CAPITAL REQUIREMENT/MONTH

RAW MATERIALS

1. Phenol 1
2. Formaldehyde
3. Curing Agent
4. Alkaline Catalyst
5. Packaging Charges

TOTAL WORKING CAPITAL/MONTH

Raw Materials	Rs.	10,37,500.00
Salary & Wages	Rs.	85,120.00
Utilities & Overseas	Rs.	82,400.00
TOTAL	Rs.	12,05,020.00

TOTAL WORKING INVESTMENT

Total Fixed Capital	Rs.	49,30,000.00
Total Working Capital for 1 Month	Rs.	24,10,040.00
TOTAL	Rs.	73,40,040.00

TURN OVER/ANNUM

By sale of 30 Mt. of Phenolic Resin
Intended for Mfr. of Floer Type foam

TOTAL	Rs.	1,95,00,000.00

PROFIT SALES RATIO = Profit / Sales x 100 = 17.83%

RATE OF RETURN = Operating profit / T.C.I x 100 = 47.36%

BREAK EVEN POINT (B.E.P) = 40.51%

44

Polyol from Propylene Oxide

Polyol is a polyhydric alcohol, ie. one containing three or more hydroxyl groups. Those having three hydroxyl groups (trihydric) are glycerols, those with more than three are called sugar alcohols, with general formula CH_2OH $(CHOH)n$ CH_2OH, where n may be from 2 to 5.

Polyurethane system camprises polyol and isocyanate used for thermoware/Non-thermoware panel (sandwich) refrigeration bloch wood imitation and commercial refrigerator, industries with or without blowing agent.

MANUFACTURING PROCESS OF POLYOL FROM PROPYLENE OXIDE

Polyol is manufactured from Propylene Oxide, which is isomerized to Allyl alcohol ($H_2C = CH\ CH_2\ OH$) in a Reactor MS (Jacketed) (Fluidized bed) containing Lithium Phosphate (catalyst) at 230 - 270°C.

Allyl alcohol is obtained as a result of above isomerization process having the following properties:-

Colorless liquid with pungent mustard like odour, BP - 96.9°C, mp - 129°C.

Density (d) = 0.8520 (20/4°C).
Bulk density (d) = 7.11 lb / gal (20°C).
Refractive index = 1.4131
Flash Point (p) = 70°F (21°C) — (TOC).
Autoignition tempt = 713°F (375°C)
Miscible with water, alcohol, chloroform, ether.

Allyl alcohol thus formed is then reacted in another Reaction vessel

MS (Jacketed) at 55°C with Peracetic acid (CH_3 COOCH), when 2,3 - epoxy -1- propanol (an epoxide) is formed.

This is then subjected to treatment with HOCL followed by hydrolysis with Alkali (NaCH / H2 O) at 40 — 45°C. Polyol (under) then formed in dilute equeous solution.

High - purity Polyol is obtained in several stages. The crude polyol is concentrated to 80% or more in Triple - effect evaporators and salt is removed by centrifuging. Additional concentration of the product, followed by desalting, yields 98% Polyol; colored substances are removed by solvent extraction and the product is refined by steam - vacuum distillation.

It is checked for quality then it is packed in MS Drums (of capacity 210 Kgs. each) then they are stored / despatched for marketing.

Plant Economics of Polyol from Propylene Oxide

Rated Plant Capacity = 10.00 MT/Day

LAND & BUILDING

(Land Area 2000 Sq.mts.) = Rs. 66,20,000.00

PLANT & MACHINERY

1. Reactor MS (Jacketed) Fluidized Bed with accessories
2. Reaction accessories
3. Triple effect Evaporator
4. Storage Tank
5. Centrifuge
6. Solvent Extraction Unit
7. Steam Vacuum Distillation
8. Boiler
9. Drum Filling Machine
10. Storage Tanks
11. Lab Equipments
12. Instrumentator & Process Control Equipments
13. Misc. equipments viz pipe fittings, valves, motor, etc.

FIXED CAPITAL

1.	Land and Building	Rs.	66,20,000.00
2.	Plant and Machinery	Rs.	1,28,25,000.00
3.	Other Fixed Assets	Rs.	22,25,000.00
	TOTAL	Rs.	2,16,70,000.00

WORKING CAPITAL REQUIREMENT/MONTH

RAW MATERIALS

1. Propylene Oxide
2. Peraceptic Acid
3. For Packing the product
4. Misc. Chemicals

TOTAL WORKING CAPITAL/MONTH

Raw Materials	Rs.	2,15,90,600.00
Salary & Wages	Rs.	1,14,380.00
Utilities & Overseas	Rs.	3,03,000.00
TOTAL	Rs.	12,05,020.00

TOTAL WORKING INVESTMENT

Total Fixed Capital	Rs.	2,16,70,000.00
Total Working Capital for 1 Month	Rs.	2,20,07,980.00
TOTAL	Rs.	4,36,77,980.00

TURN OVER/ANNUM

By sale of Polyol

TOTAL	Rs.	30,30,00,000.00

PROFIT SALES RATIO = Profit / Sales x 100 = 9.33%
RATE OF RETURN = Operating profit / T.C.I x 100 = 68.90%
BREAK EVEN POINT (B.E.P) = 26.43%

45

Unsaturated Polyester Resin

Polyester resins are prepared by reacting a dihydric alcohol with a mixture of unsaturated and saturated dibasic acids. The basic resin, so obtained is not usable because of its high viscosity and poor reactivity. It is diluted with a reactive unsaturated compound called monomer and supplied to the user. The remaining polymer chemistry is carried out at the casteomers end where with the help of a catalyst and an accelerator, the resin is further polymerized (cross-linked) to produce a three dimentlonal influsible structure.

PROCESS OF MANUFACTURE

The theorctical charge for a polyester reactions is one molar equivalent of glycol for each molar equivalent of acid. However it is common practice to use from 10-20% excess glycol to Šallow for glycol loss in the reflux condenser system and to bring the acid number doors to low value rapidly. A typical formulation is shown below.

Raw Material	Moles	Wt. lbs.	
Propylene	1.1	83.7	(10% excess)
Maleic Anhydride	0.5	49.0	
Phthalic Anhydride	0.5	74.0	
		206.7	
Losses (Estimated 10%)		20.7	
Polyester resin yield		186.0	
Styrene (30%)		79.7	
Total resin solutions		265.7	

The Raw materials are either weighed into the reaction kettle directly from their shipping container or in case of larger production operation from large storage tanks, bins, or hoppers to which materials have been previously charged. The liquid ingredients (usually the glycol) are charged to the reactor first, with the agitator running the batch is heated to 175o to 210oF and the solid components are added (Maleic, phthalic etc.) If the reaction involves a solvent reflux such as xylene, charged. a solvents reflux in removing water from the condensation reaction and serves to control the temperature of the reaction and maintain the same at the desired level.

A blanket, of inert gas should be introduced as the temperature is increased to prevent discoloration and cross-linking polymerisation through the unsaturated acid. This latter reaction is most likely to occur and where above 400oF. Once started it is almost impossible to stop and may proceed to get the entire batch.

The batch is gradually heated over a period of several hours to approximately 400oF. It is held at this temperature until, the acid number come down to the desired point. Cooking time depends upon the ingredients and can run upto 16 hrs. or even more. The condensation reaction that kept it under control occurs in exothermic and close observation. A reflux is maintained in reflux condenser and the water collected in the distillate receiver is measured to follow cause of the reaction. When a solvent such as xylene is used to aid in the removal of water, it Šcomes out as an azeotropic mixture.

In addition to the amount of distillate collected, the course of reaction is followed by taking frequently samples for acid number determination. The frequency of these samples is increased as the reaction proceeds. At a predetermined acid numbers usually less than 50, the reflux is stopped and all solvent, water and unreacted constituents are stripped from the batch. This sometimes involves vacuum stipping or blowing with inert gas.

Plant Economics of Polyester Resin

Rated Plant Capacity = 260.00 KGS./Day

LAND & BUILDING

(Land Area 300 Sq.mts.) =	Rs.	3,50,000.00

PLANT & MACHINERY

1. Reaction Kettle
2. Reflux Condenser
3. Total Condenser
4. Decantor
5. Receiver
6. Blending Kettle
7. Styrene and glycol storage tanks
8. High Pressure Boiler
9. Miscellaneous equipments
10. Generator

FIXED CAPITAL

1.	Land and Building	Rs.	3,50,000.00
2.	Plant and Machinery	Rs.	6,28,000.00
3.	Other Fixed Assets	Rs.	2,80,000.00
	TOTAL	Rs.	12,58,000.00

WORKING CAPITAL REQUIREMENT/MONTH

RAW MATERIALS

1. Polypropylene glycol
2. Maleic Anhydride
3. Phthalic Anhydride

TOTAL WORKING CAPITAL/MONTH

Raw Materials	Rs.	4,28,945.00
Salary & Wages	Rs.	21,000.00
Utilities & Overseas	Rs.	46,600.00
TOTAL	Rs.	4,96,545.00

TOTAL WORKING INVESTMENT

Total Fixed Capital	Rs.	12,58,000.00
Total Working Capital for 1 Month	Rs.	14,89,635.00
TOTAL	Rs.	27,47,635.00

TURN OVER/ANNUM

By sale of 30 Mt. of Phenolic Resin
Intended for Mfr. of Floer Type foam

TOTAL	Rs.	1,95,00,000.00

PROFIT SALES RATIO = Profit / Sales x 100 = 17.83%

RATE OF RETURN = Operating profit / T.C.I x 100 = 47.36%

BREAK EVEN POINT (B.E.P) = 40.51%

EIRI PROCESS TECHNOLOGY BOOKS

CHEMICAL/ DYES/ PETROCHEMICALS/ LUBRICANT/ ELECTROPLATING

01 Small Medium & Large Chemical Industries
02 Industrial Chemicals Technology Hand Book
03 Modern Technology of Organic & Inorganic Chemicals
04 Hand Book of Electroplating Anodizing & Surface Finishing Technology
05 Hand Book of Agro Chemical Industries (Insecticides & Pesticides)
06 Technology of Synthetic Dyes, Pigments Intermediates
07 Petrochemicals, Lubricants, Greases & Petroleum Refining
08 Hand Book of Lubricants, Greases & Petrochemicals Technology

GUMS, ADHESIVES AND SEALANTS

01 Technology Of Gums, Adhesives & Sealants With Formulations
02 Hand Book Of Adhesives With Their Formulaes
03 Adhesives Technology & Formulations Hand Book (Hand Book of Adhesives)
04 Technology of Glue and Adhesives with Adhesives Bonding and Formulations

SMALL SCALE INDUSTRIES/ STATIONERY/PAPER/ INKS/ CANDLES & EXPORT BUSINESS

01 Start Your Own Export Business (How To Export)
02 Start Your Own Small Business And Industry
03 Candle Making Processes & Formulations Hand Book
04 Stationery, Paper Converting & Packaging Industries
05 Modern Inks Formulations & Manufacturing Industries
06 Profitable Businesses To Start For Entrepreneurs
07 Modern Small & Cottage Scale Industries
08 Profitable Small Cottage Tiny & Home Industries

BIO FUEL & BIOPROCESSING

01 Technology Of Bio-Fules (Ethanol & Biodiesel)
02 Modern Technology Of Bioprocessing

PRINTING, SCREEN PRINTING & PACKAGING

01 Hand Book of Printing Processes Technologies & Industries
02 Hand Book Of Printing Technology (Offset, Screen, Flexo, Gravure, Inkjet & Digital)
03 Hand Book Of Offset Printing Technology
04 Screen Printing With Processes & Tech.
05 Hand Book Of Prepress
06 Hand Book Of Packaging Technology
07 Modern Packaging Technology for Processed Food, Bakery, Snack Foods, Spices and Allied Food Products
08 Hand Book Of Food Packaging Technology
09 Modern Technology of Printing Inks

PAINT, VARNISH, SOLVENTS, COATING & LACQUERS, POWDER COATING

01 Paint Pigment Varnish & Lacquer Manufacturing
02 Paint Varnish Solvents & Coating Technology

EIRI PROCESS TECHNOLOGY BOOKS

03 Paint, Pigment, Solvent, Coating Emulsion, Paint Additives & Formulations
04 Technology Of Coating, Resins, Pigments & Inks Industries
05 Manufacturing Technology & Formulations Hand Book On Thinners, Putty, Wall & Industrial Finishes And Synthetic Resins
06 Technology of Synthetic Resins and Emulsion Polymers
07 Technology of Paints and Coatings with Formulations
08 Powder Coating Technology Hand Book

PLASTIC/POLYMER PROCESS, COMPOUNDING, INJECTION MOULDING, ROTATIONAL MOULDING, PLASTIC FILM, FIBRE GLASS, PLASTIC WASTE RECYCLING, MOULDS, PET & RESINS INDUSTRIES

01 Moulds Design & Processing Hand Book
02 Hand Book Of Plastic Materials & Processing Technology
03 Injection Moulding Of Plastics
04 Plastic Processing and Packaging Industries
05 Plastic Waste Recycling Technology
06 Technology Of Plastic Films
07 Rotational Moulding Technology Hand Book
08 Plastic Compounding, Master Batches, Pet & Other Plastics
09 Synthetic Resins Technology With Formulations
10 Technology Of PVC Compounding And Its Applications
11 Hand Book of Polymer And Plastic Technology
12 Hand Book of Fibre Glass Moulding
13 Technology of Reinforced Plastics
14 Plastic Additives Technology Hand Book
15 Technology of Pet Bottles, Preform and Pet Recycling
16 Modern Technology of Extrusion & Extruded Products
17 Technology of Synthetic Resins & Emulsion Polymers
18 Technology of Plastic Additives with Processes and Packaging
19 Technology of Disposable Medical Products

BAKERY, CONFECTIONERY & BREAKFAST, PASTA & CEREALS

01 Hand Book Of Bakery Industries
02 Hand Book Of Confectionery With Formulations
03 Breakfast, Dietary Food, Pasta & Cereal Products Technology
04 Hand Book Of Modern Bakery Products
05 Modern Bakery Technology & Fermented Cereal Products With Formulae
06 Technology of Confectionery, Chocolates, Toffee, Candy, Chewing & Bubble Gums, Lollipop and Jelly Products with Formulations

AGRO CULTIVATION, ANIMAL FARMING, AGRO PLANTATION & AGRO CHEMICAL/ PESTICIDES/ FLORICULTURE & BEE KEEPING

01 Poultry Farming & Feed Formulations
02 Hand Book of Pig Farming
03 Agro Based Hand Book of Plantation, Cultivation & Farming
04 Agro Based Plantation Cultivation & Farming
05 Agro Chemical Industries (Insecticide & Pesticides)
06 Modern Bee Keeping & Honey Processing

EIRI PROCESS TECHNOLOGY BOOKS

07 Technology Of Modern Rice Milling And Basmati Rice
08 Hand Book Of Goat Farming
09 Floriculture Hand Book (Flowers Growing Technology)
10 Aloe Vera Cultivation, Processings, Formulations And Manufacturing Technology
11 Poultry Farming, Hatchery and Broiler Production

DAIRY FARM, MILK PROCESSING AND ICE CREAM

01 Hand Book of Dairy Formulations, Processes & Milk Processing Industries
02 Milk Processing And Dairy Products Industries
03 Hand Book Of Dairy Farming to Produce Milk with Packaging
04 Hand Book Of Ice Cream Technology And Formulae
05 Hand Book Of Milk Processing Dairy Products And Packaging Technology
06 Dairy Farming for Milk Production Technology
07 Commercial Dairy Farming with Project Profiles

HERBS & MEDICINAL CULTIVATION

01 Herbs, Medicinal & Aromatic Plants Cultivation
02 Aushidhi And Sungndhit Paudho Ka Vaysayik (Hindi)
03 Hand Book Of Aromatic & Medicinal Plants And Biodiesel (Jatropha)
04 Hand Book Of Medicinal & Aromatic Plants (Cultivation, Utilisation & Extraction Processed)

FOOD & AGRO PROCESSING, PRESERVATION, SNACK FOOD, DEHYDRATION, FRUIT BEVERAGE, POTATO, MAIZE, MEAT PROCESS

01 Fruits & Vegetables Processing Hand Book
02 Fruit Beverage & Processing With Mango
03 Food Processing & Agro Based Industries
04 Manufacturing Technology of Snacks Food, Namkeen, Pappad & Potato Products
05 Preservation & Canning Of Fruits and Vegetables
06 Hand Book of Food Dehydration & Drying
07 Meat Processing & Meat Products Hand Book
08 Technology of Food Preservation & Processing
09 Hand Book of Food Packaging Technology
10 Agro Based & Processed Food Products
11 Potato & Potato Processing Technology
12 Technology of Maize & Allied Corn. Products
13 Technology of Food Processing Industries
14 Technology of Sweets (Mithai) with Formulae
15 Modern Technology of Frozen Food Products
16 Technology of Water and Packaged Drinking water
17 Complete Hand Book on Frozen Food Processing and Freeze Drying Technology
18 Technology of Sweets (Mithai), Namkeen and Snacks food with Formulae
19 Complete Book on Banana Cultivation, Dehydration, Ripening, Processing, Products and Packaging Technology

EIRI PROCESS TECHNOLOGY BOOKS

TEXTILE, GARMENTS, DYEING

01 Modern Technology Of Bleaching, Dyeing, Printing & Finishing Of Textiles
02 Technology Of Textiles (Spinning & Weaving, Dyeing, Scouring, Drying, Printing And Bleaching)
03 Garments Manufacturing Technology

SPICES & COLD STORAGE

01 Spices & Packaging With Formulaes
02 Start Your Own Cold Storage Unit

PULP & PAPER TECHNOLOGY

01 Hand Book Of Pulp & Paper, Paper Board & Paper Based Technology

NON WOVEN TECHNOLOGY

01 Complete Technology of Nonwovens Fabrics, Carry Bags, Composite, Geotextiles, Medical Textiles, Fibres, Felts, Apparels, Spunlace and Absorbent Nonwoven

TEXTILE AUXILIARIES & CHEMICALS

01 Textile Auxiliaries And Chemicals With Processes And Formulations

PHARMACEUTICALS & DRUGS

01 Pharmaceuticals And Drugs Technology With Formulations

LEATHER & LEATHER PRODUCTS

01 Hand Book Of Leather & Leather Products Technology

BIOTECHNOLOGY

01 Hand Book Of Biotechnology

CERAMICS

01 Hand Book of Ceramics and Ceramics Processing Technology

TREE FARMING

01 Hand Book Of Tree Farming

MUSHROOM CULTIVATION/ PROCESS

01 Hand Book Of Mushroom Cultivation, Processing and Packaging

BIOFERTILIZERS & VERMICULTURE

01 Hand Book Of Biofertilizers & Vermiculture

MINERAL AND MINERALS

01 Hand Book Of Minerals And Minerals Based Industries

RUBBER CHEMICALS, COMPOUND & RUBBER INDUSTRIES

01 Rubber Chemicals & Processing Industries
02 Modern Rubber Chemicals, Compounds & Rubber Goods Technology
03 Technology Of Rubber & Rubber Goods Industries

AYURVEDIC MEDICINES

01 Ayurvedic & Herbal Medicines With Formulaes
02 Hand Book Of Ayurvedic Medicines With Formulations (A

EIRI PROCESS TECHNOLOGY BOOKS

Complete Hand Book Of Ayurvedic & Herbal Medicines)

STEEL, S.S., NON FERROUS METALS, ROLLING MILL

01 Modern Technology of Non Ferrous Metals and Metal Extraction

02 Processing Technology of Steels and Stainless Steels

03 Modern Technology of Rolling Mill, Billets, Steel Wire, Galvanized Sheet, Forging & Castings

04 Manufacturing Technology of Non-Ferrous Metal Products

WOOD, VENEER, PLYWOOD, PARTICLE, BOARD, FIBREBOARD, BAMBOO & FOREST PRODUCTS

01 Modern Technology Of Wood, Veneer, Plywood, Particle Board, Fibreboard, Bamboo & Forest Products

BIO GAS PRODUCTION

01 Modern Technology of BIOGAS Production

WASTE BASED PRODUCTS INCLUDING INDUSTRIAL, AGRICULTURE, MEDICAL, MUNICIPALITY, ORGANIC & BIOLOGICAL

01 Technology Of Products From Wastes Industrial, Agriculture, Medical, Municipality, Organic & Biological

02 Products from Waste Technology Handbook

FOOD CHEMICALS, FOOD ADDITIVES, PIGMENTS, AROMA, SWEETENERS AND FOOD EMULSIFIERS

01 Technology of Food Chemicals, Pigments and Food Aroma Compounds

02 Modern Technology of Food Additives, Sweeteners and Food Emulsifiers

SOYBEAN

01 Technology of SOYBEAN Products with Formulae

02 Technology of Soya Milk, Tofu, Hydrlyzate and allied Soyabean Products with Project Profiles

EIRI Multiple Project Reports in CD ROM

01 92 New Lucrative Project Reports In Cd

02. 45 Infotech/It, Hospitality, Hospital, College, School & Club

03. 23 Profitable Construction Projects

04. 56 Agro Based & Food Processing Projects

05. 52 Food, Dairy, Bakery, Confectionery & Snacks Foods

06. 45 New Chemicals & Allied Project Reports

07. 100 Profitable Plastic, Polymers & Allied Projects

08. 44 Textile, Garments, Hosiery & Allied Products In Cd

09. 23 Dairy Farming (Buffalo & Jersey Cow, Dairy Products & Other Milk Processing Ind.

10. 42 Paper, Pulp & Paper Converting Products Reports

EIRI Multiple Project Reports in CD ROM

11. 31 Essential Oils, Perfumes, Flavours & Aromatic Compounds
12. 28 Surgical And Disposable Medical Projects
13. 36 Profitable Printing & Allied Projects Reports
14. 63 Profitable Packaging & Allied Project Reports
15. 99 Profitable Printing & Packaging
16. 42 Electroplating, Anodizing & Allied Projects
17. 31 Profitable Plantation & Cultivation Projects
18. 55 Profitable Products From Agro And Other Industrial Wastes
19. 35 Profitable Gums, Adhesives, Sealants And Resins Projects
20. 54 Paint, Varnish, Solvents, Lacquers, Resins, Enamel, Pigments, Thinners & Powder (54 Project Reports In Cd)
21. 43 Iron, Steel, Casting, Fabrication, Wire Drawing & Rolling Mills Projects
22. 26 New Educational Projects (Schools, Colleges, Training/ Management Institute, Hostels Etc.)
23. 12 Mosquitoes Preventive Projects (Coils, Mats, Liquids, Agarbatti, Nets, Spray Etc.)
24. 21 Bakery And Allied Products
25. 67 Rubber And Rubber Goods Industries
26. 37 Aluminium And Aluminium Based Industries
27. 14 Potato And Potato Based Industries
28. 50 Electrical, Electronics And Computer Based Industries
29. 52 Cosmetics (Herbal & Synthetics) Technology Projects (52 Project Reports)
30. 10 Molasses Based Lucrative Projects
31. 24 Fruits/Veg. & Allied Food Dehydration Projects
32. 7 Power Plant Projects (Thermal, Hydro, Solar, Wind Energy And Lignite Coal Based)
33. 35 New Profitable Industries
34. 160 New Export Oriented And Profitable Projects (160 Project Reports In Cd)
35. 5 Ginger & Ginger Processing Industries
36. 13 Fish Farming And Fishery Products
37. 6 Agarbatti And Allied Projects
38. 28 Fruit Juices, Food Dehydration And Allied Products
39. 9 Tea Plantation And Processing Based Industries
40. 14 Roasted/Salted Cashew Nuts, Almonds, Namkeens, Spices Projects
41. 23 Injection Moulded Plastic Products (23 Project Reports)
42. 38 Biofertilizer, Biofuel, Enzyme, Organic Farming & Manure, Protein And Allied Lucrative Projects
43. 10 Maize & Corn Processing Projects
44. 11 Profitable Solar & Solar Based Products
45. 11 Infotech/It Projects
46. 42 Hospitality, Building Material, Power Steels, Alcohol & Other Food Products
47. 24 Soap & Detergents (Scouring Powder, Toilet Cleaner, Laundry Soap, Detergent Cake & Powder, Toilet Soap, Enzyme Based Detergents, Phenyl & Soap Coated Paper)
48. 10 Coconut And Coconut By Products
49. 22 Alcohol, Beer, Imfl, Country Liquor, Wine & Other Related Projects

ALL FOLLOWING PROJECT REPORTS ARE READILY AVAILABLE

- Steel Furnitures And Electrical Appliances
- Steel Furniture And Fire Fighting Equipments
- Steel Furniture And Room Cooler
- Steel Wire Drawing And Galvanizing
- Steel Wire/Rod
- Steel Wool
- Ston Scrusher And Screening Plant
- Submerged Arc Welded Pipes
- Submersible Pump Manufacturing
- Super Enamelled Copper Wire
- Super Enamelled Copper Wire (From Copper Cathode Rod)
- Three Wheelers
- Tie-Rod Ends
- Tin Containers
- Toolroom And Sheet Metal Products
- Trolley (Shopping) For Carrying Of Stores At Super Market And Ware Houses
- Tractor Trailers
- Transmission Power Fitting
- Tubular Poles
- Tyre Retreading By Cold Process
- Super Enamelled Copper Wires
- Trolley (Shopping) For Carrying Of Stores At Super Market & Ware Houses
- Tmt Bars
- Tubular Poles For Electrical Transmission (By Fabrication Process)
- Tubular Poles Of M.S. & High Tensile Steel
- V- Belt
- Vacuum Cleaners
- Vacuum Flask (Stainless Steel)
- Valves For Refrigeration And Air-Condition
- Vehicle Welding & Painting
- Venetion Blind
- Washing Machines (Automatic & Computerised)
- Water Controller (Automatic)
- Watch Straps/Chains/ Bracelets/Belt Brass & Stainless Steel
- Water Coolers
- Welded Wire Mesh
- Welding Electrodes
- Wheel Barrow
- Wick Stoves
- Wind Mill Window Frame (Ferrous & Non-Ferrous)
- Wrist Watch

CHEMICALS (ORGANIC & INORGANIC) WITH PETROLEUM PRODUCTS

- Acetic Anhydride
- Acetic Acid (Glacial)
- Acetic Acid From Ethanol
- Acetone
- Acetylene Black
- Acetyl Chloride
- Acetylene Gas
- Acetylene Gas & Oxygen Gas (Integrated Unit)
- Acid Black Dye
- Acid Slurry
- Activated Alumina
- Activated Bleaching Earth (Activated Fullers Earth)
- Activated Carbon From Cashewnut Shell
- Activated Carbon From Rice Husk
- Activated Carbon From Rice Husk, Coconut Shell & Coconut Powder
- Activated Carbon From Wood
- Activated Carbon Powder & Granules From Coconut Shell
- Activated Carbon & Sodium Silicate From Paddy & Rice Husk
- Alcohol From Broken Rice
- Alum For Water Treatment
- Adhesive (Fevicol Type)
- Aerosol Insecticides Spray (Baygon, Hit, Mortein Type)
- Agarbatti Synthetic Perfumery Compounds
- Alcohol From Potato
- Alcohol From Rice Grains
- Alcohol From Rice Husk
- Alcohol From Molasses
- Alcohol, Beer, Starch, Liquid Glucose, Dextrose, Sorbitol, Vitamin-C,
- Alcoholic Beverages And Vinegar From Coconut Water
- Germ Oil, Cattle Feed Etc. From Maize
- Alkyd Resin
- Alkylated Phenol Likenonyl Phenol, Dodecyl Phenol
- Alum (Non Ferric)
- Alum (Ferric)
- Aluminium Chloride From Aluminium Ore
- Alum Cake
- Alum From Aluminium Hydrate
- Aluminium Ingot By Bauxite
- Aluminium Phosphide
- Aluminium Phosphate
- Aluminium Sulphate (Non Ferric Alum) 17% - 18% Alumina Content In Granules (2 Mm To 4 Mm) And Flakes
- Amines & Allied Products
- Amino Acid
- Ammonia Gas
- Ammonia Gas Bottling
- Ammonia Liquor
- Ammonium Nitrate
- Ammonium Chloride (Pure & Technical)
- Ammonium Sulphate
- Annato Seed Extraction And Processing
- Anti Corrosion Chemicals
- Anthranilic Acid From Phthalic Anhydride
- Anesthesia (All Types) Used In Hospitals
- Aniline
- Argon Gas
- Ariel Type Detergent Powder
- Anthraquinone
- Antimony Trioxide
- Atenolol
- Auramine "O"
- Azodicarbonamide
- Baking Soda From Ash
- Barium Carbonate
- Barium Compounds
- Barium Nitrate
- Barium Peroxide
- Barium-Thio-Sulphate Banzene
- Baryte Powder
- Bar Soap (All Varieties) Using Soap Noodles
- Beer Plant
- Belt Paste
- Beneficiation Of Chromite Ore Processing Charge Chrome
- Benzyl Acetate, Benzyl Benzoate, Benzyl Alcohol
- Beta Naphthol
- Bentonite Powder
- Benzoic Acid
- Benzidine
- Biofertiliser From Mother Culture
- Bio Oil For Power Generation From Coffee Husk
- Bio Gas Plant
- Bio Gas Filling In Cylinder
- Bio Tech Unit
- Bi-Chromate Of Sodium, Potassium & Ammonium
- Bi-Functional Black Mfgr.Reactive Dye (Dye From Cotton Yarn Dyeing)
- Bio-Fuel (Jatropha Cultivation And Extraction)
- Bituminous Roademulsion
- Black Phenyl
- Black Sulphur
- Bleaching Powder (Stable)
- Blue Detergent Powder
- Bone Crushing Plant
- Bone Meal (Calcined) Enrichment With Calcium & Phosphorus
- Boric Acid
- B.O.N. Acid
- Bromine Gas Plant
- Brandy
- Butanol
- Butyl Rubber For The Manufacture Of Tubes For Truck And Car Tyres
- 1,4, Butanediol
- Butyl Acetate
- Caffein From Tea Waste
- Calcined Lime (Dead Burnt Dolomite)

Market Survey Cum Detailed Techno Economic Feasibility Report on all Projects are available Contact.
"ENGINEERS INDIA RESEARCH INSTITUTE". 4449, Nai Sarak (D), Main Road, Delhi-110006 (India)
Ph. : 09811437895, 91-11-23918117, 23916431, 45120361, 64727385 Fax : 91-11-23916431
E-mail : eiriprojects@gmail.com, eiribooks@yahoo.com • website: www.eiri.in, www.eiriindia.org

ALL FOLLOWING PROJECT REPORTS ARE READILY AVAILABLE

PAINT, ENAMEL, SOLVENTS, THINNERS, INKS & VARNISH PAINT, ENAMEL, SOLVENTS, THINNERS, INKS & VARNISH

- Acrylic Emulsion Paints
- Acrylic Cement Paint (Dry Powder)
- Aluminium Paint
- Automobile Paints
- Ball Point Pen Refill Ink
- Bituminious Road Emulsion
- Bitumen
- Bituminious Felts For Water & Damp Proofing
- Bituminious Road Emulsion Rapid Medium & Slow Setting
- Buffing & Polishing
- Cement Paint For White & Grey Cement
- Dispersant
- Dry Distemper
- Dry Distemper & Cement Paint
- Duplicating Ink Black For Gestner Duplicator
- Emulsion Paints (Water Based)
- Hammertone Paint
- Insulating Varnish & Wire Enamel
- Iron Oxide Pigments
- Insulating Varnish (Poly Vinyl Butyral Based, Ffo Grade)
- Lime Colour (Cement Colour)
- Synthetic Red Oxide For Floorings
- Solvent & Thinners
- Marking Inks (Water Proof)
- Metal Naphthanate (As Drier For Paints)
- N.C.Putty
- Offset Printing Ink
- Oil Bound Distemper Paint
- Paint Brushes
- Paint Manufacture For Rolling Coating Of Aluminium And Steel Coil
- Paint Removers
- Paint Industry
- Paint & Varnish
- Picture Varnish
- Powder Coating Paint
- Printing Inks (Offset,Flexo & Roto Gravure)
- Primer Paint & Enamel Paint
- Putty & Water Proofing Paint
- Printing Inks (Flexo-Graphic Ink)
- Putty (Metal Casement)
- Red Oxide Primer (Anti Corrosive)
- Refrectory Paint (Graphite Based)
- Screen Printing Inks
- Silk Screen Printing Ink Formulation For Plastic, Paper, Cloth
- Stamp & Pad Ink
- Stoving Paint
- Spirit Soluble Maleic Resin
- Texture Paint
- Thinners And Its Allied Products
- Toner Ink
- Varnish Thinner (Solvent)
- Vacuum Metallizing Lacquers
- Wood Primer

PHARMACEUTICAL, DRUGS, AYURVEDIC/HERBAL COSMETICS & MEDICINES, HOMOEOPATHIC MEDICINES, HOMOEOPATHIC MEDICINES, DISPOSABLE SYRINGE, DENTAL COLLEGE & FINE CHEMICALS ETC. MEDICINES, HOMOEOPATHIC MEDICINES, DISPOSABLE SYRINGE, DENTAL COLLEGE & FINE CHEMICALS ETC.

- Aromatic Pills
- Alumina From Bauxite
- Aspirin
- Ayurvedic Pain Balm Ointments
- Ayurvedic Churan And Tablets
- Ayurvedic Tablets (Hajmola Type)
- Ayurvedic/Herbalpharmacy
- Ayurvedic Sherbats
- Ayurvedic Products
- Bulk Drugs (E.O.U)
- Blood Bags
- Calcium Gluconate
- Capsule, Tablet & Injection With Modern Instruments
- Cashew Feni
- Chloroquinone Phosphate (Bulk Drugs)
- Clinical Thermometer
- Dental Clinic
- Dental College
- Dental Grade Eugenol
- Dextrose Monohydrate, Liquid Glucose
- Dehydrated Onion & Onion Powder
- Dextrose Powder (Anhydrous From Starch)
- Dextrose Saline Solution
- Distillery (I.M.F.L)
- Disposable Needles For Syringes
- Disprin
- Distilled Water
- Empty Hard Gelatine Capsules
- Fairness Cream
- Filling & Packing Of Capsules
- Glucose - D - Powder
- Glycerine
- Hair Colour Mate (Formulations And Process Only)
- Herbal Cosmetics
- Herbal Shampoo
- Herbal Shampoo And Cream
- Herbal Hair Oils (Ayurvedic)
- Homoe & Bio-Medicines With Mother Tincture
- Homoepathic Medicines
- Hypodermic Needles
- I.V. Fluids
- Ibuprofen
- Infusion & Transfusion Sets (I.V. Set)
- Injectable For Pharmaceuticals
- Injection Ampoules Packaging Box
- Integerated Surgical Cotton
- Ice Making Plant
- Ice & Cold Storage
- Lactose & By Products Processing From Milk
- Lichen (Jatamansi Charila)
- Liquid Glucose And Its By-Products
- L-Lysine Monohydro Chloride
- Liquid Glucose From Potatoes
- Medical College
- Methanol (Hpcl Grade)
- Nicotine From Tobacco Waste
- Ointment-Ayurvedic (Yellow & White)
- Pharmaceutical And Food Grade Gelatine
- Pharmaceutical Industry (Tablets, Capsules, Liquid, Gel, Ointment Powder Injectable)
- Pharmaceutical Unit (Eou) With Formulations, Injectables, Etc.
- Pyridine & Derivatives
- Salt (Iodized Salt)
- Saline & Injection Water
- Saline Water & Dextrose Solution (I.V.Fluid In Plastic Bottles)
- Sorbitol
- Starch (Maize)
- Surgical Adhesive Plaster
- Surgical Bandages
- Surgical Gloves
- Surgical Cotton
- Surgical Cotton And Bandage
- Synthetic Camphor Powder
- Tablets & Capsules
- Tissue Culture
- Tincture From Rectified Spirit
- Trimethopime
- Veterinary College With Hospital
- Veterenary Medicines (Only Formulations)
- Vitamin 'C', Sorbitol' Anhydrous Dextrose, Starch

Market Survey Cum Detailed Techno Economic Feasibility Report on all Projects are available Contact.
"ENGINEERS INDIA RESEARCH INSTITUTE". 4449, Nai Sarak (D), Main Road, Delhi-110006 (India)
Ph. : 09811437895, 91-11-23918117, 23916431, 45120361, 64727385 Fax : 91-11-23916431
E-mail : eiriprojects@gmail.com, eiribooks@yahoo.com • website: www.eiri.in, www.eiriindia.org